THE HIGH PEAK
DAMBUSTER
SERGEANT JACK MARRIOTT DFM

FRANK PLESZAK

AIR WORLD

AIR WORLD

THE HIGH PEAK DAMBUSTER
Sergeant Jack Marriott DFM

First published in Great Britain in 2022 by
Air World
An imprint of
Pen & Sword Books Ltd
Yorkshire – Philadelphia

Copyright © Frank Pleszak, 2022

ISBN: 978 1 39909 746 8

Typeset by SJmagic DESIGN SERVICES, India.
Printed and bound by CPI Group (UK) Ltd, Croydon, CR0 4YY

Pen & Sword Books Ltd incorporates the imprints of Pen & Sword Archaeology, Air World Books, Atlas, Aviation, Battleground, Discovery, Family History, History, Maritime, Military, Naval, Politics, Social History, Transport, True Crime, Claymore Press, Frontline Books, Praetorian Press, Seaforth Publishing and White Owl

For a complete list of Pen & Sword titles please contact:

PEN & SWORD BOOKS LTD
47 Church Street, Barnsley, South Yorkshire, S70 2AS, UK.
E-mail: enquiries@pen-and-sword.co.uk
Website: www.pen-and-sword.co.uk

Or

PEN AND SWORD BOOKS,
1950 Lawrence Road, Havertown, PA 19083, USA
E-mail: Uspen-and-sword@casematepublishers.com
Website: www.penandswordbooks.com

Contents

Acknowledgements

I would like to thank the many people who have posted on social media and those authors I used as reference and from whom I have learned so much.

To my wife Alison, sister Christine, and brother Lawrence for proof reading and correcting my many mistakes.

I would also like to give thanks for the help and assistance I have received from Dom Howard of Lancasterbombers.net; the Avro Heritage Museum at Woodford; Dambuster expert Charles Foster nephew of Dambuster pilot David Maltby, and in particular a special mention to 617 Squadron archivist Dr Robert Owen who has been gracious and unstinting with his time, understanding and help.

Lastly, but most importantly of all, a very special thank you to my neighbour and friend Norma Bagshaw, niece of Jack Marriott. Without all her input and gracious access to her family archives this piece of work would never have been possible.

Image Credits

Many of the images are from the internet and are available from several locations and every attempt has been made to trace the copyright holder. I would however, like to thank Norma Bagshaw for access to all her personal archives, the Avro Heritage Museum for the drawing of the Lancaster modifications, Bobbie Grew for images of Sgt Webb's logbook and Steve Pearce for images of Sgt Mortimer's Lancaster notes, and the Lincolnshire Aviation Heritage Centre for the image of the control yoke and throttle quadrant of ED932.

Preface

The 'Dambusters', or more correctly Operation Chastise, is arguably the most famous historic military operation of the twentieth century. Most people have heard of it and know of the famous 'Bouncing Bomb'. Many will know the name of the commander of the attack – Guy Gibson, and some the name of the 'Bouncing Bomb' inventor – Barnes Wallis. The raid took place during the night of 16-17 May 1943 and was immediately headline news around the world. Interest and intrigue have not diminished with the passing of time. The myth was enhanced with the release of Guy Gibson's book *Enemy Coast Ahead* in 1946 and further still when Paul Brickhill published his book, still considered by many to be a classic, *The Dam Busters* in 1951.

Not surprisingly, soon after it became a film of the same name. Released in 1955, it is quite possibly the best-loved if not most-watched war film of all time and further immortalised the legend of many of those who took part. At the time the film was being made, much of Operation Chastise was still covered by the Official Secrets Act and the film not only used 'artistic licence', it also perpetuated some popular but untrue myths in many of the

scenes. However, it does form the basis for most people's knowledge of the event, and it clearly demonstrates accurately the skill, dedication, ability, and absolute heroism of those young men that took part.

No military operation is the result of just one or two high profile names. And while Gibson and Wallis undeniably deserve the adulation and praise they have had and continue to receive, the success of the Dambusters was thanks to a multitude of people with different roles and from varying backgrounds. Typically, each Avro Lancaster would require around fifty personnel to keep it flying. These would include the seven air crew members, flying control officers, parachute packers, meteorological officers, the flight maintenance crew (fitters, maintenance and electrical mechanics, instrument and radio specialists), the bombing-up team, drivers, ground servicing engineers, armourers, gun belt fitters, petrol and oil tender crews, and mobile workshop teams.

Right: Flying and support team for a single Avro Lancaster.

Below: Some of 617 Squadron personnel in July 1943.

THE HIGH PEAK DAMBUSTER

In addition to these were the squadron, base support, ancillary personnel, and RAF management. To support Operation Chastise there would have been over 1,000 individuals involved in its planning, execution, and analysis.

The success of the Dambusters could not have been achieved without all their input and for many their hard work and long hours was just as intense as those that flew on the raid. In literature few of these are mentioned let alone identified by name, and while all but a few of the Dambusters' pilots get a cursory mention, most of the names of the other aircrew members usually only ever appear in lists of crews.

For Operation Chastise there were, including Gibson, twenty-one crews that trained for the raid. Two of the crews didn't take part on the night. Each of the nineteen Lancasters that departed for the raid had a crew of seven, so there were 133 young men, most of them not much more than boys. The average age was just 22, Gibson himself only 24. Three of the Lancasters turned back without using their 'Bouncing Bomb'. Eight crashed or were shot down and only three of the aircrew survived to be taken prisoner of war. Fifty-three young men lost their lives during the night of 16 and 17 May.

Three of those that took part that night came from the High Peak region of Derbyshire. Sergeant Jack Marriott came from Chinley, Flight Lieutenant Bill Astell a mile away at Combs near Chapel-en-le-Frith and Sergeant John Nugent from nearby Stoney Middleton.

The aim of this book is to tell, in words and pictures, the sad and mysterious story of just one member of an aircrew that were all killed after having reached both the Möhne and Eder Dams. He was Sergeant Jack Marriott, flight engineer on Lancaster Z-Zebra (AJ-Z).

I'm not going to go into the incredible science, engineering, planning or politics that went into making the raid, nor a post-raid analysis of the

Jack Marriott.

success or benefits of Operation Chastise. But it is important to describe the events that took place leading up to, and on, the night of the raid itself, together with a little post-raid history of 617 Squadron. In order to do this I have drawn extensively on the excellent works of many others to pull together a picture of what happened leading up to the operation, what happened as the night progressed, and also the fate of all the aircrew and aircraft involved. Some of the events are still speculation as in some cases the details are vague, and even those air crew members that participated on the night and were subsequently interviewed had different recollections of what happened.

I have necessarily concentrated on the activities and actions of the Lancaster AJ-Z and considered various possibilities to explain what might have occurred, even though we will never know the actual reasons. The story continued for Jack and 617 Squadron after the Dambusters. For Jack, his memory has been kept alive for more than eighty years by his niece, Norma Bagshaw.

I have outlined the story as a series of relevant facts in a chronological order. I refer to most people mentioned by their surnames and give their full names, and where appropriate their military rank, in appendices. I have also capitalised crew positions where it refers to a specific role. Where I include images of handwritten letters or typewritten documents, I include a transcription for clarity complete with any errors for authenticity.

Introduction

Even before the start of the Second World War the British Air Staff had identified strategic air targets should there be another conflict in Europe. German industrial areas were considered to be a primary target, and in particular the Ruhr Valley which was critical for production of arms and munitions.

As early as 1938 the possibility of attacking the large dams that controlled water for the Ruhr was being discussed. If these could be breached it would cause untold damage, disrupt vital production and require a redistribution of workers from other work to help in any rebuild effort. By the time of Second World War, the dams were impossible to attack. Multiple layers of floats stretched across the front of the dams which prevented the use of any surface weapons, and suspended below steel nets prohibited the use of torpedoes or submarine devices. From the air there was no suitable aircraft or bombsight capable of delivering the pin-point attack that would be needed.

The Assistant Chief Designer at Vickers Armstrong Aviation was Barnes Wallis who looked at the issues and possible solutions for an airborne attack. His initial idea was for a 22,000lb 'Earthquake' bomb that when dropped would accelerate so fast it would embed itself deep into the base of the dam, and when it exploded would shake the dam to bits. The idea was rejected as there was no means to guarantee accuracy and, more importantly, no aircraft was capable of carrying such a heavy payload.

Disappointed but undeterred, Wallis set about not only looking at other solutions to destroy the dams, but designing an aircraft capable of carrying what was essentially a 10 ton bomb. During 1940 and 1941 he began tests on model dams and determined that if the explosion was up against the wall of the dam below the water, surface pressure was not dissipated but assisted the explosion in breaching the dam wall. It also meant that a much smaller weapon would be required to cause the breach.

INTRODUCTION

Once he had discovered where the placement of a bomb needed to be, Wallis looked at how it could be delivered accurately. Famously, he took inspiration from his daughter's game of marbles to design his 'Bouncing Bomb'. Despite many failures and setbacks, he came up with the idea of the Upkeep, weighing just over 4 tons and designed to rotate backwards, skip across the surface of the water, over the torpedo nets, hit the dam wall, roll down the inner face of the dam wall and, using a pressure-activated hydrostatic trigger, explode at the optimum depth.

Although his design for an aircraft (the Vickers Windsor) was completed and eventually flew in 1943, by 1942 the Avro Aircraft Manufacturing Company had revised their disastrous twin-engine bomber, the Avro Manchester. They had replaced the two powerful but unreliable Rolls-Royce Vulture engines with four lower power Rolls-Royce Merlin engines. With very little redesign they had created the performant, fast and reliable Avro Lancaster with a huge carrying capacity.

Having committed to the weapon, the RAF were reluctant to withdraw and use a frontline squadron for its delivery. A new squadron was formed, resourced from existing No.5 Group Bomber Command aircrews and to be based at RAF Scampton in Lincolnshire, which was waiting to have a concrete runway installed and so only had a single squadron based there. The premise for the creation of the squadron was that it would use aircrews

Vickers Windsor prototype.

xiii

Avro Manchester prototype.

that had completed at least one tour of operations with some key personnel being specially selected for their ability.

Initially referred to as 'Squadron X', the new 617 Squadron came into existence on 21 March 1943. The commander was 24-year-old Wing Commander Guy Gibson. Highly decorated, he had transformed 106 Squadron into the most successfully bomber squadron in No.5 Group. Having just completed his third tour with 106 Squadron on Lancasters, he had been posted to No.5 Group headquarters ostensibly for a rest and to write a book about wartime bomber pilots. Eventually he was asked if he would consider forming and leading a new special squadron for one more low-level mission.

The top-secret operation would require incredible skills from all the aircrew members. Most No.5 Group squadrons were asked to contribute complete Lancaster crews and, contrary to popular belief, Gibson neither knew nor selected all the pilots personally. Although he brought pilots Shannon, Hopgood and Burpee with him from 106 Squadron and had briefly met Martin previously, all the other pilots were new to him. Some clearly did not match the criteria required of the new squadron. However, most of the pilots were highly skilled, some highly decorated. Flight Lieutenant Henry Maudslay, an ex-Etonian athlete from Leamington Spa was one of these, transferred from 50 Squadron he was soon confirmed as a Squadron Leader and 617 Squadron B-Flight Commander.

Again, a popular misconception is that Gibson brought with him his entire aircrew from 106 Squadron. In fact, he had a completely new crew at 617 Squadron and his bomb aimer, far from being experienced, had not flown any operations let alone a whole tour.

Maudslay, however, already had forty-two operations behind him. He had been seconded from 44 Squadron to do operational acceptance testing and service trials of the Lancaster at A&AEE[1] Boscombe Down before it entered RAF service. He was then transferred to 44 Conversion Flight where he flew three more operational missions before joining 1654 HCU[2] as a Lancaster instructor pilot. It was while there that he 'checked out' several of the eventual 617 Squadron pilots on Lancasters. Bill Astell was one of these and became one of his closest friends.

After transferring back to operational duties at 50 Squadron his crew was eventually finalised. They were experienced and highly competent and all moved with him to 617 Squadron; Jack Marriott was the sergeant flight engineer. The navigator was Canadian Flying Officer Robert Urquhart. With twenty-eight operations and a citation for a DFC, he was highly experienced and as such became 617 Squadron B-Flight Flight Navigation Officer. Sergeant Cottam, the wireless operator was another Canadian with several ops[3] to his credit. Pilot Officer Michael Fuller from Surrey was the bomb aimer, also with several ops with his previous squadron, 106 Squadron. The front gunner was Flying Officer William 'Johnny' Tytherleigh from Cambridge. He was highly experienced having completed a full tour before joining 50 Squadron, and completed a further eight ops with Maudslay. After transferring to 617 Squadron he was appointed B-Flight Gunnery Leader. The rear gunner was Sergeant Norman 'Bunny' Burrows from Liverpool who had only one op to his name before joining Maudslay's crew.

Jack Marriott

On Monday 19 January 1920, John Marriott was born at his family home of Middleton House in the tiny Derbyshire Peak District hamlet of New Smithy, near to the village of Chinley. He was the youngest of four boys and two girls.

John's father, Thomas Henry, had moved to New Smithy with their young family in 1917 from Ashover near Matlock.

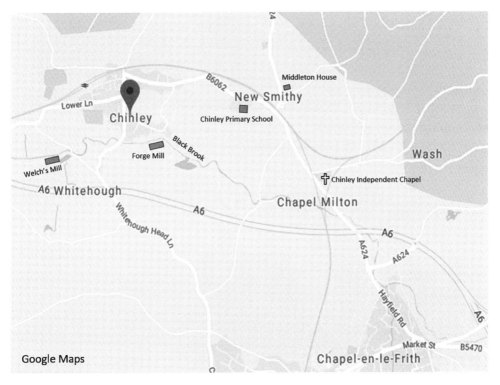

Map of Chinley.

Florence Emily (Floss) was born in 1904, Thomas William (Bill) in 1906, Edith May (May) in 1909, Joseph (Joe) in 1912, Charles (Chas or Charlie) in 1914 and John in 1920. As with most of his relatives and siblings, forenames were either abbreviated or converted into a pet-name. Thus, John became Jack to his family and close friends.

Jack's grandmother Emily Marriott (in black), father Thomas Henry (holding the pony) and grandfather Joseph Marriott (far right) near their home in Yew Tree Close, Ashover about 1900.

Jack's father ('Pop') mother Lois, elder brothers Bill (left), and Joe (right).

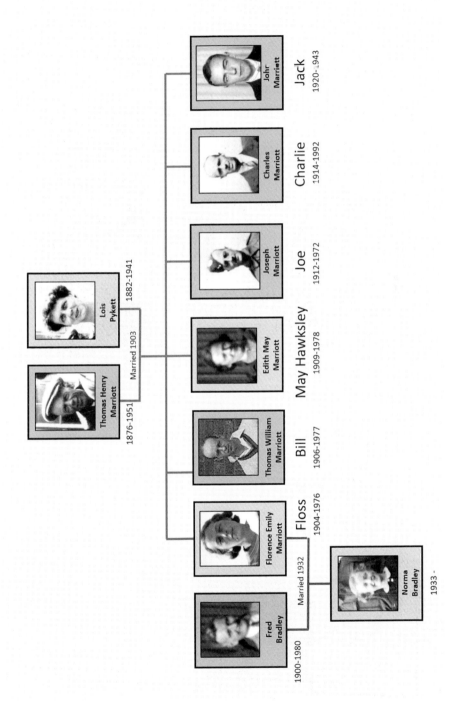

Marriott family tree.

3

Thomas Henry was a stern father, but full of character and bizarrely intriguing. A veteran of the Boer War and First World War, he worked as a labourer for Derbyshire County Council highways department where he, like his father before him, could indulge his passion for horses.

The family home of Middleton House proved ideal for their large family; a curiously long thin bedroom provided a dormitory-like accommodation for the boys while the girls shared a separate small bedroom. Access was by a separate staircase at the rear of the house.

Jack was a likeable child and he developed a special and close relationship with brother Charlie. Although several years difference in age they played, fought, and grew together, and together they developed their cheerful and happy-go-lucky characters.

As with all his brothers and sisters, Jack attended the nearby Chinley Primary school on Buxton Road. Jack was a popular child but despite being an excellent student he left school to work, like his brothers had before him, for the J.J. Hadfield Company Ltd.

J.J. Hadfield had been developing and growing their bleach works since the turn of the century at Forge Mill on the banks of Black Brook on the south side of Chinley. They were, by the time Jack started working for them, a large company employing a significant proportion of the local community.

Chinley Primary school (about 1928–1930) Jack is on the second row from the front on the extreme right.

Fire damage at Forge Mill in 1934.

In 1936 when Jack started his employment with them, they had only just fully recovered from a devastating fire that started on the Friday evening 17 August 1934.

So intense was the inferno that most of the factory was destroyed. Although Buxton and New Mills fire brigades were quickly on the scene it required additional support from Stockport and Manchester fire services to control and manage the incident. The company was back operating in a reduced capacity after six months, but full production wasn't resumed for several more months.

J.J. Hadfield was regarded as an excellent employer. They had throughout their history shown a keen interest in the welfare and wellbeing of their workforce. As their Forge Mill works was in a remote location, most of the workforce had to remain on the premises for their meals. In March 1925 a modern canteen was officially opened providing good meals at low prices.

In the evenings and at weekends the canteen was used for social events such as dances, concerts, and entertainment. Adjoining the social club, Hadfield's had a very large sports field managed by the Forge Social & Athletic Union', which provided, among others, football, cricket, bowls and tennis.

The Forge Social & Athletic Union's cricket and football teams were particularly successful, regularly topped their respective leagues and were feared and respected in equal measures. Every Saturday throughout the year the whole area was busy with sporting activities attracting teams and visitors from all over the area.

Jack was a keen sportsman and a popular member of the sports club. Though a frequent participant at both football and cricket, he never reached

The Forge Social & Athletic Union club house and tennis courts.

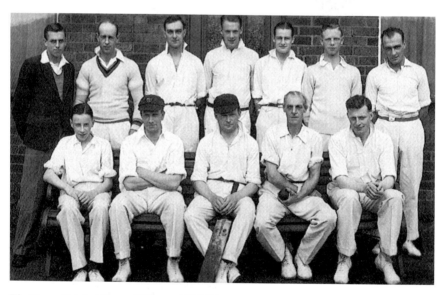

The Forge Cricket Second Eleven 1929/30 (Bill Marriott back row, second from left).

the same standard as his eldest brother Bill, who was a regular choice for the cricket second team squad.

J.J. Hadfield was a progressive employer and provided a range of other social benefits including annual trips to the seaside for their employees.

This was always a popular and eagerly awaited annual activity. Blackpool was a favourite destination. Jack relished these trips and always made the most of them.

Above left: Jack on Blackpool sands.

Above right: Jack on Blackpool's central pier.

Right: Another fun day out.

Norma Bagshaw

Jack was a family man, and apart from the special relationship with brother Charlie he also had a very close relationship with his eldest sister Floss, who had helped so much with Jack's upbringing.

Floss (Florence Emily) worked at Welch's Mill (also known as Whitehall Works) on the west side of Chinley, also on the banks of Black Brook and not too far from J.J. Hadfield's Forge Mill.

During the 1920s, Welch's main production was cotton brocades which were manufactured in various designs with the majority dyed in a wide range of chrome colours for the lucrative Indian market. Other cotton products were also produced and by the 1930s a towelling and nappy range was introduced, necessitating the introduction of a sewing machine department.

It was while working at Welch's Mill that Floss met Fred Bradley, who worked on machines that aged cotton products. Their relationship blossomed, in 1932 they were married at Chinley Church, before long they had moved to their own home Moorfield on Lower Lane in Chinley.

On 7 June 1933 Norma, their only child, was born. As with her mother, Norma soon had a strong relationship with Jack, he was fun to be with.

As Norma got older, Jack would regularly take her along when out walking with his girlfriend. The Wash, a rural area to the east of Chinley in the Peak District was a favourite destination and still holds fond memories for Norma.

Above: Norma with (from the left) her mother Floss Bradley, grandmother Lois Marriott, Aunt May (Hawksley) and father Fred Bradley.

Right: Norma with father Fred Bradley in the garden at Middleton House.

Joining the Royal Air Force

By 1940 Jack's career at the Forge was progressing but, ominously, so were developments in Europe. It wasn't long before it became obvious that further men would be required to leave their normal employment and enlist into the armed forces.

And so it was around mid-April that the 20-year-old Jack, with trepidation but also a sense of duty and pride, found himself at the local combined forces recruiting centre. We have no record of Jack's experience at the recruiting centre but it was probably similar to that experienced by many others who attended the Royal Air Force section. Likely he would have been greeted by a no-nonsense, long-serving NCO who would have asked abruptly, without any indication of warmth or interest, what Jack would like to do in the RAF. Jack no doubt suggested engineer, before having to describe his educational achievements. Seemingly, without much thought and no discussion whatsoever and his trade of engineer confirmed, he would have been whisked away for a medical examination at which he suffered all the usual medical indignities. Finally, he would have been told to hold himself in readiness for a letter telling when and where to report.

Jack's chosen (or allocated) trade was ground engineer, possibly based on his experience at J.J. Hadfields. He will have received his letter from the Officer-in-Charge of the RAF Recruiting Centre in mid- or late May of 1940. It will have been brief and to the point, basically confirming that his application for enlistment into the Royal Air Force Volunteer Reserve had been approved, instructing him to report back at the Recruiting Centre at 9 am on 7 June, and a short list of the various items he should bring with him.

He no doubt made all his farewells, promises to write regularly, collected his final wages from work and reported back to the Recruiting Centre as instructed. He will have joined a crowd of other similar new recruits aged from 18 to early 30s. En masse they were led through their oath of allegiance 'to our Sovereign King and his heirs and successors', followed by a ritual form-filling and signing exercise. Finally, he will have been allocated a railway warrant affording him travel to Padgate near Warrington.

RAF Padgate is well-remembered by thousands of young men who joined the RAF, it was their first experience of

RAF Padgate.

military life with their first taste of military discipline, ill-fitting uniforms and severe haircuts. After a short journey via Manchester, Jack arrived at Padgate train station where he was met by RAF officials and led to RAF Padgate the home of RAF No.1 Reception Unit and RAF No 3 School of Recruit Training.

The new recruits would have been arranged in three ranks while a roll call was performed, during which Jack will have become Aircraftman Second Class (AC2) John Marriott 1003474 RAFVR,[4] with a starting trade as Aircraft Hand General Duties (ACH GD). His name, number and his religion (Church of England) were stamped on two dog-tags which he will have worn permanently around his neck and his RAF Service Record started.

The recruits would then have been crudely marched carrying their suitcases and been allocated a bed in one of the many huts. The following day all the new recruits were marched from store to store and in a seemingly haphazard fashion, allocated their RAF issue clothes and equipment including knife, fork, spoon, mug and a towel. All new recruits would then have had another cursory medical to ensure they were free from any contagious diseases (known as Free from Infection, or FFI) and then undertaken a brief trade test to determine their best suitability.

Having changed into uniform the new recruits were immediately transformed from a mis-matched bunch of civvies into an even and pristine blue military group. No longer could the mill worker be distinguished from a bank clerk, farm worker or labourer; everybody was equal.

Jack was assigned to 4 Wing at Padgate on 10 June and the following two weeks consisted of RAF basic training which would have comprised mainly of drill practice. They were marched everywhere, to the mess-hall, to the sick quarters for a variety of jabs, to church, to the rifle range, to the

AC Jack Marriott RAFVR
1003474.

public baths once a week, to the local cinema for various instructional films. They went everywhere as a marching squad, sometimes in uniform, sometimes in PT kit, sometimes in fatigue overalls. They were never alone, even the most private matters were managed as a squad – privacy was a privilege confined to their past.

In addition, there was lots of cleaning of huts and barracks, polishing floors and generally tidying up around the camp. There were injections and vaccinations, haircuts and of course lectures on topics such as the organisation of the RAF, ranks in the RAF, discipline, diseases and lectures on not 'talking shop' outside of the camp. There were sports trials and bayonet practice, but after two weeks Jack was already rehearsing in full dress uniform for his passing out parade.

Basic training over, Jack's passing out parade was on Friday 21 June 1940. He then had a weekend at home and the following Tuesday, 25 June, travelled by train and reported for his next posting to No.39 Maintenance Unit (MU) at RAF Colerne in Wiltshire. It was Jack's first experience of RAF aircraft and an operational airfield.

At the time of Jack's arrival, RAF Colerne had only recently been upgraded and occupied by No.39 MU. It was used for storage and maintenance of aircraft but was also home to some aircraft of Fighter Command. Since there had been a rapid increase in personnel at the site, accommodation was at a premium. Initially Jack was billeted in a tent before being allocated to permanent accommodation. Though Jack had some exposure to aircraft, much of his time was spent on guard and patrol duties while undertaking lessons and being assessed in a series of aptitude tests. He had plenty of time to write home in which his subtle sense of humour is clearly in evidence.

Letter 15/9/40 from RAF Colerne. (Transcript on p.286)

No 1003474 a.c.2 J Marriott
Tent No 11
H Q No 39 m u
Colerne
Wilts
Sun 15. 9. 4 0

Dear Floss Fred & Norma,

First of all I must apologise for not writing before, but as your letters crossed in the post I thought that perhaps you would have written again. However as I haven't seen anything you must be waiting for me. I told mother in the letter that I posted yesterday that I should write to you Sunday night cum Monday morning. It is my turn on tonight it is now about 9. 30. I say about 9-30 because I don't know for sure as I dropped my blue pencil, four & sixpence, watch on the ruddy floor last Wednesday & needless to say it doesn't. Thanks

13

2

for the P O you sent I shall be able to put it towards another 4/-6-I dont think. And now to get on to the subject of air-raids. As you probably know last Friday was Friday the 13th. It was very windy and cloudy down here. It was about 3·30 in the afternoon. I was just going for an early tea as I was on duty at 4. I just happened to look up and I saw a plane come out of the clouds. heading this way. I thought it looked a bit different to what I'd been seeing and then I saw something drop from it and then the ruddy whistling. For a couple of seconds I was sorta rooted to the ground, then I came to and flung torso flat on floor at the same time

2

as the do das landed. there was
two dropped, so I thought I had
better be doing towards a bit
of cover (there is a sod over now)
I set off towards a trench and then
suddenly remembered I'd dropped my
knife and fork so for some
unknown reason I went back for
them and then ran like a
rabbit to the trench while
sonny boy was still sticking
around. However the ack-ack gun
started on him so he vamoosed.
When everything had got back
to something like normal we found
he had missed us by quite a
bit but it was quite near
enough to be going on with.
They must have been fairly

4

heavy bombs as one of them
knocked a few trees down and
set one on fire. Needless to say
no laxatives were needed on Saturday.
We have had very little air-
raids, during the night. It is a
bit different to what I expected as
it is full moon tomorrow. I don't
expect we shall worry if he fails
to come again. It is now ten
past one and nothing doing. I
wrote to May tonight just before
I wrote to you. I went out last
night for the first time for nearly
a fortnight. I went with two
more lads down into Box which
is a place a bit bigger than
Colerne but we have another
of those great hills to climb
infact anywhere we go to from
the camp we have to climb

5/

a hill to get back. You
will see by my address that
I am now in a tent. I dont
know for how long but I
rather like it although I only
sleep there every other night.
I have heard that we are
to be billeted out. The five
of us on our job had some
pleasant news on Wednesday.
We learned that we were to
get 6ᵈ a day extra as we are
doing Service Police work. It
will come in very handy especially as we shall get the 6ᵈ a
day for tobacco. We have
also got about 17/6 back pay
to come. I should think by
now that Joe has got to

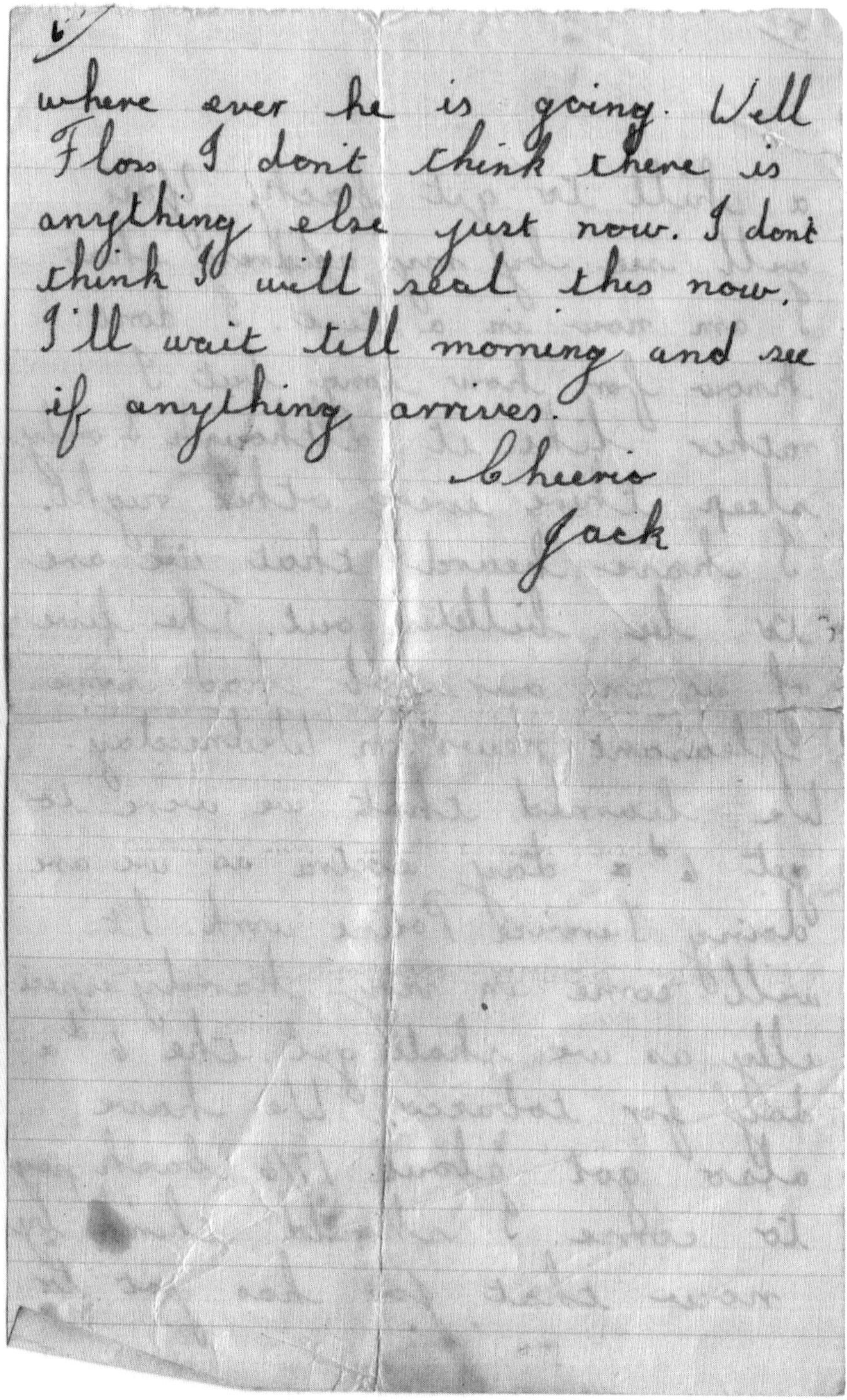

where ever he is going. Well Floss I don't think there is anything else just now. I don't think I will seal this now. I'll wait till morning and see if anything arrives.

Cheerio

Jack

Letter 16/9/40 from RAF Colerne. (Transcript on p.287)

No 1003474 .A.B.2. J Marr.
Tent No 11
S.G No 39 M U
R A F
Colerne
Wilts
16. 9. 4 0

Dear Floss,

You will no doubt be suprised to he receive another letter from me so quickly after the one I posted this morning. I told you in that letter I wrote last night that I wouldn't seal it up till I saw whether I got one, from you this morning. However there was a fellow going down to Bath at 6.30 a m so I thought I might as well send it down with him together with the one for May. Well I got the one from you that you wrote on Friday complete

2

with stamps, for which I thank you, but you needn't put any in every letter you send. I shall try and get this posted in Bath tonight so that you should get it the day after the other. I got the Reporter and a letter from Arthur as well this morning. I was glad to hear that mother has got her money through. It was funny you starting your letter with Friday 13th after me writing about same. You are right about us not being able to leave the Guard Room during raids, but I think it is as safe as any-place as there is a wall of sand-bags in front of it. It wouldn't of course stand a direct hit but there aren't

3

many places that would. We seem to have one or two fire men in the family. It should be a good show when Chas and Frank Halley get together. It will be tough if May has to wait till the cold weather comes before she can have her operation on the thyroid gland. If it is that that is making her lose weight Fred wont have to worry about his, will he? I hope you dont mind that crack Fred but I have to fill up space and get my 2½d worth. The weather is not too good today as it has rained nearly all the morning. I believe we are moving out of the tents into a big house tonight, but you can put Tent No 11 on your next letter as I shall get it O.K. Mother told me about that bloke who was on leave but it is hardly worth it for a weekend as it is all travelling. Well F loss I will close now. You can tell mother I got the Reporter & will write Wednesday unless I get a letter before.

Cheerio

Jack.

After fourteen weeks at RAF Colerne, Jack's initial training was over and his aptitude tests successful. On 1 October he was promoted to AC1 (Aircraftman First Class). After completing his roster on guard duties he returned home for a short break before travelling to his new posting on 19 October, at No.5 School of Technical Training (5SofTT) RAF Locking, just outside Weston-Super-Mare in Somerset. Jack was by then confirmed in his trade (Mustering) as ACH u/t FM/FR. He was an Aircraft Hand (ACH), under training (u/t), in Fitter Mechanics (FM) and Fitter Radios (FR).

5SofTT at RAF Locking specialised in training in the areas of Flight Mechanics Airframe, Engines and Rigging, Parachute Packing and

Jack in the garden at Middleton House.

Fabric Working. Jack's initial training was followed by further aptitude tests which honed his abilities. From 25 October his mustering became u/t FM, he was specialising as a Fitter Mechanics. His courses consisted of subjects on aircraft airframes, engines, carburettors and magnetos, electrics and instruments, aircraft engines (both radial and inline), hydraulics and propellers. After a week Jack had completed his general mechanical fitter training and progressed to u/t FM (E). He was then in training to be a Mechanical Fitter specialising in engines.

The training was intense, on 1 December Jack's RAF Service Record was updated with a character of VG (Very Good, the highest character which was awarded in the Royal Air Force Volunteer Reserve) and in the Proficiency section that he was under training. He had little time for letters, but he did manage to buy an RAF Christmas card from the NAAFI shop and send it home. His training continued and towards the end of February 1941 had qualified as FM (E).

On 12 March, after a short break at home, he was posted to 18 Squadron at RAF Massingham near Fakenham in Norfolk. Here he was working with the squadron's twin-engine Bristol Blenheim Mk.IV light bombers. At the

Engineering lesson on a Bristol Mercury radial piston engine.

same time, he was training for his grade II engine qualification (u/t F II (E)). As the training intensified, 18 Squadron relocated to nearby RAF Oulton from 3 April. A week later Jack was posted to No.2 School of Technical Training (2SofTT) at RAF Cosford between Telford and Wolverhampton to continue towards his engine grade II qualifications.

Sadly, towards the end of April, Jack's mother died. Following a short break at home Jack was back at RAF Cosford completing his training and preparing for his final assessments. By the beginning of June his training was over, and his final exams completed.

On 11 June he was a fully qualified Grade II Engine Fitter (F II (E)) having attained an 85 per cent overall pass mark. Another short break at home and then Jack was back at RAF Oulton working on the engines of their Blenheims with their Bristol Mercury radial nine-cylinder engines. On 1 November, Jack was promoted to Leading Aircraftman (LAC) and his end of year assessment as recorded in his Service Record once again showed a character of VG, and for his Trade Proficiency he was awarded a 'Superior' (could only be bettered by 'Exceptional').

Work on the Blenheims continued during the early months of 1942 and in March he undertook a Bristol company specialist training for their Mercury engines. This was completed successfully, and his Service Record Specialist Qualification section updated accordingly.

Right: Jack with brothers
Charlie and Joe.

Below: Ground crew
working on a Bristol
Blenheim Mk.IV.

Flight Engineer Training

By the spring of 1942, the Blenheim light bomber was being superseded by huge four-engine aircraft in the strategic bomber role. The Short Stirling had entered service in August 1940 and the Handley Page Halifax soon after in November. The Avro Company's medium bomber, the Avro Manchester, which was also introduced into squadron service in November 1940, had proved to be troublesome due to its unreliable Rolls-Royce Vulture engines. In a relatively minor redesign, the two Vulture engines were replaced by four less powerful but efficient and reliable Rolls-Royce Merlin engines.

The aircraft was renamed the Avro Lancaster, it was an instant success. Fast and manoeuvrable it had a huge bomb carrying capability and it went into massive production. The UK, though, had a paucity of pilots, so like all British heavy bombers it was only configured for single pilot operation (even though the Stirling had dual controls). There were no dual controls and no co-pilot, unlike all the comparable American bombers. With the increased complexity of the modern heavy bomber and the necessary management of engines and flight systems, the bomber crew became seven with the introduction in 1942 of the new role of flight engineer.

Initially flight engineer training was undertaken at squadron level. In order to formalise training No.4 School of Technical Training (4SofTT) at RAF St Athan in the Vale of Glamorgan (South Wales) was established as a flight engineer's School. The very first intake was on 30 May 1942. Typically for ab-initio (starting from the beginning) flight engineers the course took about six months to complete.

The first seventeen weeks covered preliminary airframes and engines (radial and inline), carburettors and magnetos, electrics and instruments, hydraulics and propellers. Following a short home break, a further seven weeks covered Merlin engines, advanced airframes, hydraulics, propellers, instruments, electrics and aerodrome procedures. The final course provided specific training on the airframes and engines of the aircraft to which the men were likely to get posted.

Though very little, if any, actual flight training was undertaken, simulated flight environments were created using cockpit and fuselage sections and lessons would be conducted in full flying kit. Sometimes a tethered aircraft would be provided so students could run the engines at maximum throttle and observe the effects. Topics such as damage assessment, emergency procedures, crash-landings, and dinghy drills were also covered.

As well as direct entry students, qualified ground engineers and fitters with a suitable aptitude were encouraged to apply. As soon as the opportunity arose Jack applied, his application endorsed by his 18 Squadron engineering lead. His service record was stamped with 'Recommended for training as flight engineer'. Jack was an early entry, arriving at 4SofTT on Tuesday 7 July.

For fully qualified fitters such as Jack, the course encompassed only the advanced topics and as such was condensed down to around six weeks. The training at RAF St Athan was intense. There were no course books or handouts, all diagrams and notes had to be copied long-hand into his own notebooks.

In addition to the flight engineer training, topics such as Morse Code, oxygen supply and the effects of hypoxia, physical fitness, navigation,

Flight engineer lesson on a Lancaster B.III cockpit section.

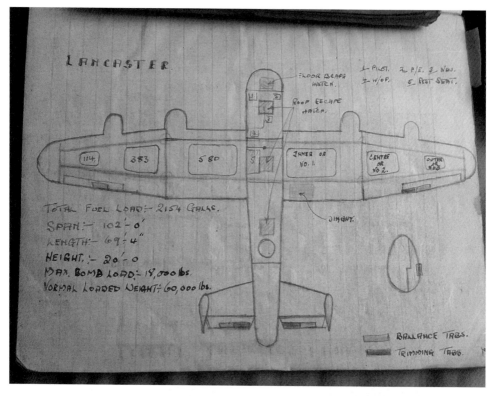

Trainee flight engineer Eric Mortimer's hand-drawn Lancaster diagram.

and armaments were also undertaken. Jack did, however, have at least one weekend off, spending it at nearby Barry Island, from where he sent a postcard home.

The conclusion of the course was two exams, one written and the other oral. Those students who achieved a pass mark of 70 per cent or more were recommended for a commission to officer rank. There were in actual fact few that achieved such a high score, it required excellent exam results together with a demonstration of discipline, leadership skills and a determination that had been demonstrated throughout the entire course. Of the 19 flight engineers that took part on Operation Chastise (The Dambusters) fifteen had passed through 4SofTT. Only two of them were Pilot Officer rank, but neither had gained it as a result of their 4SofTT course results.

Jack just missed the officer recommendation having achieved a very creditable 64 per cent. His flight engineer's logbook was duly stamped and his passing out parade was on Wednesday 19 August, at which he was presented with his flight engineer's winged Brevet. At the same time, he, together with all successful students who were now qualified in a flying trade, was immediately promoted from LAC to Sergeant.[5] Despite his background and experience with radial engines and the introduction of the Lancaster, Jack specialised in the Merlin V12 inline engine. Following his passing out parade it is no surprise that he was posted to a Lancaster squadron.

Example of flight engineer's logbook (Sergeant Webb 467 Squadron).

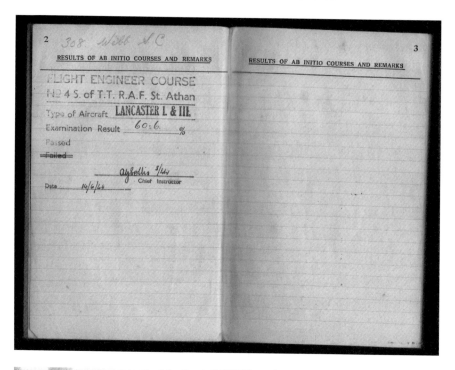

Above: Example of flight engineer's qualification stamp (Sergeant Web 467 Squadron).

Left: Jack with his winged flight engineer's Brevet.

Joining an Operational Squadron

On Friday 21 August 1942, Jack arrived at RAF Wigsley, a satellite station of RAF Swinderby in Lincolnshire to 1654 HCU. With the introduction of the four-engine heavy bombers, the Royal Air Force had created Heavy Conversion Units (HCU) to retrain crews experienced on medium bombers, and flight engineers recently graduated to operate the heavy bombers before final posting to an operational squadron.

During the initial days following his arrival at RAF Wigsley, Jack was engaged in more ground school activities. From his quarters and the Sergeants' Mess he would walk to the 'Flights', the offices and crew rooms of the HCU which contained the classrooms, parachute section and changing rooms. Typically, Jack would have been expected to get some flight time while HCU training. Some HCU crews even took part in actual bombing raids, but it seems that Jack did neither. His posting to 1654 HCU was summarily brief. It is not recorded whether he volunteered or was allocated, but less than a week later he was posted to an operational Lancaster crew of 50 Squadron based at RAF Swinderby.

50 Squadron Lancasters at RAF Swinderby 1942 (Lancaster R5689 (VN-N) in the foreground is possibly the most photographed Lancaster of Second World War).

31

Avro Lancaster Crew

It seems that Pilot Officer Drew Wyness from Sale, near Manchester, was in need of a new flight engineer. Whether his regular flight engineer was ill or had completed his operational tour isn't known, but on 25 August, just four days after arriving at Swinderby, Jack joined Wyness' crew of Pilot Officer Kauffling, Sergeant Oldridge, Pilot Officer Spedding, Sergeant Newman, and Sergeant Gurden at 50 Squadron. Jack's first-hand involvement in the war had just become much closer.

The Avro Lancaster consisted of seven crew members. Once a crew had come together they were a tight knit team, wholly dependent and reliant on each other. Typically, their strong comradeship existed from the moment they formed until they were either shot down or disbanded and existed both in the air and on the ground.

The pilot, regardless of rank, was the captain of the crew. His seat was on the left-hand side of the cockpit on a raised platform, it was the only position in the aircraft with armoured protection. He was responsible for controlling the aircraft both on the ground and in the air. The rest of the crew were totally dependent on him, his skills, and on his decision making. He was the leader and had to know the duties of all the crew members and what they were doing at all times. Gibson in his book *Enemy Coast Ahead* describes his duty as a Lancaster pilot: 'The pilot of a bomber must know everything. He must know the duties of the rest of the crew inside out, and should be able to take on any one of them should the occasion arise.'

At the right-hand side of the pilot, the flight engineer had a simple pull-down collapsible canvas seat, known as a 'second dickey'. There were no dual controls, though some flight engineers were trained to take over from the pilot and fly a Lancaster straight and level if needed. The flight engineer was responsible for the management (and running repairs) of the engines, propellers, fuel, flight, and oxygen systems. His instruments were on the main control panel directly in front and also behind on the right-hand fuselage bulkhead.

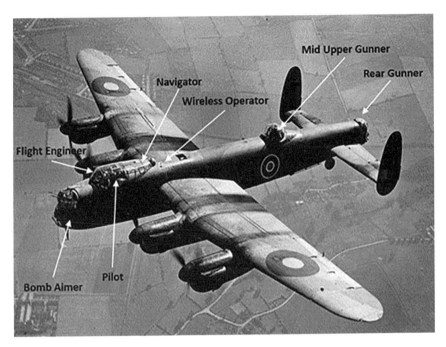

Aircrew positions in standard Avro Lancaster B.III.

Lancaster flight engineer checks the instruments on his console The second dickey seat can be seen folded in its stowed position.

Flight engineers tended to be very much overlooked as an aircrew category. They were usually non-commissioned and regarded by some, quite erroneously, as being 'blue collar' and less well educated than pilots and navigators, who were considered 'white collar'. Gibson, often regarded as aloof and dictatorial, had high praise for them however: 'The flight engineer is the pilot's mate and sits beside him watching the engine instruments. Most flight engineers were ground mechanics of Bomber Command who have volunteered to fly on operations, and a grand job of work they do too.' Yet few received the acknowledgement they deserved; they were the interface between the aircrew and ground crew, and many had some of the best technical training the RAF could provide. They also, along with the gunners, had probably the most uncomfortable position in the aircraft, with only a collapsible canvas 'perch', which many chose not to bother with for most of the time. Their view out of the cockpit, however, was excellent.

At the front of the Lancaster, the bomb aimer had two duties. His main duty was to release the bomb load accurately. His location was lying prone (or kneeling) in the Perspex nose blister, with bombsight and bomb release controls. He also acted as front gunner, climbing into the nose turret and sitting on a simple canvas seat.

Directly behind the pilot sat the navigator, facing the port side of the fuselage. He was equipped with a blackout curtain, his navigational instruments, and a desk for his charts. His primary duty was to ensure the aircraft was accurately directed to and from the target destination.

The wireless operator is often considered to have had the cosiest seat in a Lancaster. He sat behind the navigator, just in front of the wing spar facing forward and next to the heated cabin air outlet. His desk contained all the necessary radio equipment and Morse key.

The mid-upper gunner was located in the dorsal turret and was on constant alert, scanning and protecting from enemy fighters from all sides.

The rear gunner also sat for the duration of a mission protecting the Lancaster's vulnerable rear. Often (as with front gunners) when on low flying missions they would (after seeking the pilot's permission) shoot at opportunistic targets as they flew over.

First Tour of Duty

Jack didn't get much time to adjust to being in an operational squadron. It is not known if he was able to participate in any training flights, but it is assumed he did. Only four days after joining 50 Squadron his Lancaster and crew were allocated to his first operational mission, his first 'op'. I will elaborate on his duties and activities prior to and during the mission in later chapters.

During the night of 25–26 August 1942, twelve Lancasters from 50 Squadron, including Jack's, were detailed for a bombing mission to Kassel. They departed RAF Swinderby starting at around 20:30 and were part of a total of 306 assembled for the attack. The weather conditions were good and there was only a light wind. The attacking force was split into three sections. The first section contained the Pathfinders,[6] who used their flares to illuminate the most important targets in the city centre – the Henschel armaments works (codenamed Bream), the marshalling yard (codenamed Smolt) and the surrounding city block. Following these were the bombers who released their load, and finally, four selected crews surveyed the damage and results of the attack.

It was quite a costly mission, a total of thirty-one aircraft failed to return. All twelve 50 Squadron Lancasters returned safely, however, despite one of the Lancasters being fired upon (without damage) by a Vickers Wellington rear gunner when the aircraft passed under the Wellington. Jack had completed his first op successfully and received a 50 Squadron 'op Bomber Card' to commemorate the event.

There was no time to reflect. The very next night, Friday 27 August, Jack's crew were detailed for another attack on Germany. This time it was Nuremburg. However, after crossing the English Channel, Jack's Lancaster developed an (unspecified) technical fault and had to abort the mission and returned without reaching their target; they landed back at RAF Swinderby at around 00:30.

50 Squadron Commemorative Bomber Card for Kassel 25-26/8/1942.

He had no ops over the following weekend and found time to start writing a letter home. Interestingly, the letter describes how his crew were given 'Wakey Wakey' pills to keep them awake while on a mission. These were more than likely Caffeine tablets, but may have been the amphetamine-based Benzedrine. Whatever they were, they had worked effectively on his first op the previous Thursday night, but because he had returned early on the Friday, he couldn't get to sleep and spent hours playing snooker to try and tire himself out. He finished his letter on the evening of Monday 30 August, after an op planned for that night was cancelled due to bad weather, and he gloats that he was able to get a full flying supper despite the mission being cancelled.

Letter 29/08/42 from RAF Swinderby. (Transcript on p.288)

1003474 Sgt J Marriott
Sergeants Mess
R.A.F Swinderby
Nr Lincoln, Lincs

(Saturday)

Dear Flos Fred & Norma,

Just a few quick lines to let you know I have not forgotten you although I'll bet you will be thinking I have. But since arriving back here on Tuesday things have certainly moved.

I expect you will know I did my first op on Thursday night. (Monday night) I will try & finish this off now. Upto half an hour ago we were due for a trip tonight but the weather over most of the course was or is lousy so we don't play.

I received four letters today the only ones I've had since I came here apart from one that was re-addressed from Barry.

I would have written before but with being moved around

so much I didn't get chance I have however ben to Lincoln once or twice & to Newark which is about the same distance away I had hoped to arrange a meeting with Arthur in Lincoln but from May's letters he is going to Scotland. I believe Alf is some where near Newark though so may-be I shall see him. I'm hoping to get a 48 on the 10 or 11th of this month & as I'm not all that far off it should be worth it. I saw one of Lowe's waggons from Whaley in Lincoln the other night so for once I am within striking distance of home.

Well there doesn't seem much else to say. I'm afraid your parcel is still following me around as I have not seen anything of it.

Being in the Sergeants Mess the grub is quite good. We had bacon, egg & fried bread at 8 o'clock tonight. You only get these kind of suppers when you are due for ops though. We diddled them tonight with not going. ~~~~

We get biscuits, chocolate raisens & chewing gum to take with us & also coffee. We can also take some kind of pill to keep you awake. I had one on Thursday which was OK, but on Friday when we set off & had to come back after a couple of hours the one I had kept me awake so I had to play snooker when we got back at about 12.30 to try & get tired.

Anyway folks I'll call it a day now.

So Cheerio
Love - Jack.

The following night, Tuesday 1 September, Jack was back on ops, detailed for a night bombing mission to Saarbrücken. Jack's crew were once again one of twelve 50 Squadron Lancasters included in the 205 aircraft on the mission. The 50 Squadron Operational Record Book (ORB) states that visibility was excellent, the raid was virtually unopposed by flak,[7] fighters or searchlights, and all twelve Lancasters returned successfully. However, this was possibly due to the fact that the Pathfinders had marked a town which they believed to be Saarbrücken, which the main force bombed vigorously. But the town bombed was in reality Saarlouis, thirteen miles to the north-west and situated in a similar bend of the River Saar. The small, non-industrial town and its surrounding villages were heavily damaged while no bombs fell on Saarbrücken. One of the pilots from 106 Squadron was Guy Gibson, who sustained flak damage to his starboard wing.

Ops were coming thick and fast. The very next night, Wednesday 2 September, Jack's crew was one of nine Lancasters provided by 50 Squadron to a force of 200 bombers that attacked Karlsruhe. This time the Pathfinders were spot on and the attack successful. Defences were reported as being very quiet and all nine 50 Squadron Lancasters returned safely to base.

Two days later, on Friday 4 September, 50 Squadron provided sixteen Lancasters for a concerted attack of 251 bombers on Bremen. Despite

50 Squadron Commemorative Bomber Card for Karlsruhe 2-3/9/1942.

heavy defences only one of the 50 Squadron Lancasters sustained minor flak damage, but all sixteen returned safely.

During this time the squadron continued to reorganise. 50 Squadron Conversion Flight was being absorbed into 1654 HCU and as it expanded, more and more Lancasters were being delivered straight from the Avro production lines.

Saturday 5 September was a rest day, but the following day Jack was again on ops, part of ten 50 Squadron Lancasters allocated to a bomber force of 207 aircraft for a night bombing mission to Duisburg. One of the Lancasters was overturned after flak exploded beneath it, fortunately it was recovered by the pilot performing a diving roll. Another suffered flak damage to the port-inner engine which was feathered, causing hydraulic failure; two holes were also made in the tail and rudder. All ten Lancasters returned to base but for Jack, the realities of war were coming ever nearer.

Tuesday 8 September was only two weeks after Jack had joined 50 Squadron, but it was already his seventh op. Eleven Lancasters from 50 Squadron formed part of 249 aircraft taking part in a raid on Frankfurt. Gibson with 106 Squadron also took part in the raid. Although the Pathfinder force had dropped their flares, scattered ground haze and a very dark night made for poor bombing accuracy. Flying Officer Calvert in one of the other 50 Squadron Lancasters commented in his Logbook 'Too many searchlights – Shaky Do.'

A day of rest was followed by another op on 10 September. Eleven Lancasters from 50 Squadron were part of 479 aircraft that took part that night on a raid to Düsseldorf. The Pathfinders successfully marked the target using 'Pink Pansies' flares.[8] The conditions were good and visibility excellent. Over 100,000 bombs were dropped in less than an hour. All eleven Lancasters returned safely, though one had turned back before releasing its bombs due to faulty guns.

A very short break followed during which the whole of 50 Squadron posed for a team photograph in front of one of their Lancasters and framed by RAF Swinderby's distinctive twin water towers. Several members of the squadron in the photograph were also later to be transferred to 617 Squadron

Ops resumed on Friday 18 September when another eleven Lancasters from 50 Squadron undertook 'Gardening' (mine laying) operations. A total of 115 bombers participated, 50 Squadron provided two at 'Nasturtium' (Copenhagen, Denmark, Sound North), two at 'Elderberry' (Bayonne, France), two at 'Pollock' (Bornholm, Denmark), three at 'Willow' (Sassnitz, Germany), one at 'Daffodil' (Copenhagen, Denmark, Sound South), and one at 'Quinces' (Kiel Bay, Germany).

50 Squadron Commemorative Bomber Card for Düsseldorf 10-11/9/1942.

50 Squadron RAF Swinderby – August 1942 1-Jack Marriott 2-Drew Wyness 3-Mick Martin 4-Jack Leggo 5-Bob Hay 6-Frank Martin 7-Tammy Simpson 8-Henry Smith 9-James O'Neill

The destination of Jack's Lancaster is not recorded, but one of the Lancasters at Nasturtium had mechanical problems and was unable to open its bomb doors, and another R5689 (VN-N) crashed on final approach when it returned to RAF Swinderby. Its port inner engine had failed and the crew mistakenly feathered (shut-down) the port outer causing the Lancaster to crash and burst into flames killing four members of the crew. It must have been a sobering realisation for Jack of how delicate and important his role was within the crew, and how maximum concentration must be maintained at all times from start-up to final shut-down.

Jack didn't have time to dwell on it. The very next night eighty-nine bombers attacked Munich. Jack was in one of five aircraft provided by 50 Squadron Lancaster; W4117 (VN-R) returned after only fifteen minutes, but the other four completed their mission successfully.

Jack's next op was on 23 September. The target for a total eighty-three bombers, with eleven Lancasters from 50 Squadron, was the Baltic city of Wismar and the nearby aircraft factory of Norddeutsche Dornier-Werke. There was low cloud, no moon and poor visibility. Several aircraft were hit by flak and only five aircraft managed to bomb the target with any degree of accuracy; one of the Lancasters failed to return.

Lancaster R5689 (VN-N) after crash landing on return to RAF Swinderby 18 September 1942.

Following the attack on Wismar, Jack had a break from ops. 50 Squadron and 1654 HCU continued to develop and grow. On 3 October, Flying Officer Henry Maudslay arrived as an instructor to 1654 HCU. He had completed a tour with 44 Squadron, had helped test the Lancaster's suitability during pre-service introduction trials at A&AEE Boscombe Down, and though officially posted to 1654 HCU in June he had been seconded back to 44 Squadron. A serious motorbike accident on 9 August kept him away from flying, but having recovered from his accident he began conversion training for Lancaster pilots. He checked-out several pilots (Astell, Barlow, Brown, and Munro) who were later to join him at 617 Squadron. He struck up a particularly strong friendship with Bill Astell, whose home was in the Derbyshire village of Combs near Chapel-en-le-Frith. It was just over a mile from Jack's home in New Smithy.

On Monday 5 October Jack was again on ops. He was one of ten 50 Squadron Lancasters from a force of 257 bombers detailed for an attack on Aachen. Despite flares dropped by the Pathfinder force there was poor visibility over the target area, and heavy flak caused considerable difficulties. Fortunately all aircraft returned, though Lancaster R5733 piloted by S/L G.H. 'Hughie' Everitt was hit by flak and lost both starboard engines. He nursed his Lancaster homeward but made a 'belly landing' at RAF West Malling in Kent.

Osnabrück was the next target on 6 October for 237 bombers, of which nine were provided by 50 Squadron. Jack's aircraft took off just after 19:30. Visibility over Osnabrück was poor with lots of ground haze. There was little flak activity, all nine Lancasters released their load and arrived safely back at RAF Swinderby around midnight.

On 11 October, Flight Lieutenant Harold Brownlow (Mick) Martin, one of the senior 50 Squadron pilots with a reputation for his low flying skills and meticulous pre-flight preparation, left the squadron. He had completed his tour of operations and was posted to 1654 HCU to undertake pilot training. After being awarded a DFC he happened to meet Guy Gibson, who was receiving a DSO, during their investiture at Buckingham Palace in February 1943. Gibson was impressed with Martin's knowledge of low-level flying so it is not surprising that Martin was one of the few pilots that Gibson actually personally invited to join 617 Squadron

On 12 October, Wismar was once again the target for fifty-nine bombers of No.5 Group. 50 Squadron provided eleven aircraft which departed RAF Swinderby around 18:00. Seven were detailed to bomb the town of Wismar, and the other four the Norddeutsche Dornier-Werke factory. Lancaster

W5154 returned early at around 20:00 with problems with one of its turrets. The targets were obscured by cloud, but the Norddeutsche Dornier-Werke factory was believed to have been heavily damaged, while some of the crews reported bombing the nearby city of Lübeck. Unfortunately, R5902 (VN-T) piloted by Sergeant Howard Rawlins was either hit by flak or a night fighter. The aircraft entered a tight spin and exploded. All but one of the crew were killed immediately.

The following night 288 bombers attacked Kiel. 50 Squadron provided nine Lancasters, it was the final operation flown by 50 Squadron from RAF Swinderby. The aircraft departed at 18:50, the weather and visibility were good en route and over the target. Opposition at Kiel was light, and all aircraft returned without damage or casualties. By this time Jack had flown sixteen ops since arriving with 50 Squadron less than two months previously.

50 Squadron returned to their former base at RAF Skellingthorpe which had been upgraded to a Class 'A' standard airfield. It had had a 350-yard extension to the main runway and the addition of further accommodation sites. During the move back no active ops were undertaken. However, the squadron, including Jack's crew, had for some time been in special training for a secret mission. Along with other No.5 Group aircraft they had practised low-level daytime formation flying.

On Saturday 17 October, the day following the completion of the move back to RAF Skellingthorpe, 50 Squadron Lancasters took part in Operation

Lancasters taxi for take-off

Robinson. A total of ninety-four aircraft took part in a top secret attack on the Schneider heavy industry and armaments factory at Le Creusot in the Burgundy region of eastern France. Previous RAF experience of daylight bombing at Augsburg and Danzig had been unsuccessful but with specialist training it was believed such a large force could be successful.

Eighty-eight of the bombers attacked the Schneider factory, while six attacked a power station at nearby Montchanin. All nine of No.5 Group squadrons supplied Lancasters. The operation was led by Wing Commander L.C. Slee, the CO[9] of 49 Squadron. Following his squadron out over the Atlantic was 9 Squadron, 44 Squadron, Jack's crew in one of twelve Lancasters provided by 50 Squadron, 57 Squadron, 61 Squadron, 97 Squadron, 106 Squadron and 207 Squadron. Guy Gibson led twelve Lancasters from 106 Squadron, which included pilots John Hopgood and Dave Shannon, all three of whom were later to join 617 Squadron with Jack. Gibson and Hopgood piloted two of the Lancasters that attacked the power station.

The aircraft started taking off around 12:00. Coastal Command Whitley bombers flew fifteen minutes ahead of the Lancasters to attack any German submarines, forcing them to remain submerged so they would not see the Lancasters and signal warnings. Fighter Command and aircraft from No.2 Group also attacked targets along the French coast in order to distract attention.

The nine squadrons joined up in a loose formation as they flew south from Land's End down passed Brittany and over the Bay of Biscay before turning inland south of Saint Nazaire. The formation was unescorted but met no opposition whatsoever. They flew at heights of between 50 and 500ft before most climbed to their bombing height of 4,000ft as they approached the town of Nevers, about fifty miles to the west of Le Creusot. Those detailed for the attack on the power station bombed from about 500ft. Gibson received superficial flak damage, Hopgood flew so low that the blast from his own bombs damaged his aircraft, and the only aircraft lost on the whole mission W5774 of 61 Squadron flown by Squadron Leader William Corr, which crashed into the power station.

As the sun was setting over Le Creusot more than 200 tons of bombs were dropped in less than ten minutes. One of the 50 Squadron Lancasters was unable to open its bomb doors so had to return complete with its bomb load, while all others returned individually by the fastest route. By the time the aircraft arrived back in Britain the weather had deteriorated and many Lancasters had to divert to airfields in the south of England. All 50 Squadron aircraft returned safely to RAF Skellingthorpe by 23:00 after flying for

No.5 Group Lancasters flying at low level over Montrichard on the River Cher in France towards Le Creusot.

about ten hours, except W4161 which had to divert to RAF Hinton-in-the-Hedges in Northamptonshire.

Though the mission was regarded as a great success, post-raid photographs revealed that destruction was not as complete as had been hoped, and many bombs had over-shot the target and destroyed many houses in a civilian workers' housing estate. Despite this, the attack was prominently reported in the daily newspapers.

On Monday 19 October the leader column in *The Daily Dispatch* featured a detailed description of the raid complete with a photo of Jack's pilot, Flying Officer Drew Wyness, and a group photo of 'Navigators, Machine-gunners, Wireless Operators, and Flight Engineers who took part in the Creusot raid'. Jack may well be one of them, but it is not possible to identify him.

Following the Le Creusot raid Jack was given a few days off. There were no 50 Squadron operations until 21 October, but Jack's next sortie was not until Saturday 24 October with another daylight mission, this time to Milan. 50 Squadron provided nine aircraft to a No.5 Group formation of seventy-one Lancasters. The aircraft took off just after 12:00 and despite

The Daily Dispatch 19/10/1942

MONDAY, OCTOBER 19, 1942

Some of the officers who took part in the Creuzot raid:— Back row (left to right): Flt.-Lt. Abercromby, Sqdn.-Ldr. Moore, D.F.C., and Sqdn.-Ldr. Everitt, D.F.C. and bar. Front row: Flying-Officer Wyness and Flying-Officer Calvert, D.F.C.

Left and below: The Daily Dispatch 19/10/1942.

A group of navigators, machine-gunners, wireless operators and flight engineers who just took part in the Creusot raid.

good visibility they encountered little defensive activity; Lancaster R5691 (VN-K) failed to return having crashed into the English Channel and W4135 was hit, having descended to treetop level to escape flak. All seven other aircraft dropped their bombs and successfully returned to base by 22:00.

It was then nearly two weeks until Jack's next sortie. Italy was again the target on Friday 6 November, and a night bombing mission to bomb the city of Genoa. 50 Squadron provided five aircraft which departed RAF Skellingthorpe from around 21.30 to complete a total of seventy-two Lancasters. The heating in a Lancaster was basic. The wireless operator was usually OK as the heater vent was by his position, but for the rest of the crew it was woefully inadequate. Jack, as with most flight engineers, was more often than not stood in the exposed cockpit during the high-altitude night operations and was often cold. Over 115 tons of bombs were dropped on Genoa and although two aircraft were shot down all five 50 Squadron Lancasters returned safely.

There was no rest for Jack. After a few hours sleep it was time for a briefing and then he prepared for another night sortie back to Genoa. It was the fourth and heaviest bombing raid of the war so far on the Italian city.

In total, 175 Lancasters had taken off with twelve provided by 50 Squadron. The weather was good and in total 237 tons of bombs were dropped on the city and the Ansaldo shipyard. Six Lancasters were lost but all twelve of the 50 Squadron aircraft had returned by 02:00, though three had been damaged by flak. Squadron Leader Moore in R5687 was hit in the port wing, damaging both engines. The port-inner had to be shut-down, with reduced power on the port-outer. His flight engineer suffered oxygen starvation due to the damage and was near to collapse, but still managed to help the Lancaster limp back to base. It must have been a stark reminder to Jack of the dangers he was facing. Lancaster W4267 was hit by flak which caused the aircraft to go out of control for a period, and another W4135 received flak damage to the rear turret and starboard tail.

Two days later Jack was back on a night-bombing sortie of Germany. The target was Hamburg, and the weather conditions were reported to be bad with heavy cloud and limited visibility.

Nine 50 Squadron Lancasters were part of a total force of 213 aircraft. One returned early because of engine problems and four of the Lancasters had to use 'dead reckoning'[10] to determine the drop zone and it is believed they may have bombed Hanover rather than Hamburg. Flak defences over the target were very aggressive, and fifteen aircraft were lost, including one Lancaster from 50 Squadron

In addition, Lancaster R5702 (VN-S), named 'Taipo', was hit by flak. Shrapnel and shattered Perspex peppered the aircraft and crew, cutting off the intercom between crew members. The pilot, Pilot Officer Roy Calvert, was hit in the face and arm and the aircraft started flying left-wing low due to loss of aileron trim and rudder bias systems. The navigator, Flight Sergeant Medani, RNZAF, was very badly wounded, and the wireless operator, Sergeant Lewis Herbert Austin RAAF, was killed outright, with the wireless and numerous other navigation aids put out of action while over the target. The crew managed to nurse the Lancaster back to Britain where it crash-landed at RAF Bradwell Bay with no further casualties.

Jack then had a break and managed to get a weekend pass. On Saturday 14 November he decided to have a weekend at home in New Smithy. He managed to get from 'Skelly' to nearby Lincoln and buy a train ticket to Sheffield. But without enough money for a ticket from Sheffield to Chinley he sneaked onto the Sheffield to Manchester train. Avoiding the guard wasn't difficult in a train packed with rowdy servicemen. As the train passed slowly over the Hayfield Road bridge on the approach to Chinley station, Jack climbed out and scrambled down the embankment. He was less than 100yds from home.

Floss was horrified that he had risked the journey without a ticket and wasn't going to let him go back by the same method and bought him his return ticket to Lincoln. Floss was also concerned that he had been cold on his missions, so she lent him one of her husband Fred's thick knitted

New Smithy from Hayfield Road bridge. Middleton House is behind the low wall on the right just after the Crown and Mitre.

pullovers. It wasn't quite the right size, but fortunately it was air force blue, so suitable for RAF aircrew. Floss promised to knit Jack a sweater of his own and swap it back for Fred's.

Following his break, Jack was again detailed for a night attack on a German target. On Sunday 22 November, a mixed formation of 222 aircraft including ninety-seven Lancasters, fifty-nine Wellingtons, thirty-nine Halifaxes, and twenty-seven Stirlings attacked Stuttgart. 50 Squadron supplied nine Lancasters, but two had to return home with technical issues. The remaining seven released their bombs and most dropped leaflets ('nickels') before returning safely to base with no reported casualties. Jack, though, was a little more comfortable with his new non-standard item of flying clothing.

There was another break of a week before Jack was detailed on 28 November for a night raid on Turin. It completed his raids on Italy's so-called 'industrial triangle' of Milan, Genoa, and Turin. It was the third 'area bombing' raid on the Italian city and from a total of 228 bombers, Jack was one of the six from 50 Squadron. In total, 371 tons of bombs were dropped on the Fiat Plants and on the city, including the 8,000lb blockbuster bombs used for the first time in Italy. Visibility was good and flak was intense. Three aircraft were shot down but all six 50 Squadron Lancasters landed safely, though one was hit by flak and returned on three engines.

Jack's next op was just over a week later on 6 December, with a night raid on Mannheim. Ten Lancasters of 50 Squadron departed RAF Skellingthorpe, but four were detailed for Gardening and to drop sea-mines in the 'Nectarine' area. The other six, including Jack, joined a force of 272 aircraft in the strategic bombing of Mannheim. Jack's usual navigator, Pilot Officer Spedding, was ill and replaced by a Sergeant Gurney. One of the Lancasters failed to reach the target because a crew member became ill due to lack of oxygen and the Lancaster returned early. All ten aircraft returned to base, though one had diverted to RAF Wyton.

Two days later Jack took part in the fifth area bombing raid on Turin. Pilot Officer Spedding had recovered and returned. Ten Lancasters of 50 Squadron departed to join a force of 133 bombers. One returned early with technical issues and the other nine dropped their bombs damaging the city centre, university, and the Fiat factory. One Lancaster was shot down over Turin, but the nine 50 Squadron Lancasters all successfully returned to base.

Jack was one of ten 50 Squadron Lancasters the following night that returned to Turin. Again, one Lancaster returned early with technical issues but the other nine joined another 123 aircraft. Though visibility was good, and flak was light, smoke from the previous night's raid restricted accurate bombing. A total of 393 tons of bombs was dropped and three aircraft lost, but all 50 Squadron Lancasters returned to base successfully.

It was Jack's last op with Drew Wyness and the crew with whom he had formed a strong bond, both professionally and socially, over the fifteen weeks since he joined 50 Squadron. Most of the crew had finished their thirty-op tour of duty. Jack had almost completed a tour, having taken part in twenty-six operations. On 11 December his Service Record was updated. Once again, his character assessment was VG, his Proficiency Column A (trade ability) was 'sat' (satisfactory), and as it was his first review since becoming a sergeant, Proficiency Column B (supervisory ability) was also 'sat'.

Confusingly, even at the end of 1942, the length of an operational bomber tour was not formalised. A tour was usually regarded as being thirty ops, however it could sometimes be granted for fewer ops. Similarly, the length of time on non-operational duties between active ops was of an undefined period of time, though it was usually considered to be up to nine months for flying crew members. After his last op on 9 December Jack had a short leave break. To ensure he travelled home legally, Floss had sent him the cost of a return train ticket. He returned Fred's blue pullover – proudly announcing in his jovial, cocky manner that it had been touring over Turin.

On his return to RAF Skelligthorpe, Jack waited to be allocated to a new crew. 50 Squadron continued on ops, though weather restricted the number of flights through December and into January. Crew reorganisations continued. On 1 January 1943, Henry Maudslay who had been promoted to flight lieutenant, joined the squadron from his pilot training duties at 1654 HCU. Two days later Wyness (who Jack had confided to his family that he held in high respect) was posted the opposite way, joining 1654 HCU as an instructor.

It's not recorded what Jack's activities were through the January and February of 1943. Maudslay, though, undertook nine missions, including ops over Germany, Italy and France, during which time he was finalising his operational crew. Jack joined the Maudslay crew toward the end of February. His first flight with Maudslay, perhaps a check out, was on Sunday 21 February, when they flew in Lancaster W4823 on a short flight to RAF Waddington.

There was no immediate return to ops for Jack because the following Wednesday his new pilot left for a week's leave. Maudslay returned on 2 March and the following night, with his finalised crew, was included on the night's Battle Order. The target was once again Hamburg. Maudslay, presumably accompanied by Jack, undertook a short air test of about thirty minutes during the afternoon and following their briefing, took off in Lancaster W4823 (VN-F) with seven other 50 Squadron Lancasters at 19:00.

They were part of a force of 417 aircraft. One of the 50 Squadron Lancasters (ED483) had a technical problem and had to return early. The 50 Squadron Lancasters avoided a mass of search lights to the north of Hamburg and though they had departed RAF Skellingthorpe into a cloudless night, by the time they reached their target there was poor visibility and significant ground haze.

Their Pathfinders had marked the wrong target, mistaking a mud bank for the docks with their recently introduced H2S[11] radar. Maudslay had been briefed to bomb the large Altona railway station but as with many of the bombers that night they released their load downstream from the centre of Hamburg, around the small town of Wedel causing considerable damage. A total of ten aircraft were lost but all 50 Squadron Lancasters returned safely.

As Jack's flying logbook doesn't exist there is no record of his non-operational flying activities. However, as he was confirmed as Maudslay's permanent flight engineer we can assume he accompanied Maudslay during all his flying activities. So, on Friday 5 March he and Maudslay were driven the short distance to RAF Waddington to collect a new Lancaster ED693.

The next day they were flying in Lancaster ED478 (VN-G) on fighter affiliation, air firing, and 'Tinsel Tests'.[12] This was followed on 7 March flying again in ED478 (VN-G) performing air tests and multi-engine shutdown.

They were flying again during the day of 9 March, putting Lancaster W4161 (VN-J) through an air test. No sooner had they landed than they were briefed for a mission that night. Their target was deep into Germany to attack the southern city of Munich.

In Lancaster ED415 (VN-C), Jack joined another nine 50 Squadron Lancasters were among 142 Lancasters, 81 Halifaxes, and 41 Stirlings. Two of the 50 Squadron Lancasters returned early, the others pressed on against strong headwinds and suffered intense flak. Bombing from 12,500ft was only partially successful as the area was obscured by smoke. One of the 61 Squadron Lancasters was shot down over Munich and seven others failed to return, but once again all 50 Squadron Lancasters returned to base.

Jack's crew had a day off flying, then on 11 March the whole crew undertook an air-firing exercise which gave all of them, and particularly the gunners, practice at shooting target drones towed by single-engine Miles Martinet target tugs.

Miles Martinet target tug.

It seems that following the exercise Maudslay vacated his pilot's seat and gave members of the crew the opportunity to take control of the Lancaster. No doubt Jack would have relished the opportunity, but in Jack's case it would have served to ensure that should Maudslay be severely injured and unable to fly while on a mission, Jack would at least have had some experience of handling the heavy aeroplane.

That night the Commanding Officer of 106 Squadron, Wing Commander Guy Gibson, completed his final op of his third tour from RAF Syerston in Nottinghamshire. It was an eventful trip to Stuttgart as he had to shut-down one of his engines and rather than return to base he continued his mission on three engines, flying low throughout the raid. He had expected to go on leave to Cornwall and was surprised to be summoned to HQ No.5 Group where he was told he was being posted, ostensibly, to write a book, (as he describes in *Enemy Coast Ahead*) 'for the benefit of the would-be bomber pilot'.

Jack was back on the Battle Order the following night. 50 Squadron provided ten Lancasters in a raid of 457 aircraft on a night-bombing raid to Essen. Jack's crew were in their familiar Lancaster ED415 (VN-C), and with the rest of No.5 Group, bombers attacked the huge Krupps heavy armaments factory. Maudslay attacked towards the end of the raid at around 21:40. Twenty-three aircraft failed to return from the raid, including 50 Squadron's Lancaster B. Mk. III ED449 (VN-T).

From 15 to 21 March 1943 crews were briefed on six consecutive days but operations were cancelled at the last minute due to fog and early morning mists. Jack's crew, though, were able to undertake further air tests and training exercises in Maudslay's previous Lancaster ED475 (VN-D).

Three 'old' 50 Squadron Lancasters which hadn't been used on ops since February had been flown over to nearby Scampton, home of 57 Squadron. At 09:15 on 15 March they were destroyed by fire on the ground in the morning fog. They had been stored close to where several 57 Squadron Lancasters had been parked in preparation for take-off the previous evening, nose to tail, around the airfield perimeter track after fog had come down, making it too hazardous to taxi the aircraft back to their dispersals. 57 Squadron Lancaster W4834 had returned with its bomb load and as it was being removed, it seems its 4,000lb 'Cookie' exploded.

It was completely destroyed, as were the three 50 Squadron Lancasters W4112 (VN-L), W4196 and W4823 (VN-F), along with two further 57 Squadron machines (ED306 and ED594). A further five 57 Squadron Lancasters (R5751, W4376, W4797, W4822, and ED706) were also damaged. It was the worst incident of its type in 1943 and illustrates one of the benefits of having widely separated aircraft dispersals. It is believed that the three 50 Squadron aircraft had possibly been flown to Scampton to

The devastation from an exploding 4,000lb bomb after a Lancaster crashed on take-off from RAF Croft.

participate in ops on 14–15 May, but there is some speculation they were there in preparation for the creation of the (at that time secret) 617 Squadron

On Monday 22 March, Jack's crew were flying and practising 'Beam Approaches'. This was an early form of ILS[13] and required close cooperation between Jack and Maudslay during their airfield approaches. This was followed by a practice bombing exercise at the Wainfleet Bombing Range just off the Lincolnshire coast. When they got back to Scampton, they learned that they were detailed for ops again that night.

It was another night-bombing raid and the target was the Kriegsmarine U-boat pens at St Nazaire on the French coast of Brittany. Ten of the 50 Squadron Lancasters formed part of a large force of 357 aircraft from No.3, 4, 5, and 6 Groups. Most of the Stirlings provided by No.3 Group were recalled early and one of the ten 50 Squadron Lancasters returned with technical problems. All the others reached the target, but two found their bombs had 'hung-up' (failed to release). The remaining seven attacked their designated targets but with unclear results.

On their return they found that the poor weather that had restricted ops during the previous days had returned and most of the Lancasters had to land at airfields in the south of England. Maudslay landed at RAF

50 Squadron March 1943.

Abingdon in Oxfordshire where the crew spent the night, returning to RAF Skellingthorpe during the morning of 23 March.

The weather once again restricted ops from 23 to 25 March, but the lack of flying presented the opportunity for a new squadron photo – complete with a backdrop of the impressive Avro Lancaster.

By this time Gibson had spent some days at No.5 Group HQ at Grantham. It seems that there was no work done in the preparation of his book and he was called in to see the recently appointed CO of No.5 Group, AVM Ralf Cochrane, who wasted no words and asked, 'How would you like the idea of doing one more trip ... a pretty important one.' Gibson's character is well documented, so it's no surprise that he accepted the offer.

Gibson writes in his book that he heard nothing more for a few days, then he was called in to see Cochrane again. This time he was given a little more detail but not the actual target, though he suspected it was the German battleship *Tirpitz*. Cochrane went on to say that special low-level training over water would be required, and a dedicated squadron with the best possible crews would be set up. Scampton only had a single squadron (57 Squadron) so was selected as the base, all No.5 Group squadrons would provide crews and donate Lancasters.

Squadron X

Gibson arrived at RAF Scampton during the afternoon of Sunday 21 March 1943. The airfield was waiting to have its grass runway extended and converted to concrete. He was allocated Hangar No.2 with the squadron offices in a two-story, long, flat-roofed annex attached to the north side facing the runway. Gibson's office was at the far west end of the corridor on the first floor. He immediately set about the process of creating a new squadron. While a number was being formalised the new squadron was temporarily, as with all new squadrons without a confirmed number, known simply as Squadron X.

One of his first tasks was to arrange for the crews. For a squadron comprising two flights of ten aircraft, he needed twenty additional crews. Contrary to popular myth, Gibson neither knew all the pilots nor selected them all himself, despite writing:

> It took me an hour to pick my pilots. I wrote all the names down on a piece of paper ... I had picked them all myself because from my own personal knowledge I believed them to be the best bomber pilots available. I knew that each one of them had already done his full tour of duty and should really now be having a well-earned rest; and I knew also that there was nothing any of them would want less than this rest when they heard that there was an exciting operation on hand.

It's true that he knew Hopgood and Burpee from 106 Squadron, Shannon had also been with him at 106 Squadron and on completion of his tour had been transferred to 83 Squadron. Gibson had also met Martin and discussed low flying at their medal investiture, but the rest were either recommended by their squadron CO or had responded to a request posted to all No.5 Group squadrons for volunteer crews for a special mission.

The preparation for this special mission had been going on for some time. Seven reservoir dams had been identified, five in the industrial Ruhr Valley (Möhne, Sorpe, Lister, Ennepe, and Henne) and two further to the east in the Weser Valley (Eder and Diemel). The Möhne, Eder and Sorpe Dams were the primary targets and all the others were secondary.

It was believed that if these could be destroyed it would significantly disrupt German industrial war production and electricity supply, cause significant and untold disruption below the dams, reduce morale, and then during their repair, divert German resources away from other military construction programmes.

Though the idea of attacking German and Italian dams had been considered as early as 1937, there were several issues preventing a realistic attack plan. First, any bomb would have to be considerably heavier than any contemporary RAF aircraft were capable of carrying. Second, conventional bombing would have required an accuracy impossible to achieve. Torpedo nets in the water prevented any type of torpedo attack.

By 1942 the aircraft engineer Barnes Wallis had come up with a unique design for skipping a bomb across the water of the reservoir, over the torpedo nets to hit the dam wall and then sink in contact with the dam wall to a depth where the water pressure would assist the explosion in breaching the dam. His testing, famously, had started with marble experiments, had progressed through experiments in water tanks at the National Physics Laboratory, scale model dams at the Building Research Establishment and

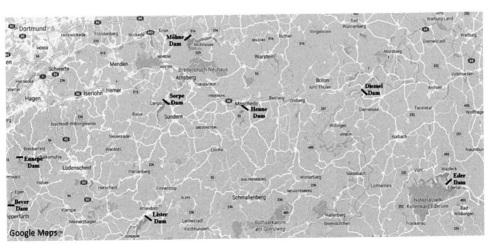

Location of the seven initial target dams (and the Bever Dam).

the Road Research Laboratory, to a successful test explosion on an unused dam at Nant-y-Gro Reservoir in Wales. Two types of bomb were being developed, the Highball for use against ships, and the larger version that was given the codename 'Upkeep' for use against dams. Test releases from a specially converted Vickers Wellington started badly but were eventually successful.

The 'Bouncing Bomb' thus came into being. However, though it is always known as this, it is a convenient but misleading term! In the first instance, the Upkeep wasn't technically a 'bomb', as these are explosive stores that detonate on impact, or following impact with a delayed fuse. It is usually described as a 'mine', but again this is a misleading term as a mine is an explosive device that is placed in a location and detonates on contact with, or in proximity to, its target. The Upkeep was more correctly a 'depth charge', which is a weapon that explodes at a predetermined depth using a hydrostatic trigger. For the Upkeep, Wallis determined that this was 30ft below the reservoir water level for maximum destructive power. Nor did the Upkeep 'bounce', which is a physical property whereby there is a change in direction after hitting an obstacle; the Upkeep didn't change direction, it skipped or skimmed across the water following its release. By adding backspin, it aided the skipping process but more importantly, it ensured that the Upkeep stayed in contact with the inner face of the dam wall as it sank to its predetermined depth before exploding.

The Upkeep was developed and produced by the Vickers Company as the Vickers Type 464 modifications. Initially, it had been designed with a wooden spherical casing which surrounded a cylindrical metal core containing 6,600lb of Torpex high explosive. But in trials, the outer casing shattered on impact with the water leaving the central cylinder to continue. Its overall weight was over 4 tons and it had three hydrostatic pistols. There was also a 'self-destruct' detonation by a fuse, which could be armed automatically as the bomb was dropped from the aircraft, or manually if it had to be jettisoned.

The final operational version of the Upkeep was a cylinder 60 inches long with a diameter of 50 inches. Fortunately, by May 1943 the Lancaster heavy bomber had been in service for over a year. It was reliable, fast, and capable of carrying a massive load. However, it required extensive and elaborate modifications in order to deliver the Upkeep. The Lancaster's manufacturer, Avro, worked in close collaboration with Vickers to produce twenty-three modified Lancasters. These were taken straight from the production line at Avro's Woodford facility and converted in a secret hangar. Their designation was the Avro Lancaster B.III Type 464 Provisioning, to denote that they had been provisioned for the specific task of carrying the Vickers Type 464 Upkeep.

The modifications were extensive. The huge bomb bay doors were removed, and a pair of aluminium and steel V-shaped callipers were installed to carry Upkeep, which would be swung apart to release Upkeep. Backspin was provided by a Vickers Variable Speed Gear motor forward of the callipers, operated from the wireless operator's position. The ventral turret position (which was only present in a few of the Lancasters) was fared over, as were the parts of the bomb bay forward and to the rear of the callipers. The dorsal mid-upper turret was also removed to save weight with the gunner, which was normally a permanent position moving to the front turret. Because of the very specific nature of the operation the role of the crew differed slightly to that of a standard Lancaster, with additional roles undertaken when attacking the target.

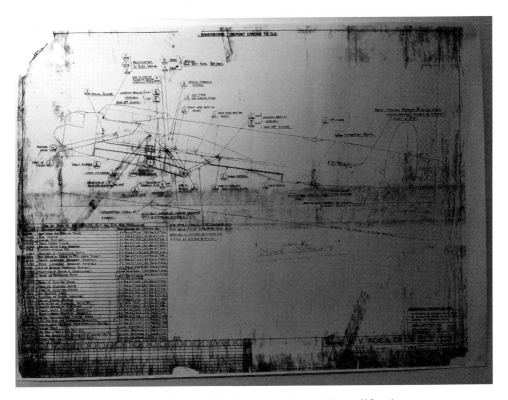

Avro original drawing of some of the Lancaster Type 464 modifications.

The crew positions of the Lancaster Type 464 also changed in order to accommodate the changed and additional roles required in the delivery of the Upkeep.

Standard Lancaster	Lancaster Type 464
Pilot	Pilot
Flight Engineer / co-Pilot	Flight Engineer / co-Pilot
Navigator	Navigator / height monitor
Wireless Operator	Wireless Operator / controlling Upkeep
Bomb Aimer / Front Gunner	Bomb Aimer / co-Navigator
Mid-upper Gunner	Front Gunner
Rear Gunner	Rear Gunner

Internally, few of the converted Lancaster Type 464s were identical as additional equipment and minor modifications were undertaken up until the night of the raid. All had the manual Upkeep release though, which was a T-shaped handle just in front of the pilot's trim controls, and an additional super-sensitive altimeter at the pilot's eye level on the dashboard so he didn't need to look down when flying at low level. Most were eventually fitted with 'fighter-type' VHF radio sets to enable communication between aircraft during the mission.

By the time Gibson arrived at Scampton the development of the Upkeep, its method of delivery, and the modified Lancaster to carry it, was well under way, but none of it was complete and it was all still top secret. In order that Squadron X could start their low-flying practice, ten standard Lancasters were transferred (albeit eight temporarily) from other No.5 Group bomber squadrons as below.

Reg.	617 Sqn. code	Date allocated	Providing squadron	Lancaster version	Manufacturer
W4921	AJ-C	26/03/1943	106 Sqn.	B.I	Metropolitan-Vickers
W4926	AJ-Z	27/03/1943	97 Sqn.	BI	Metropolitan-Vickers
W4929	AJ-J	26/03/1943	61 Sqn.	B.I	Metropolitan-Vickers
W4940	AJ-B	27/03/1943	57 Sqn.	B.I	Metropolitan-Vickers
ED329	AJ-T	27/03/1943	207 Sqn.	B.I	Avro Chadderton
ED437	AJ-N	27/03/1943	50 Sqn.	B.III	Avro Chadderton
ED735	AJ-R	27/03/1943	44 Sqn.	B.I	Avro Chadderton

Reg.	617 Sqn. code	Date allocated	Providing squadron	Lancaster version	Manufacturer
ED756	AJ-H	30/03/1943	49 Sqn.	B.III	Avro Chadderton
ED763	AJ-D	02/04/1943	467 Sqn.	B.III	Avro Chadderton
LM309	AJ-X	27/03/1943	9 Sqn.	B.I	Avro Yeadon

On Wednesday 24 March, Gibson was taken to meet Barnes Wallis in secret at Burhill near Weybridge. Though Wallis was frustrated that he could not reveal the actual targets, he nevertheless outlined the requirements and showed Gibson films of the Upkeep trials.

The same day over at RAF Skellingthorpe, Maudslay, much to his surprise, was notified that he was being promoted to squadron leader and posted to a new squadron at Scampton with his complete crew, where he would be a flight commander. It seems that he hadn't responded to the request for volunteers, and although neither Jack nor the rest of the crew realised it, they were about to join the RAF's most elite squadron. They travelled the short distance from RAF Skellingthorpe to Scampton by road the following day.

Several crews were already there, the rest arrived over the following week or so. Maudslay was particularly pleased to be sharing his mess with his good friend Bill Astell, who was already at Scampton having transferred over from 57 Squadron. Again, contrary to popular belief, not all crews (including some of the pilots) were either experienced or tour expired. It is true that some were, and many were highly decorated, but some had only completed a few ops and for some, Operation Chastise would be their first mission. It appears that Gibson was even concerned that some of the crews may have been recommended just to get them off their previous squadron and probably were not up to the task in hand.

Most of the remaining crews arrived by the end of March, though it wasn't until the beginning of April that 617 Squadron was complete with Gibson, two flights of ten crews and a spare crew.

	Pilot	Previous Squadron	Date joined 617 Sqn.
1	Gibson	106 Sqn.	21 March 1943
2	Byers	467 Sqn.	24 March 1943
3	Anderson	49 Sqn.	25 March 1943
4	Barlow	61 Sqn.	25 March 1943
5	Hopgood	106 Sqn.	25 March 1943
6	Knight	50 Sqn.	25 March 1943

	Pilot	Previous Squadron	Date joined 617 Sqn.
7	Maltby	97 Sqn.	25 March 1943
8	Maudslay	50 Sqn.	25 March 1943
9	McCarthy	97 Sqn.	25 March 1943
10	Munro	97 Sqn.	25 March 1943
11	Wilson	44 Sqn.	25 March 1943
12	Astell	57 Sqn.	26 March 1943
13	Lancaster	57 Sqn.	26 March 1943
14	Lovell	57 Sqn.	26 March 1943
15	Shannon	83 Sqn.	26 March 1943
16	Townsend	49 Sqn.	26 March 1943
17	Young	57 Sqn.	26 March 1943
18	Burpee	106 Sqn.	29 March 1943
19	Brown	44 Sqn.	30 March 1943
20	Martin	1654 HCU	31 March 1943
21	Rice	57 Sqn.	01 April 1943
22	Otley	207 Sqn.	04 April 1943

Within days the squadron was allocated 617 Squadron number, with codes AJ. It is arguably the most famous RAF squadron number. Training started immediately. Astell was sent on the first sorties in one of the temporary Lancasters on Saturday 27 March and the following day to fly over, and take photographs of, all the lakes and reservoirs in England. The reason given was that it was to assist in the development of cross-country exercises. Young, previously with 57 Squadron, was A-Flight Commander, and Maudslay B-Flight Commander; between them they organised the crews, the structure of the squadron and prepared training schedules.

Gibson was away much of the time in secret discussion with his superiors, during which time Maudslay and Young managed the squadron between them. He did, however, assemble the whole of 617 Squadron for a meeting to briefly outline their mission, which ended with him saying 'You're here to do a special job.' Maybe then Jack realised, for the first time, that he was part of an elite squadron.

To simulate night flying during the day Lancaster ED763 previously with 467 Squadron was installed with 'Two Stage Blue'. This was a navigational training aid in which the front section of the cockpit and the bomb aimer's blister were covered with blue Perspex, which would simulate night flying during the day when used in conjunction with orange-coloured flying goggles. All crews had the opportunity to familiarise themselves with this technique, though some found it difficult to adjust to.

Gibson outlines some of the logistic and organisational problems and how they overcame them in his book, but he did manage to get some flying in. In late March or early April, he took Hopgood as a co-pilot and Young as a passenger to assess the practicalities of low-level flying at 150ft over water before he asked all the pilots to do it. They flew to a series of reservoirs in the Peak District to the east of Sheffield. The three reservoirs were (from upstream): the Howden Reservoir and Dam, completed between 1901 and 1912; Derwent Reservoir and Dam, completed between 1902 and 1916; and the (at that time incomplete) Ladybower Reservoir and Dam.

Lancaster fitted with 'Two Stage Blue' to the cockpit front.

Pilot's view low over the Derwent Dam.

The Derwent offered the best practice and Gibson hurtled down the Derwent valley at 240 mph, dropped down to as near to 150ft as the three pilots could collectively guess over the Derwent Reservoir and dam, banked round over what would eventually be the Ladybower Reservoir and made several more approaches, of which he noted 'in the end found it more or less fairly easy'. As the daylight faded into dusk they made another approach. The visibility had drastically reduced, mist was forming in the valley, the waters of the reservoirs that had appeared blue during the day had by then turned an unforgiving black. The limited visibility was disorientating, and judging the height was impossible, so much so that they nearly hit the water of Derwent Reservoir before pulling up sharply. It could have been disastrous, Gibson writes:

> Even Spam [Spafford – Gibson's bomb aimer] said, 'Christ! This is bloody dangerous', which meant it was. Not only that. I said to Dinghy [Young] there and then, that unless we could find some way of judging our height above water, this type of attack would be completely impossible. 'But why must we fly at this dead height?' Asked Hoppy [Hopgood]. 'I'm afraid that's the snag. The scientist I met told me that in order to make his weapon work we would have to fly within a few miles an hour at the right airspeed and within a very few feet of the right height. That's our problem.'

On 29 March, Gibson was at No.5 Group HQ where he was told the actual targets and shown scale models of the Möhne and Sorpe Dams, though significantly not for the Eder Dam. At least he then knew it wasn't going to be the *Tirpitz*. Afterwards, he flew down for another meeting with Wallis at Weybridge. At the meeting Wallis gave details of the targets, elaborated on the plans and described the tests and developments of the Upkeep. He confirmed that the dams must be attacked when the reservoirs were full of water, which meant there was only a small window of opportunity between 13 to 19 May. It was only six weeks in which to finalise the testing of the Upkeep, building of the Lancaster Type 464s, developing a mechanism for accurately releasing the Upkeep, working out how to maintain a constant low altitude at night, and most importantly, the training of the twenty-one crews. Although Gibson had nearly killed himself and two of his senior pilots the night before, he rejected any suggestion of a daylight raid.

In the absence of Gibson much of the planning and development of the training was undertaken by the two flight commanders, Young and Maudslay.

This unfortunately meant that they flew less than the other pilots. However, on 31 March many of the crews, including Jack's, undertook cross-country navigation exercises flying at about 500ft. Since Jack's flying logbook doesn't exist, I have assumed that he accompanied Maudslay on all his flights. Their mission in Lancaster LM309 (by then with 617 Squadron Code AJ-X) was almost three hours, which included low-level bombing practice from 100ft just off the Lincolnshire coast south of Skegness at the Wainfleet Bombing Range where wooden panels had been erected, unbeknown to the crews, to simulate the towers on the Möhne and Eder Dams.

The method of determining the correct distance from the dams was developed by Wing Commander Dann from A&AEE Boscombe Down, using a simple triangular-shaped sight to line up with the towers on the dams. This appears to have been used by some crews, although others found that with the vibration of the Lancaster it was too difficult and preferred to use their own methods, including string and marks on the bomb aimer's window.

While most of the crews were by then undertaking longer and lower training flights, Maudslay's time with preparation and planning restricted his flying time. His next flight was 2 April in W4926 (AJ-Z) with a short session of circuits, possibly as an air test. The following day he participated in another two-hour daylight navigational exercise at 500ft in Lancaster LM309, culminating in further bombing practice from 100ft.

By early April, Gibson had learned that their targets would be dams around the Ruhr valley and that the height for the attack would be at a mere 150ft. With the unreliability of conventional altimeters at such a low level he had continued to ponder the difficulties in maintaining a height of 150ft at night over water. A bizarre option considered was trailing a weight to touch the water at the correct height and airspeed, a jerk on the wire would indicate the correct height. It was quickly discounted as being impractical. Far from the popular myth, it wasn't Gibson's idea after watching stage lights on dancing girls that provided the answer. Benjamin Lockspeiser, the Deputy Director of Scientific Research at the Ministry of Aircraft Production, proposed the 'spotlight altimeter', an idea that had been first used during the First World War and used earlier in the Second World War, which used two spotlights. These would be positioned to shine down and when the two beams of light came together, the aircraft would be at the correct height.

Maudslay flew Lancaster W4926 (AJ-Z) to RAE[14] Farnborough to have test spotlights fitted on 4 April. One Aldis light was attached in the bomb aimer's camera mount on the port side of the nose. Another was fitted into an aperture to the rear of the bomb bay which had been provisioned for a ventral machine gun. Both had shrouds to prevent light shining other than in the direction of the light beam. They were positioned to shine down and to starboard so they could be seen by the navigator from the starboard cockpit blister. The installation took three days to complete and Maudslay returned to Scampton on 8 April. Before they departed RAE Farnborough, the crew may have noticed the arrival of an odd-looking Lancaster. The first modified prototype of the Lancaster Type 464 ED765 without bomb bay doors but complete with a dangling calliper mechanism for holding the Upkeep had arrived for flight trials. That evening with a team from the Royal Aircraft Establishment Maudslay tested the spotlights flying over The Wash. The lights worked perfectly, they returned to base after about an hour and then completed several runs over the airfield where the height was accurately assessed by ground teams with theodolites.

Two days later the second prototype Lancaster Type 464 ED817 (AJ-C) was flown from Avro at Woodford to RAF Manston in Kent to be prepared for Upkeep trials. Maudslay's crew finally got a long low-level exercise in Lancaster W4926 (AJ-Z) on 11 April with a four-and-half-hour cross country flight which ended with another low-level bombing exercise.

The following day Jack accompanied Maudslay on a short air test of Lancaster ED329 (AJ-T) while Gibson travelled south by car to Manston with the squadron bombing lead, Bob Hay.

Avro Lancaster B.III Type 464 – ED817 showing V-Shaped Callipers for holding the Upkeep.

On 13 April, the Maudslay crew undertook a short daylight flight cross country, but Gibson and Hay had arrived at Reculver on the north Kent coast to witness testing of the Upkeep. Wallis and Lockspeiser were already there, among others. High speed cameras had been setup to record the events while policemen patrolled the barbed-wire perimeter of the test site. Before their arrival, testing of the smaller Vickers Highball had failed.

At 09:20 a converted twin-engine Wellington (BJ895) flown by Vickers test pilot Bob Handasyde flew parallel to the beach from east to west. As it approached two white aiming marker buoys it dived to gain speed and levelled off at about 80ft, with a half-scale test Upkeep spinning at 520 rpm. The Upkeep was released and hit the water; the wooden outer casing shattered but the cylindrical metal core that would hold the explosive on the live versions continued to spin and skip. It was a positive result for Wallis, who exclaimed 'Excellent' as he set off to collect fragments for analysis.

At 11:08, Lancaster Type 464 ED817 (AJ-C) approached, flown by Squadron Leader Maurice 'Shorty' Longbottom, an RAF Officer seconded to Vickers for test flying. The Lancaster levelled out, at around 250ft and 210 mph. The Upkeep, painted black and white was released, created a huge spray of water as it struck the flat calm sea, whereupon it shattered and disappeared. Wallis adjourned the trials while an Upkeep was strengthened for another trial later that evening.

While the modifications were being carried out, Gibson and Hay managed to borrow a Miles Magister (T9908), an open cockpit two-seat trainer from 137 Squadron. Gibson writes that it was to fly back to Scampton, though other reports suggest it was so he could fly over and have a look at the test area.

Whatever the reason, they had climbed to about 300ft near Margate when the engine cut out as Gibson describes:

> When an engine stops in a four engine aircraft you do not have to worry much about it – you have always got three others, but when it happens in a single-engine aircraft, then the long finger of gravity points to mother earth; and so we began coming down. In ordinary parts of the world this is quite

Lancaster ED817 dropping a wooden cased Upkeep at Reculver.

easy, but at Hell's Corner they make quite certain that aircraft do not land safely in fields. There were abundant wires and other devices because German glider-borne troops were not very welcome. So we fell into the trap…. After the aircraft had rolled itself into a ball and we had stepped out of the dust a man came running over to see if we were hurt. His words were memorable. 'I think they teach you young fellows to fly too early', he said. Then a policeman arrived and took a statement. 'I'm glad to see our anti-aircraft landing devices work,' he said without sympathy.

Gibson and Hay made their way back to Manston but returned to Scampton without waiting for the next Upkeep test. Just after 19:00, Lancaster ED817 (AJ-C) approached the white marker buoys at Reculver but this time instructed to release the Upkeep at just 50ft. Again, the outer wooden casing shattered on impact with the sea, but the cylindrical metal core again continued skimming across the sea.

Around about the same time ED817 (AJ-C) was making its final flight over Reculver, Maudslay and crew were getting airborne in Lancaster LM309. It was their first long night exercise and lasted almost five hours, but training wasn't going well for all the crews.

While Gibson was at Reculver the squadron adjutant Harry Humphries had written that Flight Sergeant Lovell, from 57 Squadron, had not 'come up to the required standard necessary for this squadron'. He was immediately posted back across the airfield to 57 Squadron and replaced by Sergeant Pilot Divall.

Maudslay was flying again on 15 April. During the morning a short air test in Lancaster LM309 was followed that evening by a night cross-country exercise in ED437 (AJ-N). The flight took four-and-half-hours, which incorporated a route to the north of Scotland and was undertaken at 50ft.

Unsuccessful tests with the revised Upkeep without the wooden outer casing continued at Reculver. But at Scampton, Gibson had removed another crew from the squadron. George Lancaster's crew were also sent back to 57 Squadron. It wasn't Lancaster himself that had been the concern, but his navigator. Lancaster objected to the sacking, and Gibson, not known for his tolerance, sent the whole crew back.

Training flights continued at the same intensity. Maudslay may have flown more, but his next recorded flight was on 22 April, a 20-minute air test in ED437 (AJ-N). The same day, however, the third Lancaster Type 464 ED825

(AJ-T) was delivered to A&AEE Boscombe Down but significantly, the first three of the twenty converted Lancaster Type 464s ED864 (AJ-B), ED865 (AJ-S), and ED887 (AJ-A), arrived at Scampton. Their unusual looks were no doubt much to the bemusement and curiosity of the crews that were going to use them. A further five ED886 (AJ-O), ED906 (AJ-J), ED909 (AJ-P), ED915 (AJ-Q), and ED921 (AJ-W) arrived the following day. The crews must have realised that the date for the operation was getting nearer. They were not immediately able to replace the loaned Lancasters, as various further modifications were undertaken in the Scampton hangar.

Night flying and map reading at 150ft was generally considered fairly easy, even though pilot McCarthy was furious on one exercise flying at 100ft when another Lancaster, piloted by Munro flew beneath him. The original ten standard Lancasters were getting so much use shared between the crews they frequently received minor damage and were rapidly approaching their maximum hours when a major inspection and/or maintenance would be required. Maudslay was back in the air on 24 April in standard Lancaster W4926 (AJ-Z) in which he completed two bombing exercises. As he returned following the second exercise, the Lancaster's tail wheel was damaged on Scampton's grass runway. The aircraft was assessed as Cat.Ac – 'Repair is beyond the unit capacity but can be repaired on site by another unit or a contractor' – and didn't return for use by the squadron until 15 May.

Gibson's flight that day was not as the pilot of a Lancaster but as a passenger in a DeHavilland Mosquito when he was transported down to the Vickers site at Weybridge for a meeting with Wallis. After further Upkeep tests, evaluations and calculations Wallis had determined that the release needed to be not at the 150ft but at a mere 60ft and asked Gibson if it could be achieved. It was a huge ask. A 30 ton Lancaster, flying at 230 mph, at night, over water in the face of an aggressive enemy at just 60ft – less than the length of the Lancaster itself.

Much has been written about the character of Gibson, but what he definitely was was positive, brave, and determined. He would never ask of others actions that he couldn't, or wasn't prepared to, do himself. He was just 24 years old at the time, maybe his youth made him fearless, but undeniably he had all the attributes of a great leader. He returned to Scampton to ensure that 617 Squadron were in a position to fulfil the requirements. If he had had any doubts then it is likely that Operation Chastise, 'The Dambusters', would never have taken place.

On 25 April Maudslay's crew completed another daylight low altitude bombing detail in Lancaster LM309. Accompanying them was the

Squadron's medical officer, Flying Officer Malcolm Arthurton. The weather was gusty and the Lancaster experienced severe buffeting throughout the flight, so much so that Arthurton documented that he was airsick after just ninety minutes.

The weather prevented any flying until 27 April when Maudslay completed a night tactical-training detail in Lancaster ED437 (AJ-N), no doubt at the new height of 60ft. It seems that Gibson was satisfied with the conversion to the lower level as he communicated his confirmation of 60ft to Wallis. There was no flying logged for Maudslay on 28 April, but a further Lancaster Type 464 ED910 (AJ-C) arrived at Scampton as Wallis began more Highball and Upkeep trials at Reculver.

On 29 April Gibson again departed Scampton for Reculver to observe the trials as Maudslay once again took Lancaster ED437 (AJ-N) on a daylight bombing exercise at Wainfleet. Because of his organisational tasks as B-Flight Commander, both his daytime and night-time flying was only about half that of the other crews, most of whom had done around forty hours daylight and fifteen hours night flying. Only Young had done as little flying, and Gibson had considerably fewer hours.

Wallis had completed some more tests with the Highball the previous day but at 09:15 watched with Gibson as Longbottom, flying parallel to the shore, dropped a full-size cylindrical Upkeep from 50ft, spinning at 500 rpm. It skipped six times over a distance of 670yds and veered slightly to the left. Wallis and Gibson then travelled for meetings in London, but Wallis returned to Reculver to conduct further tests. These, together with experimental work at Vickers and A&AEE Boscombe Down, satisfied Wallis that the Upkeep was ready for the operation as planned.

Maudslay ferried ED909 (AJ-P), one of the new Lancaster Type 464s, down to RAE Farnborough on 30 April for further modifications. It seems that Jack didn't accompany him because by the beginning of May most of the crews were given a few days leave. Maudslay took the train back and stopped off at his home. Jack most probably spent the time relaxing and/or studying around Scampton and Lincoln. The same day, another five Lancaster Type 464s arrived at the airfield, these being ED918 (AJ-F), ED924 (AJ-Y), ED925 (AJ-M), ED929 (AJ-L), and possibly the most famous Lancaster ED932 (AJ-G) which was Gibson's aircraft. It's believed it was chosen for him because it was the initials of Gibson's father, Alexander James Gibson.

There was little flying at the beginning of May as the crews took some well-earned rest. Gibson was sufficiently happy with the progress that by

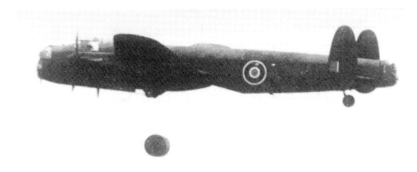

Lancaster dropping a cylindrical Upkeep at Reculver.

1 May he had telephoned Wallis to confirm his confidence that the operation would succeed.

The Maudslay crew reconvened on Monday 3 May, just as another batch of four Lancaster Type 464s were delivered to Scampton by Avro ferry pilots. The four were ED912 (AJ-N), ED927 (AJ-E), ED934 (AJ-K), and the aircraft that was allocated to the Maudslay crew, ED933 (AJ-X). All were whisked away into the hangar for further modifications. The same day Gibson reported to his superiors that the squadron was 'ready to operate'.

Jack was flying again on 4 May. As can be seen in his navigator Urquhart's logbook, it was in Lancaster Type 464 ED909 (AJ-P). They took off in the dark at 11:10 for an hour's night tactics mission.

They also flew on the following day in the standard Lancaster ED437 (AJ-N), during which a daylight cross-country flight of two hours and forty minutes was completed. In the secrecy of HQ No.5 Group a meeting had convened and decided that the operation would go ahead – and must take place as close to the night of 14 May as possible. It was just over a week away!

Final Upkeep trials were also undertaken at Reculver. On 6 May during testing, only one release was considered to have been satisfactory. However, adjustments to the callipers and spin mechanism were undertaken overnight and the following day some of the Upkeeps were released perpendicular to the shore so that as they skipped along they climbed the inclined beach and crashed into the pasture beyond. The tests confirmed the release

Robert Urquhart's flying logbook.

requirements for the Upkeep and showed that the main issues associated with it had all been resolved.

That evening Gibson had a discussion with the pilots and explained all the tactical and technical aspects of the mission. Without identifying the actual targets, he told them – stressing the need for secrecy – that the operation would take place within the following two weeks. He confirmed his satisfaction with low-level navigation, how to maintain a final bombing run at 60ft, how to determine the release distance, and also that the Upkeep was available.

He went on to describe that they would be using VHF (Very High Frequency) radio sets as fitted in fighter aircraft for communication between the Lancasters while over the target so that the attacks could be controlled and coordinated efficiently.

Finally, he notified the pilots that they would start dress rehearsals that evening. Nine aircraft flying in groups of three, they would make mock attacks at the Eyebrook Reservoir (sometimes quoted as Uppingham Lake) between Leicester and Peterborough. Although its dam was more similar to that at the Sorpe Dam, scaffolding towers were erected to give it the appearance of the Möhne Dam. It proved excellent for honing their difficult bomb-aiming techniques. The aircraft were then to fly on to Abberton Reservoir just south of Colchester, which was supposed to look like the Eder Reservoir from the air (even though the surrounding area is virtually flat). Six of the crews were selected to conduct parallel approaches at the Derwent Dam (which in reality was more like the Möhne Dam) to simulate attacking the Sorpe Dam. The remainder would form a mobile reserve and would practise bombing runs over the wash.

Maudslay took off at 20:15 with the group of nine Lancasters. It was logged in navigator Urquhart's flying Logbook as one hour fifteen minutes night cross-country, bombing and tactics.

The following day, 7 May, Maudslay's and Young's allocated Lancaster Type 464s were installed with the latest VHF Type TR 1143 radio equipment. Classrooms were also setup in the crew room, complete with TR1143 radio equipment so that the pilots and wireless operators could practise and familiarise themselves with the procedures and operation of the new radio kit.

By late the following afternoon the two Lancaster Type 464s complete with TR1143 radios were ready for use. Maudslay took off in ED933 (AJ-X) at 17:40 alongside Young in ED887 (AJ-A) they tested the equipment at varying heights and distances apart and found that though some minor adjustments were necessary the equipment worked well, even over larger distances than they would be expecting. By 9 May all eighteen Lancaster Type 464s delivered to Scampton had been successfully installed, including two sets in Gibson's ED932 (AJ-G) just in case one failed.

There is no record of Jack's crew flying on either 9 or 10 May, but elsewhere at No.5 Group HQ senior staff members had drawn the draft operation and dispatched it to the Scampton base commander Group Captain Charles Whitworth for review and revision, to be returned by 16:00 on 12 May. It included a priority list of targets, how the twenty aircraft of the squadron would be split into waves to attack the targets, reserves, likely defences, and exit routes.

Gibson provided detailed comments removing the proposal that the Lancasters should climb to 3,000ft to cross the coast, recommending they remained low level all the way. He also removed a suggestion that Mosquitos make a diversionary raid as he considered it would alert the defences and make their task harder.

It seems strange now that the Eder Dam was a primary target, given that it was strategically less important than those dams that supplied water to the Ruhr Valley. In hindsight it seems that it was probably chosen as it was considered easier to breach than the other dams and as such would have a considerable effect on morale, positively for the Allies but also negatively for the German population.

On 11 May live Upkeeps began arriving at Scampton, another reminder to those that saw them that their mission was nearing. Despite most crews having had a short break they must have been exhausted, both physically and mentally. The training had been tough and intense but few of the crews had taken ill, and fortuitously there had been no serious accidents. There was no let up, crews started positioning to Manston in groups using the aircraft they were going to use on the operation. They took turns dropping inert Upkeeps (filled with concrete) towards the shore at Reculver. Gibson flew ED932 (AJ-G) and noted in his logbook 'Low level. Upkeep. Dropped at 60ft. Good run of 60yds'.

After his test release he landed at Manston and made his way to the beach at Reculver where he joined Wallis in observing the spectacle of the Upkeeps crashing up the foreshore.

Maudslay took off for the crew's first proper flight in ED933 (AJ-X). He departed at 11:35 on a daylight cross-country exercise that lasted four hours and five minutes. They no doubt used the time as an extended air test, and it gave the crew chance to familiarise themselves with the aircraft they were going to use on the operation and ensure that it was running as expected.

The same day, Jack's Service Record was updated. Once again his character assessment was VG, his Proficiency Column A (trade ability) was 'sup' (superior), and Column B (supervisory ability) was 'sat' (satisfactory).

Above left: Gibson in ED932 flying low over Reculver after releasing a test Upkeep.

Above right: Successful Upkeep release rolling up the beach at Reculver. Wallis is second from the left (waving his arms in front of an observer in uniform), Gibson is second from the right.

12 May 1943 – Reculver: Trials and Tribulations

On 12 May the 19th and penultimate Lancaster Type 464 ED936 (AJ-H) was delivered to RAF Scampton. That evening Maudslay, Shannon, Knight, Barlow and Munro took off at 18:30 for an exercise which incorporated their opportunity to release an Upkeep at Reculver. The five aircraft maintained a loose formation, flying low, and eventually made their way down the Thames Estuary and out towards Reculver.

At around 19:30 Shannon in ED929 (AJ-L) made his approach. His height and speed seemed about right to observers on the shore but Sumpter, his bomb aimer, released their Upkeep about 40yds too early. It skipped a few times and then sank into the sea. Had it been on the actual operation it would not have reached the dam. Gibson, observing, was not impressed, the following day he called Shannon and Sumpter into his office for a reprimand.

Munro flying ED921 (AJ-W) was next. His speed looked about right but the Upkeep was released too low.

As it hit the water a spume of water crashed into the underside of his Lancaster damaging the underside and knocking off a fairing that covered the bomb bay. It was a stark warning of the importance of getting the correct height. Fortunately, the damage was minor and soon repaired back at base.

It was then Maudslay's turn. This gave them the opportunity to really get used to their aircraft, but it mainly gave them experience of releasing an Upkeep and the effect it would have on the flying controls and engines, so Jack and his pilot would have been especially watchful on the handling changes at the transition of height, speed, and releasing the 4-ton Upkeep.

Maudslay circled round waiting for his turn while keeping a watchful eye on those Lancasters who were ahead in their turn to release their Upkeep. Cottam, the wireless operator, will have started spinning up the Upkeep and been crouched in the narrow Lancaster alleyway watching

Above left: Damage to Munro's ED915 (AJ-W) at Reculver.

Above right: Damage to Maudslay's ED933 (AJ-X) at Reculver.

the dial as the rotation steadied at 500 rpm. Most of the crews reported a noticeable vibration through the airframe as the Upkeep gathered speed. It was then their turn, Maudslay banked round to port nosing down to get the Lancaster to 60ft, he levelled off perpendicular to the shore, aiming for two marker posts with Jack tweaking and caressing the throttles in an attempt to maintain the correct approach speed of 232 mph. Unfortunately, the spotlight altimeters that worked so well at night were of no use at all during the day as Munro had previously experienced – the height had to be guessed – almost impossible at the height and speed with which they approached the shoreline. Fuller, the bomb aimer, oblivious to the height and speed peered intently through his personalised bombsight, waiting for the two marker posts to sit exactly within his sight.

To observers on the shore, it looked as though the Lancaster was too low and possibly too slow, but at 450yds, with one marker post visible in each eyepiece of his sight, Fuller pressed his release button. The two calliper arms swung open, the spinning Upkeep hurtled towards the sea. Maudslay instinctively resisted the tendency of the Lancaster to pitch nose up and Jack similarly further tweaked the throttles as the four Merlin engines compensated for the reduced weight and drag.

A split second later the Upkeep hit the water almost directly under ED933. The initial plume of water lurched upwards and forwards, smashing into and enveloping the rear of the fuselage and tailplane. The noise and impact must have been hugely disconcerting, probably like being hit by flak. Maudslay clearly fought with his Lancaster as it then lurched nose down. As he pulled it through the water spray, several large sections were seen to break away from his Lancaster, but he was able to gradually pull the nose up and gently climb away with water streaming from the rear of the aircraft.

The Upkeep skipped towards the shore, fortunately the successive plumes of water were less intense and behind the struggling Lancaster. After several skips the Upkeep sank into the sea without reaching the shoreline.

Knight in ED912 (AJ-N) and Barlow in ED927 (AJ-E) then each made a satisfactory approach and release. Their Upkeeps skipped across the sea and ran up the shore.

Maudslay had maintained a heading straight ahead inland as the crew assessed the damage. Burrows in the rear turret, shaken and thoroughly drenched, was fortunately uninjured and confirmed that both fins, rudders, tailplanes, and elevators were still attached but severely bent. The engines were undamaged so Maudslay nursed the struggling Lancaster back to Scampton rather than landing at nearby Manston.

Throughout training, many of the Lancasters had incurred damage. Most had suffered stress damage, and some had even returned to base with twigs attached to their tailwheels or embedded in the engine cowlings. Martin had suffered a little damage during his trials at Reculver and even Munro's damage there was relatively minor, but to ED933 the damage to the rear fuselage section was serious and there was probably large sections of the wings, central section of the fuselage, and the Upkeep release mechanism that were also badly damaged.

Following inspection, the damage was officially categorised as Cat.Ac – 'Repair is beyond the unit capacity but can be repaired on site by another unit or a contractor.' The best estimates were that the work would take a minimum of five days. Despite the best efforts and round the clock work of the groundcrews, it was five days they didn't have.

Successful Upkeep release at Reculver.

Gibson officially recorded that the 'pilot misjudged his height', and later wrote in his book

> Everything ran smoothly and there was no hitch; that is, no hitch except that six out of the twelve aircraft were very seriously damaged by the great columns of water sent up when their mines splashed in. They had been flying slightly too low. Most of the damage was around the tails of the aircraft; elevators were smashed like plywood, turrets were knocked in, fins were bent. It was a miracle some of them got home.

The station commander and an internal Court of Inquiry, taking into consideration the special training and circumstances, concluded that the cause was due to low-level bombing and no further action was taken. However, it has been suggested by some that Gibson was privately unhappy with the accident; if true, it is significant and noteworthy, and possibly a factor in him choosing Hopgood rather than Maudslay as deputy in command for the attacks on the Möhne and Eder Dams should he get shot down. If true, it must have been demoralising, and a blow to the ego and confidence of Maudslay who had worked hard as B-Flight Commander.

On 13 May Vickers test pilot Longbottom flew one of the Lancaster Type 464s used for trials with a live Upkeep five miles out to sea from Broadstairs in Kent. In another Lancaster the other Vickers test pilot, Handasyde, flew a

Live Upkeep trial 13 May.

safe distance away with a film crew and Gibson as an observer. Longbottom released the Upkeep at 75ft spinning backwards at 500 rpm. It skipped seven times, covered about 800yds maintaining a straight course then sank and a moment later exploded with a huge plume of water that rose to over 1,000ft. It was the only test of a live Upkeep that was ever undertaken.

There was no time for Maudslay to dwell on the incident at Reculver. That night he and his crew were flying again. Taking off at 22:30 they were back to using the standard Lancaster ED437 (AJ-N). A three-and-half-hour night cross-country, tactics exercise culminated in another bombing detail.

The last Lancaster Type 464 ED937 (AJ-Z) was delivered to Scampton on 14 May. It had been delivered from Avro to 39 Maintenance Unit at RAF Colerne on 6 May and had all the necessary modifications added before being ferried to Scampton. Without Lancaster ED933 (AJ-X), Maudslay was allocated the newly arrived Lancaster which was ready for testing by the early evening. Taking off at 19:15 the crew probably performed a twenty-minute air test, though Urquhart records the flight as being a 'night flying test and bombing exercise' in his logbook.

Later that night, in what was to be Jack's final training exercise, a full-dress rehearsal was undertaken. It was planned to simulate the operation as much as possible and used simulated routes to Eyebrook for the Möhne Reservoir, Abberton for the Eder Reservoir and Derwent Reservoir for the Sorpe. Unfortunately, not all crews could participate for various reasons, but Maudslay in AJ-Z took off for the exercise which lasted almost four hours.

Gibson recorded in his logbook 'Full dress rehearsal on Uppingham Lake [Eyebrook Reservoir] and Colchester Res. [Abberton Reservoir]. Completely successful.'

15 May – One Day to Go

There was little flying on Saturday 15 May. A few crews performed air tests on their Lancasters and others conducted a bombing practice at Wainfleet. Maudslay was still B-Flight commander and had plenty of final planning to complete so he and his crew did not fly at all.

There was still a live Upkeep at Manston from the Reculver trials, and Handasyde flew with it direct to the same location as the previous live drop off Broadstairs to dispose of it. It had no hydrostatic or self-destruct mechanism and was to test whether an Upkeep would explode just with a violent impact of contact with the surface of water. For safety reasons it was dropped from over 500ft and it did not explode when it hit the sea.

Key Locations.

During the morning AVM Ralf Cochrane No.5 Group AOC[15] travelled from HQ No.5 Group Grantham to Scampton to inform Group Captain Whitworth and Gibson that the operation would take place the following night, 16 May. Wallis also arrived from Weybridge in a white Coastal Command Wellington.

At about 16:00, Gibson travelled with Cochrane on his return to Grantham. Here he discussed the draft operation order with Group Captain Satterly SASO[16] and Wing Commander Dunn, No.5 Group's chief signals officer. It was also decided that Munro and McCarthy be moved from Wave 1 to Wave 2.

Gibson returned to Scampton, where he held a meeting at 18:00 in Whitworth's house and, together with Wallis, briefed Young and Maudslay, his two Flight commanders, Hopgood the deputy leader, and Hay, the squadron's bombing leader.

Sunday 16 May: Up to Boarding

Sunday 16 May 1943 was bright and sunny. The forecast was ideal for the raid. Jack and most of the crew members were in the RAF Scampton messes around 08:00 and had a hearty breakfast of porridge or cereal followed by sausages, potatoes and toast and marmalade. They were still oblivious that their day had finally arrived.

Gibson had been up since 05:30 having had no more than about five hours sleep. He had much on his mind. The raid was looming, there was still lots to do and on top of that he had lost his best friend, his black Labrador, who was killed in a road accident the previous night. Above all he was mentally, physically and emotionally drained. He was a sick man. At 09:00 he was with the squadron doctor; gout was causing him extreme pain and discomfort in his foot. The remedy, medication which would have prevented him flying that day, was rejected. He would just have to tolerate the pain.

The final Operation Order arrived, delivered by hand, at around 11:00. The plan had been finalised. The number of Lancasters was reduced from

Pilot list for Operation Chastise.

twenty to nineteen and would be used in three waves of attack. The plan indicated outbound and inbound routes, timings and areas with known anti-aircraft batteries to avoid. Wave 2 had been adjusted to include more experienced crews to specifically attack the Sorpe Dam which required a different bombing approach. Take-off was scheduled to begin at 21:00.

At 12:00 all the pilots and navigators were called into a briefing with Gibson and Wallis, while the wireless operators had a separate briefing. All were surprised to finally learn their targets: three primary targets, Möhne, Eder and Sorpe Dams and three secondary targets Lister, Ennepe and Diemel Dams. The Henne Dam had been removed from the list of targets.

As they looked at models of the Möhne and Sorpe Dams. Gibson outlined the battle order, stressed the importance of getting the job done to avoid having to go back and try again, and confirmed the crews that would be involved. Of the twenty crews, Divall and Wilson who had joined the squadron later than most of the other crews would not fly in Wave 3. Officially they, or members of the crew, were ill or injured, but it's widely believed that Gibson did not consider them to have sufficient experience to be capable of performing the job in hand.

Brown's crew had not been due to fly on the mission but were included and added to Wave 3, though his front gunner, Sergeant Buntaine, was ill and replaced for the operation by Divall's front gunner, Sergeant Allatson.

It has been written that initially, McCarthy and Munro and their crews were a little disconsolate as it seemed they had been demoted from Wave 1. Although there are suggestions it may have been due to poor results in bombing practice, it wasn't the case; their low flying expertise and bombing prowess were considered more suited for the different bombing approach required at the Sorpe Dam, even though they had not actually practised for it.

Wave 1   Nine aircraft in three groups
Gibson, Hopgood, Martin
Young, Maltby, Shannon
Maudslay, Astell, Knight.
Task 1 – attack Möhne Dam until destroyed then
Task 2 – those aircraft with unused Upkeeps to attack Eder Dam then
Task 3 – any aircraft with unused Upkeeps to attack Sorpe Dam.

Wave 2   Five aircraft
McCarthy, Barlow, Munro, Byers, Rice
Task 1 – attack Sorpe Dam.

Wave 3 Five aircraft
        Ottley, Burpee, Brown, Townsend, Anderson
        Task 1 – act as an airborne reserve to attack targets as instructed.

Around the airfield a small army of engine and airframe fitters exhaustively checked and rechecked every part of the aircraft, armourers examined and tested turrets and guns. At the bomb dump the Upkeeps were made ready and loaded onto the trolleys for delivery to each aircraft at their remote dispersal bays. At the various sections of the base specialist officers finalised the signalling procedures, examined weather forecasts and target information.

By 13:00 Scampton, which had increased in activity the previous day, was bustling. The perimeter track, so often quiet and deserted had turned into a busy motorway with trucks, trailers, tractors, buses, bicycles and a variety of personnel bustling about their business to and from the aircraft scattered around dispersal. The special Lancasters around dispersal were frantically being worked on. Fuel and oil were being topped up.

The loading of live Upkeeps from the bomb dumps had started the previous day, it was a time-consuming job, they were delivered on specially converted bomb trailers pulled by a tractor. The front fairing of the bomb bay was swung open to enable the trailer to be positioned beneath the V-shaped calliper carrying arms, and then the Upkeep was winched up into position. The callipers were then closed, rotation tests performed and compass deviation[17] calculated. 18,000 rounds of ammunition, all with 100 per cent daylight tracer (to give the impression of a heavier weight of fire than there

Fuel and oil bowsers.

was in reality), were also being installed into the two gun positions, 3,000 for each of the machine-guns.

Though most of the 617 Squadron crews still didn't know their targets, or even that they would be flying on their mission that night, it must have been obvious to them all that tonight was the night.

Inside No.2 Hangar there was feverish activity. Squadron Adjutant Harry Humphries was frantic with the amount of work he still had to do: logistics – transport of all the crews to their aircraft and transport of the crews once they returned from their mission, pre-flight checks and any last minute maintenance for the operational aircraft, meal times for the crews before take-off and on return, rations for the crews to take, safe keeping of cash and precious items, help with wills and letters to next of kin, making sure aircrew dogs were looked after – the list must have seemed endless.

The Lancaster usually flown by Jack's crew, ED933 (AJ-X), was still being worked on; the damage was substantial, and the repairs proved very difficult and time consuming. In fact, the aircraft would not be completed to be used that night. As Divall and Wilson had been stood down, and only replaced by Brown, there was one spare Lancaster, ED937 (AJ-Z), that had the required Type 464 modifications, and as Maudslay's crew had been using it since their incident at Reculver it was allocated to them to use. It wasn't ideal, crews get used to a particular aircraft, its foibles, peculiarities, they knew how to handle it, they had confidence in flying it regularly even though they had only used ED933 (AJ-X) for a few training exercises. At least they had some experience of AJ-Z. Hopefully, it wasn't going to be a painful reminder of the incident at Reculver where the test dropping of an Upkeep went disastrously wrong. They will have taken the chance to clean and polish the Perspex of the canopies and gun turrets; they knew any smears or blotches could be deceptive, especially when under attack.

By early afternoon Jack, with the rest of 617 Squadron aircrew, would have been at their aircraft checking it and ensuring everything was ready for any flying or testing they would be doing that day. As the flight engineer Jack was responsible for fuel management so would have been very particular that the fuel, oil, and coolant tanks were filled. Massive AEC Matador fuel trucks each carrying 2,600 gallons of fuel busied about, delivering 2,154 gallons to each Lancaster, filling two of the six fuel tanks simultaneously. Similarly, the oil bowser would have been used by a separate set of Erks to ensure the 150 gallons of oil were topped up.

AEC Matador 6x6 fuel bowser refuelling a Lancaster.

A further Lancaster Type 464 ED825 (AJ-T) was still at A&AEE Boscombe Down where it had been used to complete loading trials. An order was sent for a ferry team to deliver it to Scampton immediately.

Mick Martin's team were at their Lancaster ED909 (AJ-P), their live Upkeep had been loaded; somebody inadvertently pulled the Upkeep manual release handle. This was quite a large T-shaped trigger which was basically a repurposed glider release mechanism that could be used by the pilot if the bomb aimer's electrical release failed. It's not clear what happened, the manual release was just forward of the flap selection handle and a similar size. Perhaps the manual release was pulled by mistake when checking the flaps were working satisfactorily, maybe it was just snagged as Martin was getting in or out of the pilot's seat. There are some references to WAAF Fay Gillon being onboard at the time and accidentally pulling the release when climbing into the pilot's seat. Whatever happened, the V-shaped callipers swung open and the 4½ ton Upkeep crashed down, embedding itself into the tarmac hardstanding.

For the groundcrew, known perhaps disparagingly as Erks, and those onboard the aircraft there was a momentary freeze before the aeroplane and the immediate vicinity was rapidly vacated. Martin jumped into a nearby car and sped over to the armaments officer, Pilot Officer 'Doc' Watson, who declared that 'if it was going to explode it would have already done so'. After inspecting the mine Watson declared it safe and had it winched back into position.

At 14:30 all bomb aimers and navigators were summoned to a briefing where they were shown the models of the Möhne and Sorpe Dams, large-scale maps and lots of aerial photographs. The main concern raised was the routes in and out of the targets and Flight Sergeant Sumpter of ED929 (AJ-L) stressed the point that Dutch overhead power cables were very high, up to 100ft, and would have to be carefully avoided by flying over – or even under.

The bomb aimers were reminded of the approach needed for the dams, while crews assigned to the Sorpe Dam were given details of the alternative technique needed because it was an earthen dam so the Lancaster would need to fly parallel along the dam and drop the Upkeep vertically, without spinning, centrally on the water side of the dam so that it would roll down before exploding. But for those that would attack the Eder Dam there were no models, just maps and aerial photographs, and even those made the task seem a daunting prospect.

Lancaster Type 464 ED825 (AJ-T) arrived from A&AEE Boscombe Down at around 15:30. The ferry pilot had problems with No.3 engine, it would only run smoothly with the fuel booster turned off. As soon as it landed the Erks set to work to make it available as a spare, resolving the engine and other issues, but there wasn't time to have either the VHF radio or the spotlight altimeters fitted.

Activity around the airfield continued through the afternoon and into the early evening when, at 18:00, the Scampton public address system announced that all 617 Squadron aircrew were to report to the briefing room on the upper floor of the sergeants' mess immediately.

Amid the tightest security Jack will have taken his seat on the wooden benches with the rest of his team. With trepidation, fear, and undoubtedly a sense of relief, he waited for Gibson to begin. The temperature had only just begun to drop, the doors were shut tight and sentries stood on guard, windows were firmly closed, many were smoking; the tension must have been phenomenal.

The whole room stood as Gibson arrived with AVM Cochrane, Barnes Wallis and several other senior squadron officers. Gibson, Wallis and the officers sat at the front on a raised platform. Behind them huge maps with routes marked in red tape and reconnaissance photos adorned the wall.

Gibson began the briefing. He introduced the targets and then handed over to Barnes Wallis, who described the economic importance of dams and the development of the Upkeep, before using the blackboard to explain the principles and operation of the Upkeep and stressing the importance of spinning it at 500 rpm, releasing from a height of 60ft, an air speed of 220 mph, and at 475–450yds away from the dam.

AVM Cochrane went on to describe that it would be an historic raid, but stressed the importance of not talking about it after the raid in case the same technique needed to be used again.

Gibson then continued for almost an hour, standing all the time despite the ongoing pain from his gout. He detailed the running order, R/T procedures,[18] details of enemy defences, known flak hot spots, and night-fighter units and airfields. He stressed the importance of accurate map reading and keeping to the designated routes and turning points. He was followed by the squadron Met Officer,[19] who confirmed that the weather was forecast to be good, clear with a full moon, and light winds over the designated route. Everybody then synchronised their watches to the BBC clock.

In summary the route to the dams would be undertaken at minimum height all the way to and from the targets. Wave 1 and Wave 3 would take a south-easterly route over East Anglia to Southwold, crossing the North Sea to the Dutch Coast over the Sheldt Estuary and then taking an easterly direction, weaving around known flak positions and air bases to the Ruhr Valley. Wave 2 would set off first and take a slightly longer, northerly route, flying due east to Mablethorpe, crossing the Dutch coast about 100 miles north of Waves 1 and 3 over the small island of Vlieland, before taking a south-easterly course over the Zuiderzee to cross the German border at roughly the same location as Waves 1 and 3. Wave 3 would take-off after the success of Waves 1 and 2 were known so they could be directed to a target

Typical scene at an RAF Bomber Command briefing.

dam as appropriate. Homeward-bound aircraft would use a predefined return route, almost the reverse of Wave 2's outward route, back through Holland and over the Zuiderzee, before turning west towards their Lincolnshire base.

Gibson would attack the Möhne Dam first then control the attacks of the other aircraft. In case of issues with Gibson, Hopgood (No.2 of the first section) would take over the leader's role, and then if necessary, No.3 of the First section (Martin) would become leader. For the attack on the Eder Dam, Gibson would control the attack, but Young (No.1 of the second section) would assume leader responsibilities and if required, No.1 of the third section (Maudslay) would be stand-in leader for the attack on the Eder Dam.

The briefing finished around 19:30. I can't imagine how Jack and all the crews were feeling, the stress and anxiety must have been intense, but there was only about one-and-a-half hours before the first aircraft were due to take-off. As they dispersed, there would have been a gaggle of discussions as they headed for their respective canteens and messes. Supper, by all accounts, was a quiet and subdued affair. Those flying were given their standard pre-flight meal of two eggs and bacon.

Many had a sense of impending doom, concerned that this could be their last flight, and prepared instructions to have their affairs put in order. Many wrote letters, some tried to sleep, and others went to the hangar or crew room. Knowing there was going to be a long, hazardous flight ahead, nerves were strained, and the tension must have been almost unbearable. Some crews played football, others cricket with ground personnel, some chatted, some played cards, others just sat and smoked cigarettes. Some even tried to snatch a few moments' sleep. Most were frightened, all tried to hide their fear, and many felt physically sick. Most bomber crews regarded the last hour before take-off as the worst moments of the whole trip. Worse than the take-off, the outward journey, the bombing run, the fighters, or even the flak. The intense training and secrecy of the previous few months only intensified the feeling and as the minutes ticked away the level of anxiety, even for the most level-headed and seasoned bomber crews among them, would have heightened to an almost unbearable level.

By 20:00 flying rations were ready and the crews collected their flying clothes from the crew room. After collecting flight bags and flying rations, they were given their few items of escape equipment: miniature compass, silk maps, fishing line, and German and Dutch money. Some crews made their own way to their aircraft. Buses, trucks and other transport started to assemble ready to deliver the crews to their aircraft. Most were sat outside on the grass or in deck chairs; it was still a hot day, and many remained in shirt sleeves. Outwardly it might have looked calm, but tension was mounting, stomachs were churning.

Gibson arrived and, hiding his fear and nerves, casually announced 'Well, chaps, my watch says time to go.' The crews from Waves 1 and 2 collected their flying kit, and carrying their flying clothes clambered aboard their transport. Dave Shannon, reputedly a laid-back individual, had returned to his room for something and had to be called for, which increased the tension on his already stressed crew. These young crews at the peak of their abilities, honed by their extensive training, would have changed from their youthful exuberance of only a few hours previously. They were now highly focused professionals with their thoughts firmly fixed on their task ahead.

Around the peri-track[20] the nineteen converted Lancasters sat at dispersal, waiting. ED933 (AJ-X) was still being repaired and ED825 (AJ-T) the spare was available, though without either VHF radio equipment

Lancaster crew of No 57 Squadron at Scampton board a van to take them to dispersal and their waiting aircraft, February 1943.

or spotlight altimeters. The only other two Lancaster Type 464 conversions were at Manston where they had been used for bombing trials, but were not available even if they were needed.

Gibson arrived at his aircraft ED932 (AJ-G) before 20:30 in his own Humber car cramped together with his crew, by which time the crew buses, vans and other transport had pulled up outside No.2 Hangar. Having completed their external pre-flight checks, they gathered around the entrance hatch just about to climb aboard when AVM Cochrane arrived with an official RAF photographer. Cochrane wished Gibson and his crew the best and the photographer took a picture of Gibson and his crew of AJ-G.

Astell's crew arrived at their Lancaster AJ-B and Abram Garshowitz, the wireless operator, chalked on the Upkeep: 'Never has so much been expected of so few.' He was hoping it wasn't a bad omen. Many of the crews followed the time-honoured flying ritual of 'watering' the tailwheel.

Gibson's crew climb aboard. (from the left Trevor-Roper, Pulford, Deering, Spafford, Hutchison, Gibson and Taerum).

Jack and AJ-Z Prepare for Take-Off

Jack, his skipper Henry Maudslay, and the rest of the crew arrived at their aircraft ED937 (AJ-Z), which they had used for the previous three days since their disastrous incident in ED933 (AJ-X) during bombing trials at Reculver. The Erks were still busily readying the aircraft. The crew chief would have been ready with Form 700, completed by the Erks, for signing, but the team will have wanted to double check anyway. Apprehension, building since the end of the briefing, was now really stretched.

Undoubtedly Jack, as the flight engineer, will have gone round with the groundcrew fitters and riggers ensuring he was happy with his aircraft. He would have checked a 'trolley-acc'[21] was available and wheel chocks were in place, then checked that the wheel, engine, and pitot and static vent covers were removed, flying controls were OK and locks removed. Then visually checked the engines and other systems for leaks of fuel, oil, or engine coolant, and ensured all the fuel and oil tanks were full. He would have also confirmed that all engine cowlings, inspection panels and the wing leading edge were secured. The whole team would have taken time with Fuller the bomb aimer to curiously (perhaps intriguingly) review and check the 4½ ton Upkeep hanging below the Lancaster.

External checks complete, Jack would have carried his parachute, a flight bag which probably contained engine and system performance information, notes made at the briefing, and leather flying helmet among other items. He would then have climbed up the primitive steel step ladder through the small square entrance hatch on the starboard side near the tail plane. Because of the cramped crew positions, he would probably have entered the aircraft after pilot Maudslay, bomb aimer Fuller, and front gunner Tytherleigh. He would have turned right through the small entrance hatch then clambered forward through the thin cramped fuselage over the wing spars, stowed his parachute in the bulkhead receptacle and continued past the wireless operator's and navigator's positions. He would then have been followed by navigator Urquhart, wireless operator Cottam, and lastly, rear gunner Burrows, who closed and locked the hatch.

The distinctive smell of a Second World War bomber, a peculiar melange of paint, dope, metal, oil, coolant, petrol and leather, was to be their home for the next five or six hours. It was enough to upset some of those even with the strongest disposition, but it had to be ignored. The moment of truth had finally arrived, these young men, 133 of them in nineteen Lancasters, now faced the stark reality that all the training was behind them and this was it. Fighting back feelings of fear, voices no doubt increased to a nervous pitch and with dry mouths, they continued.

Once at his position next to the pilot, Jack would have connected his intercom then begin checking the onboard systems. It's unlikely that he will have pulled down his fold-away seat, the 'second dickey', as his instruments were both forward of him on the main control panel, and behind on the starboard side of the fuselage bulkhead. Jack would then have followed his flight engineer pre-flight checks.

It was Jack's 30th op, it would complete his tour of duty. His procedure was one that he and the rest of the crew knew so well. This time was different, it was a special op. Each task would have been completed with

Standard Lancaster Instrument panel (See appendix 5 for details).

Standard Lancaster flight engineer's panel (See appendix 5 for details).

special attention, switches that were normally just observed being in position would have been touched for added confirmation, just to make sure the checklist was followed to the letter. I'd bet that not a single check was overlooked or not given the maximum attention however trivial:

Parachutes stowed and secured
Check security of emergency escape hatches
Fireman's axe fire extinguisher & first aid kits are in position
All hatches closed & secure
Flame floats and equipment properly stored
Oxygen main cock 'ON'
Check emergency air bottle, normal pressure 1200 psi

Check hydraulic accumulator, static pressure 220 psi
Turn Master switch to 'FLIGHT'
Check fuel cross feed cock 'OFF'
All idle cut-off switches 'OFF'
Switch fuel contents gauge 'ON' & check fuel contents
Test fuel pumps by ammeter one at a time
Main fuel cocks to No.2 (centre) tanks 'ON'
Leave master cocks and No.1 (inner) & No.2 (centre) fuel
    pumps 'ON'
Switch on undercarriage & flap indicator switches & check
    indicators
Switch on fuel contents gauges switch & check fuel contents

Then, together with pilot Maudslay, they would have started their onboard systems checks. Jack would have read from his checklist and Maudslay repeated each check as he carried it out:

Seat secure
Adjust rudder pedals to suit leg length & ensure pedals are
    adjusted evenly
Test that full rudder to port and starboard can be applied from
    normal sitting position without extending legs fully
Test all control for full movement & put automatic pilot 'IN'
Brakes 'ON' (Note pressure min. 120 psi)
Test elevator trimming tab control movement – full and free
    set to neutral
Test rudder trimming tab control movement – full and free set
    to neutral
Test aileron trimming tab control movement – full and free set
    to neutral
Cold air
Mixer box to I/C position
Flap gauge & indicator light switch 'ON'
Set altimeter to 'ZERO' – QFE
Propeller Pitch controls 'FULLY FINE'
Supercharger in M (Medium) ratio
Flap lever 'NEUTRAL'
Undercarriage lever locked 'DOWN'
Master switch to 'GROUND'

Gibson's crew completed their pre-flight checks then just after 21:00. Observing radio silence, Robert Hutchison, his wireless operator, fired a red Very pistol. It was the signal for all Wave 1 and Wave 2 aircraft to start their engines. Around the dispersal Lancasters began spluttering into life.

Having completed the pre-start-up checks pilot Maudslay, together with Jack and the groundcrew designated as the starter (stood just ahead of the port wingtip clearly visible to the pilot), would then have initiated the engine start-up procedure, revisiting some of the previously completed checks.

Maudslay would have settled himself in his raised pilot's seat then through his open window would have shouted the order:

'Ready for starting.'

The starting crew member would have responded with:

'Undercarriage locked down', 'Brakes on', 'Switch to ground.'

Jack would then have double checked the undercarriage lever between him and the pilot was in the down position, the undercarriage switch at the top centre of the control panel was on and the control panel undercarriage lights directly ahead of the pilot's control column showed green (locked down) for both left and right undercarriage, then replied 'Undercarriage locked down.' Maudslay would then have double checked that the brake lever on his control column yoke was on and locked, and replied, 'Brakes on', before turning around and checking the master switch on the bulkhead behind him was in the Ground position, after which he would have replied 'Switch to ground'.

One of the Erks would have climbed via the main wheel beneath No.3 engine nacelle to balance precariously on footrests on the undercarriage oleo leg to access the starboard priming station. The trolley-acc would have been connected with the Erk waiting for the engine to start turning.

No.3 engine, the starboard-inner, was always started first; when running, it charged the pneumatics and hydraulics for the brakes and other essential services. The starting crew member would have raised his left arm, pointing skyward, and with his right hand pointed at the starboard-inner engine and then made revolving motion with his index finger and shouted to the Erks:

'All clear', 'Contact starboard-inner.'

Maudslay, peering over Jack's shoulder at the groundcrew, would then have gone through the start sequence and issued the following commands, which Jack would have checked and/or set before repeating the command back to Maudslay to confirm it had been completed.

Master fuel cocks – OFF
Slow-running cut-out controls – ENGINE RUN
Throttles – SET ½ INCH OPEN
Propeller pitch – FULLY FINE
Supercharger control – M RATIO, warning lights out
Slow-running – IDLE CUT OFF
Air intake heat control – COLD
Radiator shutters[22] – AUTOMATIC
Fuel tank selector cocks (port & starboard) to No.2 (centre) tanks – ON
Fuel pump switches No.2 tanks (port and starboard) – ON
Master fuel cocks – ON
Ignition – ON
Booster Coil – ON

Jack will have leaned forward and flicked the two toggle magneto ignition switches for No.3 Engine into the ON (up) position and switched on the adjacent booster coil switch. The crew chief signalled 'ready to start' with a thumbs up and pointing at No.3 engine. Jack would then have lifted the switch guard and pressed the start button for No.3 engine. The Erk standing on the undercarriage pumped the fuel through to the priming nozzles and repeatedly pressed the priming pump until the engine coughed and banged then burst into life as the carburettors picked up.

The beautiful, reliable and resilient Rolls-Royce (Packard[23]) Merlin engines would have flashed a burst of fire (despite their flame suppressors covering the exhaust pipes), coughed thick bluey-black sooty smoke, and then burst into life with that deep guttural purring immediately recognisable as the Rolls-Royce Merlin.

The groundcrew would then have given a thumbs up with one hand while pointing at the engine with the other to confirm the engine was running OK. Onboard Jack would have been monitoring the process and as soon as the engine was firing regularly, he would have tweaked the throttles gently and reset the slow-running cut-out switch to the engine running (up) position.

The process would then have been repeated with No.2 port-inner engine then by No.4 starboard outer, and finally No.1 port outer. When all the four engines were running, Jack would have leaned forward and switched off the booster-coil switch. Beneath the Lancaster the Erk would have locked the priming pumps and moved to safety. The crew chief would have issued the command 'Switch to flight'. Maudslay would have turned round and flicked the main switch to the aircraft batteries and repeated 'Switch to flight', and the Erk disconnected and wheeled the trolley-acc to a safe distance. The wash from the propellers would have rushed over the tail plane making the rear of the Lancaster bounce lightly on the tailwheel and the whole machine to throb rhythmically and noisily.

Jack would have gently eased the four throttles forward until the rev-counter on the front console was showing a steady 1,200 rpm. He would have turned to his flight engineer's console on the starboard fuselage side and carefully monitored the oil pressure, oil temperature, and coolant temperature gauges for the four engines while ensuring that the fuel pressure warning lights were not illuminated. He would then have switched the four electric fuel booster pump switches to the off position to ensure the engine driven pumps were operating normally.

As the engines were warming up, Maudslay in the pilot's seat would have leaned forward and switched his DR Compass[24] on and adjusted it as required for the flight. He and Jack together would have checked that the hydraulically operated flaps lowered and raised satisfactorily.

Once the oil temperature had reached 15°c (yellow gauges on the flight engineer's panel) and coolant temperature 40°c (blue gauges on the flight engineer's panel) and Jack and Maudslay were happy the engines and systems were running satisfactorily, they would have started the power checks, known to the crews as 'giving the gun'. Jack would have flicked the RAD shutters switches to open and eased the four throttle levers forward to 1,500 rpm. He would then have leaned forward and flicked the No.1 magneto switch for No.1 engine down to the off position checking that the revs did not drop more than 150 rpm, then back up to the on position followed by the No.2 magneto switch for the same engine to the off position checking that the revs did not drop below 150 rpm or with a difference of 100 rpm between the two magnetos. This would have been repeated in sequence from left to right using the eight magneto switches for the four engines. If any engine failed this test the aircraft would have to be reported as unserviceable and would not be able fly. Fortunately, all engines behaved; the op was on.

The throttles would have been moved even further forward till the red boost gauges in the central control panel showed +4 psi and then Jack would have leaned forward and tested the superchargers, even though they were unlikely to be used in this mission, by switching the two supercharger switches down to the S ratio and ensuring a fall in the engines rpm and the red warning light came on, before returning the switch to the M ratio.

The propeller speed control levers below the throttle controls would have been pushed fully forward to 3,000 rpm, the aircraft would have tensed and pressed itself into the wheel chocks, desperate to move forward, and then the levers would have been moved back to an engine boost of +9 psi and the magnetos tested for each engine again as a precaution.

On completion of the tests, with the engines sweetly ticking over at 800 rpm, Jack will have reported 'All engines OK', which Maudslay would have repeated to acknowledge. By this time the airframe would have throbbed and rattled, pushing against the wheel chocks like a thoroughbred racehorse braced, tense and fired up, desperate for the off.

I love the sound of Merlin engines, it's a beautiful noise. What a joy the cacophony of the fifty-six Merlins of the fourteen Wave 1 and 2 Lancasters must have made. But it was not something to be admired or enjoyed by those involved that night. I doubt if any of the aircrew or groundcrew even noticed. This was the serious business of making sure they were running properly and were ready for the difficult night they knew would be coming.

But for the seven crew onboard AJ-Z the checks continued. Maudslay as captain would have announced to the crew 'engines OK', and then gone round the remaining five other crew members in turn.

> To Michael Fuller the bomb aimer:
> 'Intercom OK.'
> To Johnny Tytherleigh the front gunner:
> 'Turret elevation & rotations OK, intercom OK when turret rotated, feed (bullets) clear.'
> To Robert Urquhart the navigator:
> 'Instruments & lights OK, 'GEE'[25] set off & check spotlight altimeters (assumed check).'
> To Alden Cottam the wireless operator:
> 'Wireless OK, spare batteries OK & Upkeep rotation locked (assumed check).'
> To Norman Burrows the rear gunner:
> 'Turret elevation & rotations OK, intercom OK when turret rotated, feed (bullets) clear.'

Each of the crew would have checked their equipment and repeated the command so Maudslay knew everything was OK to proceed. All the checks must have been satisfactory and the crew happy that AJ-Z was ready for the action ahead.

The Form 700, basically a logbook of airworthiness, was signed by Maudslay indicating he was happy with the aircraft. It was then passed back to the crew chief. The ladders were pulled aboard, and the entrance hatch closed and locked. AJ-Z and the Maudslay crew were ready to go.

Around them the thirteen other Wave 1 and Wave 2 Lancaster crews had gone through the same process. Like Jack's aircraft all were similarly issue free – with the exception of one aircraft: AJ-Q. It was piloted by the American Joe McCarthy, the checks had gone satisfactorily up until the power checks were started. No.4 engine, the starboard outer, had developed an issue with the coolant temperature. It appears that a leak had developed in the coolant system and the engine had to be shut-down. This was a serious issue; the aircraft couldn't be risked as there was the possibility that the engine could seize or even catastrophically explode.

McCarthy was scheduled to be the first aircraft airborne; he was desperate not to miss the most significant mission of his life and having shut the engines down yelled to at his crew as he frantically clambered out of AJ-Q: 'For Christ's sake, get into that spare aircraft before some other bugger gets there and we don't get to go!' They disembarked and rushed over to the only serviceable spare aircraft ED825 (AJ-T) which had arrived that afternoon. Fortunately, AJ-T had been fixed and loaded with fuel and an Upkeep. But it hadn't had a flight test, nor did it have a VHF radio installed or the spotlight altimeters, ordinarily this would have meant it couldn't be used on the mission, but this was no ordinary raid; McCarthy was in Wave 2, so no VHF or spotlight altimeters were required, and the ground power checks would have to suffice for a flight test. They intended to go on the mission whatever.

Rushing through the pre-flight for a second time that evening he discovered another issue. The compass deviation card, an essential requirement for navigation, was missing from its little cradle at the top of the dashboard. McCarthy, already stressed and no doubt cursing and swearing once again, clambered out of his pilot's seat and jumped into the nearest van and sped off back to Hangar No.2. On arriving he leapt out of the van, threw his parachute to the ground and ran into the hangar where he was met by the chief ground engineer, who listened to his abusive tirade then hurried off to find the missing compass card.

Around the airfield the thirteen Lancasters hummed like a swarm of bees in the fading daylight. Observing strict radio silence, at about 21:20 Barlow's Lancaster AJ-E started to move around the peri-track towards the southerly threshold of Scampton's grass runway. They were immediately followed by Munro in AJ-W, Byers in AJ-K, and Rice in AJ-H. McCarthy looked on disconsolate as the four Lancasters approached the take-off holding point.

At 21:28 the black-and-white chequered airfield flight-control caravan parked just off the runway flashed its green Aldis Lamp. Barlow's engines roared, the Lancaster accelerated over the grass and was soon airborne. Munro followed at 21:29, Byers at 21:30, and Rice at 21:31. The four Lancasters of Wave 2 banked round to starboard onto an easterly setting for Mablethorpe on the Lincolnshire coast.

Except for McCarthy, all Wave 2 aircraft, which had a longer flight, were airborne. The first flight of Wave 1, led by Gibson, were already making their way to the runway. Jack, at his position alongside Maudslay in AJ-Z, would have pulled up his dickey seat and connected the primitive back support and sat vibrating in symphony with his massive aircraft as it throbbed rhythmically. While waiting for their turn to move, he would have been anxiously watching his engine gauges, ensuring there were no last-minute issues.

At 21:39 the flight controller's Aldis flashed green again. Gibson (AJ-G), with Hopgood (AJ-M) on his right, and Martin (AJ-P) on his left-hand side opened their throttles simultaneously and began their take-off. Gibson slightly ahead in a loose three-ship vic formation, climbed slowly away.

One of the few photos taken on the night of Operation Chastise by official Air Ministry photographer Flying Officer W Bellamy. Believed to be Barlow in AJ-E.

Flight 2 of Wave 1 were taxiing, and McCarthy had finally been given his compass correction card. He raced back to the waiting van, grabbing at his parachute on the way. But in his haste, he missed the canvas loop handle and snatched the D-ring of the ripcord, which sent his parachute silk billowing across the airfield. In temper he threw the now useless parachute pack to the ground cursing 'Goddamit, I'll go without one.' Fortunately, the crew chief quickly grabbed a spare and managed to push it through the window before McCarthy sped off to AJ-T to start his engine power checks.

At 21:47 a green Aldis was flashed from the control caravan. Young (AJ-A) leading Shannon (AJ-L) on the right, and Maltby (AJ-J) on the left took off also in a loose vic formation.

McCarthy had finally got his engines started and was going through his power checks.

Lancaster takes off past an airfield Control caravan.

Jack and AJ-Z Taxi for Take-Off

Even before the second flight led by Young were airborne, Maudslay had revisited some of checks.

Master switch – 'FLIGHT'
Nav lights – 'ON'
Altimeter – 'set to QFE' – airfield elevation
Radiator shutters – OPEN
Brake pressure – sufficient
Autopilot – checked
DR compass – set
Pitot head heater – on

Flight engineer gives thumbs up to the groundcrew.

Chocs away.

He would then have waved his hands to and fro to the groundcrew on the port side to signal the removal of the wheel chocks. Jack would have given the thumbs up to those on the starboard side. Once the chocks had been removed to a safe distance the crew chief would have given a thumbs up with both hands, indicating the aircraft was clear to taxi.

Maudslay released the brakes on his control column with a squeal and rush of air and opened the throttles to around 1,000 rpm until the huge heavy Lancaster started to move forward. He would have used careful pressure on the brakes and, by using differential power on the outboard engines, manoeuvred his way to the holding point at the southern end of the runway.

As they made their way, the final take-off checks and take-off configuration were carried out. It's probable that Maudslay would have shouted the instructions with Jack carrying out the check or making the setting before repeating the instruction to confirm.

Pilot Command – 'Response'	Equipment Location
Elevator trim tab – 'Two notches forward'	On a pedestal between pilot's and flight engineer's seats
Rudder trim tab – 'Neutral'	On a pedestal between pilot's and flight engineer's seats
Aileron trim tab – 'Neutral'	On a pedestal between pilot's and flight engineer's seats
Propeller pitch – 'Fully Forward and locked'	Central at the bottom of the control panel between pilot's and flight engineer

Pilot Command – 'Response'	Equipment Location
Fuel Contents – 'Checked'	On the flight engineer's panel on the starboard side and just behind the flight engineer's seat
Master engine fuel cocks – 'On'	Central at the bottom of the control panel between pilot's and flight engineer – port fuel cocks to the left and starboard fuel cocks to the right of the throttles
Fuel Tank Selector cocks – 'Checked – port and starboard on tank 2'	On the flight engineer's panel on the starboard side and just behind the flight engineer's seat
Cross Feed cock – 'Off'	Marked as 'Balance Cock', on the floor just forward of the main spar, visible through a hole in the spar cover
Booster pumps – 'No.1 and No.2 tanks On'	Switches on the flight engineer's panel on the starboard side and just behind the flight engineer's seat
Superchargers – 'M ratio'	Switch at bottom of the control panel above starboard fuel cocks
Air Intake – 'Cold'	Port side of pilot's floor, so would have been done by Maudslay
Radiator shutters – 'Automatic'	Switches on small panel on the starboard fuselage side next to control panel
Flaps – '20° down'	Push/pull flap selector on a pedestal between pilot's and flight engineer's seats in front of trim tabs, indicator on central console above throttles

Behind Astell and Knight, the last two aircraft of Wave 1 followed closely. By this time Barlow, Munro, Byers and Rice had already crossed the English coast above Mablethorpe heading eastwards across the North Sea to Vlieland.

Jack Takes Off

Just before 21:55, Maudslay, Astell and Knight moved onto the southern end of Scampton's grass runway. They moved a few yards forward to straighten their tailwheels, throttled back to 2,000 rpm on all engines, tightened the throttle tension enough to hold its position and not slip when released, applied their brakes and anxiously watched the flight control caravan, staring intently waiting for the green Aldis lamp.

McCarthy had completed his power checks and was also taxiing for take-off.

AJ-Z's checks were all in order, the crew were ready. Maudslay's right hand cradled the four throttle levers, his little finger and thumb controlling the outboard engines and the palm of his hand the inners. Jack's left hand fitted around Maudslay's, ready to take over once they were airborne.

The training was complete, these highly trained and skilful airmen were at the pinnacle of their readiness, their fear had transformed into intense concentration. Their palms were sweaty, their mouths dry. They had all flown around thirty missions before, but that didn't count now. They were focused on the job in hand and the first part was to get their Lancaster safely airborne. Taking off in a Lancaster was a two-man job, the flight engineer was equally as important as the pilot.

At one minute to ten the runway controller's Aldis flashed green. Most people would have taken a deep breath and gulped, there might have been a murmur 'Here we go'. Together, Maudslay and Jack eased the four throttles to zero boost with the brakes on to check the engines were responding evenly. The throttles were then eased back, the aircraft throbbing with power vibrating and straining against the brakes. Maudslay released the brake lever on his control column with his left hand. The Lancaster lunged forward, and together with Jack he advanced the throttles forward.

The engines roared as the huge Lancaster moved forward, as the speed built up Maudslay instinctively tweaked the left throttle levers for the

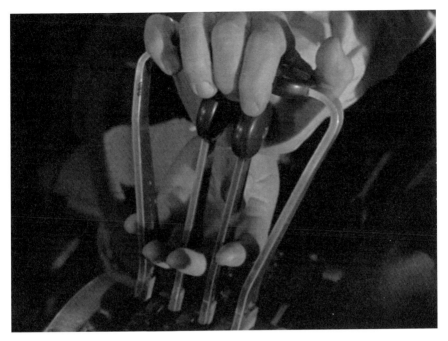

Flight engineer's right hand and pilot's left hand on throttles during take-off (Clip from The Dambusters film).

port engines slightly ahead of the starboard to counteract the Lancaster's tendency to swing to port on take-off. Although Jack was a master of the engines and controls, it was the pilot who could feel the swing and make the necessary engine adjustments. Jack carefully watched the boost and rpm needles swing round.

Knight on Maudslay's port quarter and Astell on the starboard watched as Maudslay edged forward, and then followed. The three Lancasters lumbered down the undulating grass runway. Slowly at first but as the speed built up the heavy controls became more responsive and Maudslay instinctively pushed the control column forward to bring the tail up. He could then use the rudders to keep straight, so removed his right hand from the throttles and asked Jack for 'Full power'. Jack moved the throttles fully forward through the gate and then tightened the throttle lock to keep them in place.

It was a heavy aeroplane, almost 30 tons. The noise of the engines was deafening even through the leather flying helmets. The Lancaster rattled and creaked and bumped and bounced. Urquhart the navigator carefully watching his ASI,[26] possibly shouting the speed as it built up. As the airspeed increased and approached 90 mph, Maudslay started heaving back on the control column, it was the point of no return. It took some effort, even with both hands, but the bounces got less and less, longer and longer, until around 110 mph when finally, one last bounce and they were airborne. Jack carefully scanned his engine gauges on the front console ensuring each engine was developing the +14 psi[27] boost and 3,000 rpm of the specially uprated engines. If there was going to be a problem, it would be the boost gauges that would give the first signs of engine troubles, so he would have watched these like a hawk. Thankfully, all was well. About a minute after releasing the brakes AJ-Z was flying.

All Maudslay's strength, expertise and coordination were required in just holding the aircraft in a shallow climb. Jack still held the throttles fully open; AJ-Z used the maximum take-off run. It seemed that they only just cleared the hedges as they crossed the northern boundary of the airfield.

Even before the final three Lancasters of Wave 1 cleared the northern airfield boundary, McCarthy was powering down the runway. He was half an hour behind the rest of Wave 2, desperate to make up some of the lost time.

Safely airborne, Maudslay dabbed the brakes to stop the main wheels spinning and gave the instruction 'Undercarriage up'. Jack turned to his left,

Take-off scene from The Dambusters film.

released the undercarriage safety bolt and moved the large red undercarriage handle backwards to the up position. As the undercarriage folded away backwards into the inboard engine nacelles and the undercarriage doors closed, Jack will have carefully watched the undercarriage position indicator as the green lights showed red as the undercarriage retracted and then finally no lights to show undercarriage successfully locked up. Although the indicator was immediately in front of Maudslay's control column and clearly visible to the pilot, Jack will have confirmed 'Undercarriage up and locked'.

With the reduction in drag the nose of the aircraft pitched slightly up, but Maudslay knew the feel of a Lancaster so well and without even thinking about it, eased the control column forward and retrimmed the elevators and called for 'Climbing power'. Jack unscrewed the throttle lock, eased the throttles back to 2,850 rpm +9 psi boost and relocked. He probably had a quick look over his shoulder at the flight engineer's instrument panel to check the oil pressure was around 70 psi, the oil temperature 90° and the coolant temperature 125° on all four engines and then confirmed 'Climbing power, temps and pressures OK'.

Route to the Dams

Maudslay held the nose down letting the airspeed build up. As they were going to fly low level all the way when the airspeed passed 145 mph, he called 'Flaps up'. Jack pulled the flap selector lever and watched for the flap indicator on the main console to read 0° before confirming 'Flaps up'. Maudslay automatically trimmed the elevators backwards to compensate the nose pitching down. AJ-Z was now 'clean' and flew smoothly. Jack checked that with the increase in speed and power reductions, the oil and coolant temperatures came down.

Maudslay, Astell and Knight in their loose vic formation levelled off at about 100ft. Maudslay called for 'cruise power'. Jack set the throttles to 2,650 rpm +7 psi boost, and even before he could confirm 'cruise power', Maudslay had instinctively retrimmed the Lancaster's nose level. The three Lancasters banked round to port and made a circuit of the Scampton airfield. Navigator Urquhart set his instruments and gave Maudslay the heading of 125°, their track to their exit point at Southwold on the Suffolk coast.

Once settled into a steady cruise at 180 mph Jack flicked off the electric fuel booster switches on his flight engineer's panel and then checked the contents of the fuel tanks. He would have tweaked the engine revs, listening by ear, making fine adjustments till all four Merlins were in phase and purring sweetly.

Though Maudslay would have contacted each member of the crew periodically for a cursory check-in, the trip was probably generally quiet with little chatter. This was serious business, each and every one of the crew needed to be highly alert. Jack will have settled in, without thinking, to his normal mission role of lookout, scanning the sky and ensuring no aircraft other than Astell's and Knight's could be seen. Fuller, the bomb aimer, was key, assisting the navigator with his own maps and shouting out landmarks and obstacles. At such a low altitude and fast speed, it was relentless pressure and an absolute necessity.

Lancaster Flight engineer flicking the fuel contents switch to check fuel levels.

After ten minutes they were already above their training ground of The Wash, and a few minutes later over the Norfolk countryside. By this time Gibson's trio were approaching the English coast, but further north over the North Sea McCarthy, who was trying to make up some time, was 'gunning' his Lancaster and taking one of the return routes – a slightly more southern route to Holland. It wasn't going smoothly, he was having more problems. His radio had stopped working but as he was to attack the Sorpe Dam without an airborne controller he wouldn't have the need for a radio, so he decided to press on.

At 22:48 Maudslay's three ship vic reached Southwold. Urquhart gave a new heading of 115°, Maudslay banked gently round to port and picked up the new heading. Still flying at 100ft AJ-Z passed over the North Sea.

The Lancaster had little sophistication, it was built for the delivery and dropping of bombs and it needed continual flying. Maudslay was an experienced and top-class pilot, but as he concentrated on keeping the aeroplane straight and level while scanning the horizon, he may have been troubled by two incidents that undoubtedly played on his mind. The incident at Reculver, together with the fact that as B-Flight commander he had been overlooked by Gibson in favour of Hopgood for the role of deputy commander in the event of a problem with Gibson at the Eder Dam. Maybe he doubted his own abilities and considered his performance in training hadn't come up to scratch, and perhaps he thought that Gibson didn't consider him up to the job.

Thirty minutes ahead of them, Gibson was approaching the Dutch coast. At one point over the English Channel he had selected the autopilot, but it didn't work correctly, it pitched the Lancaster violently nose down. Gibson quickly disengaged it and pulled the nose back up. He then eased off the control column and tried to light a cigarette. Again, the nose pitched down, much to the horror of Hopgood and Martin flying alongside. The Lancaster, especially flying so low, required continual concentration. At the same time Barlow, the first of the Wave 2 aircraft, was also approaching the Dutch coast, but 130 miles to the north.

The North Sea was calm and after a few minutes out over the sea Maudslay's trio descended to 60ft. The crews kept their watchful sentry scanning the horizon and their relevant instruments. They were all busy. Maudslay with both hands on his control column keeping the aircraft straight and level as it buffeted gently in the airstream. Jack would have kept a look out while perpetually running his eyes over his engine instruments. Fuller, the bomb aimer, alert and watching ahead for landmarks and obstacles, periodically reporting back to Urquhart. The gunners, Tytherleigh in the nose gun, and Burrows in the tail gun, scanning from left to right and up and down, periodically checking the rotation of the turret and maximum elevation of their guns. Urquhart the navigator will have switched off the IFF[28] equipment as it was no longer of use outside UK airspace and he would have been monitoring his Gee and API[29] navigational equipment. He most likely released some flame floats periodically, from which Burrows in the rear turret could determine the drift and advise if the course needed to be adjusted. Cottam, the wireless operator, alert for any radio or Morse code messages probably stood with his head in the Perspex bubble-like astrodome at the back of the cockpit canopy helping with the lookout.

At some point Urquhart would have switched on the spotlight altimeters, stood up from his seat behind Maudslay and looked through the blister on the starboard side of the canopy to check that the two lights were both working and the Lancaster was flying along at 60ft so that Maudslay could ensure his altimeter was calibrated accurately. It's interesting to note that in his book *Henry Maudslay – Dambuster*, Robert Owen reports that 'Sutherland, the front gunner in Knight's Lancaster AJ-N, stated that his flight engineer Grayston [who would have had a clear view of Maudslay's AJ-Z just ahead and to the right of him] noted that one of the other two Lancasters, possibly AJ-Z, appeared to be about 20ft below them when they had levelled off at 60ft.'

As Maudslay continued on, the Lancasters of Wave 2 flying closely but not together, had arrived at the Dutch coast over the southern Wadden Islands and immediately encountered problems. At 22:57 the first of the Dambusters was lost. Barlow (AJ-E) had passed safely over Vlieland but a previously unidentified flak unit was alerted and targeted Munro (AJ-W), who was hit by flak. In order to determine the severity of the damage Munro circled over the Waddensec and shouted with his flight engineer, Appleby, with difficulty as the intercom and VHF radio had been damaged. The wireless operator, Pigeon, was sent to investigate. At the same time Byers, flying AJ-K, had been affected by the stronger than forecast northerly wind and drifted from a track that would have taken him over the lightly defended island of Vlieland. He appeared to climb as he approached, perhaps to confirm his location. It seems that he had crossed the heavily defended island of Texel and was engaged by heavy anti-aircraft fire. The Lancaster burst into flames crashing into the Waddensee, killing all seven crew members. He was the least experienced of all the pilots that night having flown on only four previous operations.

Rice in AJ-H following just behind possibly saw the two aircraft ahead of him succumb to anti-aircraft fire so remained very low. So low that at 23:00 his aircraft hit the surface of the sea just south of Vlieland. The Upkeep was ripped free which smashed into the tailwheel, pushing it up into the tail of the aircraft which flooded with water. Rice fought to maintain control of the Lancaster. Fortunately, the Upkeep wasn't fused and didn't explode. Nobody was injured and as water poured from the back of the Lancaster Rice had no other option but to turn for home.

Just as Rice turned for home Gibson's trio crossed the Dutch coast. The northerly wind that had affected Wave 2 had also forced Gibson slightly south of track over the former island of Walcheren, just north of Middelburg.

At 23:05 in AJ-W, the wireless operator, Pigeon, had returned to Munro with bad news. Although all crew members were uninjured there was a huge hole in the rear fuselage. The master compass had been destroyed which,

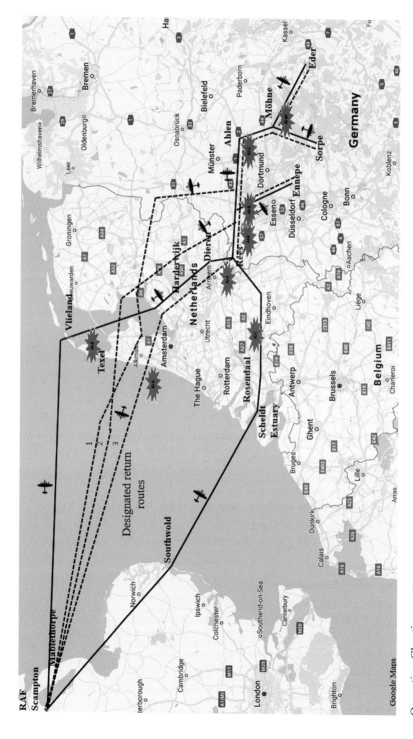

Operation Chastise route map.

together with the loss of radio, confirmed their worst fears – they would have to return to Scampton without completing their mission.

Wave 2 were down to two aircraft. Though nobody was aware, it was already looking unlikely for success at the second most important target, the Sorpe Dam.

Just over five minutes later, Young, Shannon and Maltby reached the Scheldt Estuary, but unlike Gibson they were greeted by searchlights and flak, alerted when Gibson's trio had flown over. None of the three Lancasters were hit. About the same time, McCarthy reached Vlieland to the north but avoided being hit by the same flak team that had ended Munro's participation. McCarthy had made up almost ten minutes; ahead of him, Barlow had tracked halfway down the Zuiderzee to his checkpoint of Stavoren.

By 23:15 Maudslay was approaching the Dutch coast. Remaining low, Knight and Astell eased from the tight vic formation to make themselves a more difficult target for the German defences. Urquhart turned round and, using the pull-handle on the starboard fuselage wall, armed the self-destruct fuse on the Upkeep. It was a top-secret weapon, and should they get shot down it was imperative it didn't fall into enemy hands.

As they crossed the Dutch coast at 23:21 they were right on track over the Scheldt Estuary between Schouwen and Walcheren. Fuller confirmed the Dutch coast and Urquhart called a course correction. Maudslay brought the Lancaster round to the port and Jack tweaked the throttles. They were flying at just 100ft. A minute later they were over mainland Europe. The whole crew maintained their look out, which intensified with the prospect of enemy defences and the Dutch overhead electrification system. To the north of them, Barlow had crossed into mainland Europe making a slight course correction at Harderwijk for the next waypoint of Dieren.

In bright moonlight visibility was excellent, but flying so low and fast required maximum concentration by all. There would have been heavy buffeting and little room for error. Maudslay was a top-class pilot. He was skilled at flying Lancasters in all conditions, but this was a tough ask, as it was for all those flying on Operation Chastise that night.

No anti-aircraft fire appears to have opened up as they made their way towards their next checkpoint at the town of Roosendaal. But up ahead, Gibson had reached the canal junction at Beek en Donk. Both his and Young's trio had both encountered flak. To the north, McCarthy was halfway down the Zuiderzee and Barlow was flying southeast near the waypoint of Dieren approaching the German border. Munro and Rice were flying west, back over the North Sea on their way home.

Maudslay reached the checkpoint of the large railway junction at Roosendaal at 23:35 and a further course correction was made to bring them round to an almost due-east direction, taking them to the south of the German night fighter airfields of Gilze-Rijn (between Breda and Tilburg) and north of the Eindhoven night fighter base. The whole crew would have been on maximum alert straining their eyes for any signs of night fighters and anti-aircraft activity. This was the area in which Young's trio had been subjected to flack ten minutes earlier. Maudslay's vic may have also been targeted, but there is no mention in any subsequent documentation.

Working as a team they flew across the very flat countryside alert, watching – and concerned about the power lines as much as worried about enemy defences. Fuller, with his detailed maps marked with known positions, shouting out as they approached each one so Maudslay could haul the Lancaster up and over with the purr of the four Merlins changing into a growl as they lifted the nose up and over.

At about 23:45 Gibson entered German airspace slightly off track. He flew north up the River Rhine to Rees, where he banked round to the right, flying almost due east. Young was approaching Beek en Donk, and Barlow from Wave 2, having done the long route south through Holland, was also approaching Rees, where he made a sharp turn to port.

Maudslay had picked up the Wilhelmina Canal which came south east from Tilburg and then turned in an east-west direction at Haghorst. Maudslay, like Gibson and Young ahead of him, will have found it easy for navigation in the clear moonlight. Flying along it at about 100ft, Fuller watched intensely for those dreaded power lines. Maudslay would have periodically 'bunted' over, and possibly sometimes dived beneath, the deadly cables, each time Jack's four finely tuned Merlins complained noisily at the sudden change in the aircraft's attitude.

Five minutes later as Maudslay was passing north of Eindhoven, still following the Wilhelmena Canal up ahead Barlow fell prey to the deadly 100,000-volt power lines. It's not known if he had been hit by flak or whether his Lancaster AJ-E flew directly into them, but the Lancaster was horribly snared in the power cables and took a nosedive into a field north of Haldern, exploding on impact with the ground and killing all seven crew members.

Unfortunately, the Upkeep may not have been fused and rolled clear of the crash site coming to rest without exploding, it was soon disassembled and analysed by German scientists. Wave 2 were now down to the single Lancaster of McCarthy and not one of the dams had yet been reached.

Maudslay was soon at the canal junction south of Beek en Donk and the waypoint at the distinctive junction of the Wilhelmena and Willemsvaart canals. It's believed he climbed briefly to about 300ft to get a positive identification, followed by a slight course correction before descending back down to 100ft and tracking for the Dutch-German border near Boxmeer on the River Meuse.

German officials inspect Barlow's unexploded Upkeep.

As 16 May became 17 May, Gibson's trio were at their final turning point at the small town of Ahlen, twenty miles north of the Möhne Reservoir. They had experienced searchlights and increased flak activity since crossing over the Rhine.

South-east of Dülmen Hopgood's Lancaster had been hit in the fuselage and quite badly in the port wing, causing the port outer engine to burst into flames, which some reports state as being feathered.[30] Hopgood was wounded in the head, Burcher, the rear gunner, had slight injuries to his groin and stomach, Minchin the wireless operator was more seriously hurt and couldn't move his legs, and front gunner Gregory failed to respond to calls and was believed to have been killed.

Gibson instructed his wireless operator, Hutchison, to break radio silence and notify No.5 Group HQ of the flak concentrations. Young's trio followed ten minutes behind and much to the consternation of Maltby and Shannon, Young persisted in flying much higher than the other two at around 500ft.

By 00:05 No.5 Group HQ had retransmitted the flak warning, by which time Young had passed Rees heading for Ahlen, and Maudslay had passed Boxmeer and was approaching the Rhine. Back at Scampton Wave 3 crews were ready for take-off.

At 00:09 Ottley became airborne in AJ-C, two minutes later Burpee followed in AJ-S, a minute later Brown in AJ-F, then two minutes later Townsend in AJ-O, and finally, the last of the Dambusters to leave Scampton, Anderson in AJ-Y was on his way at 00:15. They followed the same route as Wave 1 on the southern route, but as they made their way, they still didn't know which their target dam was going to be.

As Anderson became airborne at Scampton, Gibson was approaching the Möhne Dam. The final route from Ahlen had been more over difficult terrain to traverse. Gone were the flat lands of Holland which had made navigation easier, to be replaced by undulating hills, valleys, and forests.

The tight three-ship vic formation that Gibson's trio had maintained from the start became difficult to hold and Gibson seems to have lost his way for a short period, enabling Martin in AJ-P to arrive at the Möhne Reservoir first at 00:15. Gibson arrived a minute or so later as he described in his book *Enemy Coast Ahead*:

> 'We're there,' said Spam.
> 'Thank God,' said I, feelingly.
> As we came over the hill, we saw the Möhne Lake.[31] Then we saw the dam itself. In that light it looked squat and heavy and unconquerable; it looked grey and solid in the moonlight, as though it were part of the countryside itself and just as immovable. A structure like a battleship was showering out flak all along its length, but some came from the power-house below and nearby.
>
> There were no searchlights. It was light flak, mostly green, yellow and red, and the colours of the tracer reflected upon the face of the water in the lake. The reflections on the dead calm of the black water made it seem there was twice as much as there really was.

Hopgood arrived as Young's group were at the waypoint of Ahlen, but Maudslay's trio had encountered problems. There are no accurate records, but there are suggestions that the formation that had reached Rees in a close formation had become separated and spread out. It seems that Knight had increased his speed slightly and was actually ahead of Maudslay.

Astell's crew may not have been able to identify the turning point over the Rhine near Rees and carried on their original track for a while before making the course correction and getting back on track. It meant, however, that he had fallen behind slightly, so rather than a tight vic, they were then flying individually one behind the other.

At the same time as Gibson arrived at the Möhne Reservoir, Knight and Maudslay were making their way towards Ahlen. Thundering low over the rooftops of a farm just to the west of the village of Marbeck, they heaved their Lancasters up over powerlines.

Above left: Möhne Dam.

Above right: The wreckage of Astell's AJ-B.

Right: Sorpe Dam.

A minute or two later Astell, by then back on track, for whatever reason failed to spot the deadly obstacle. Whether he was preoccupied with trying to catch up the other two, or whether it was a lack of concentration we'll never know. The Lancaster smashed into the top of a 90ft electricity pylon causing the aircraft to erupt in flames; 30 tons of burning aircraft hurtled for 500yds over a farmhouse before smashing into a field beyond.

The Upkeep ripped free and rolled forward until the self-destruct fuse detonated the device 100yds further on. Operation Chastise was now down to fourteen aircraft.

Elsewhere McCarthy, despite no VHF radio and problems with his compass, had arrived at the Sorpe Reservoir. Having made up considerable time he had been slightly ahead of Gibson, which had possibly alerted the flak and searchlight defences between Rees and Ahlen that had cost Barlow's aircraft and made the rest of Wave 1's transition so uncomfortable.

Rice had arrived back over Scampton and was circling while his crew sorted out hydraulic issues and made preparations for a difficult landing in the damaged Lancaster with no tailwheel. Munro was approaching the English coast on his final leg home.

Attacking the Möhne Dam

At the Möhne Dam it was a bright, moonlit night. It was still warm in the Lancaster cockpits; Gibson was still in his shirtsleeves, his concentration intense, despite the continual pain in his feet. The three Lancasters circled at about 600ft over the hills and forests on the southern section of the Möhne Reservoir (known as the Hevesee) while the crews noted the landmarks and reviewed the plan of attack. As they did so the flak emplacements on and around the dam started firing using various colours of tracers. Though they were out of range it enabled an estimate of the number of guns; Gibson concluded there were twelve, though in reality there were only six. As expected, there were no barrage balloons or searchlights to contend with, but the flak increased in intensity whenever the Lancasters got too near the dam.

Although it has never been confirmed, it seems that despite the intensity of flak, it was decided that the best approach was from the southeast over the promontory of the north bank of the Hevesee, over Heveberg spit with a direct run towards the dam.

About 00:20 Gibson announced over VHF radio for the others to circle anti-clockwise while he made a trial approach. Flying low and fast over the calm reservoir with flak coming almost horizontally towards his Lancaster he made a successful pass over the dam and re-joined the circling Martin and Hopgood.

Just after 00:25, Young and Maltby arrived and joined the circuit of circling Lancasters. Shannon arrived a few moments later and approached the Möhne Dam over a ridge from the north, almost directly above the dam. He was immediately targeted and hit by flak from the right-hand tower causing a small hole in the fuselage.

Maudslay had turned south-easterly at the last waypoint of Ahlen, climbed to about 1,000ft in compliance with Operation Orders, which required the leader of each section to listen on VHF 'channel A'. Although they were still

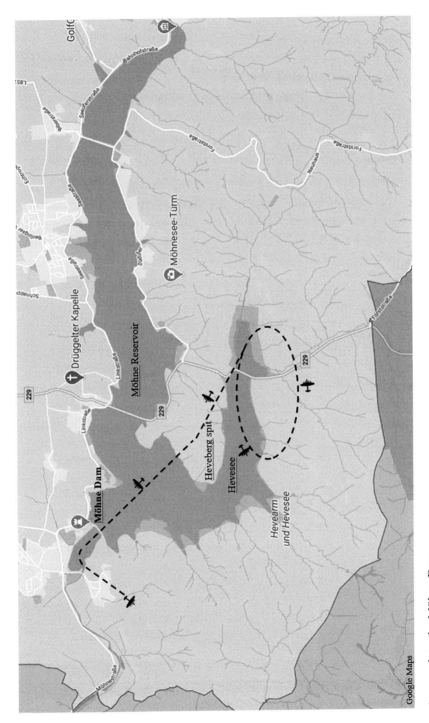

Approach to the Möhne Dam.

over five minutes from the Möhne Reservoir they will have heard the radio chatter of the six Lancasters ahead of them.

At 00:28 Gibson announced those famous words. Words so familiar to me from being very young, indelibly etched into my subconscious from seeing the film and reading Paul Brickhill's book. I could probably type them even now without referring to the book. But to be accurate I won't, because it's more appropriate to use Gibson's thoughts and impressions as he made his attack (extract from *Enemy Coast Ahead* by Guy Gibson).

'Well, boys, I suppose we had better start the ball rolling.'

'Hello all Cooler aircraft. I am going to attack. Stand by to come in to attack in your order when I tell you.'

'Hello, M Mother. Stand by to take over if anything happens.' Hoppy's clear and casual voice came back. 'O.K., Leader. Good luck.'

Then the boys dispersed to the pre-arranged hiding-spots in the hills, so that they should not be seen either from the ground or from the air, and we began to get into position for our approach. We circled wide and came down moon, over the high hills at the eastern end of the lake. On straightening up we began to dive towards the flat, ominous water two miles away. Over the front turret was the dam silhouetted against the haze of the Ruhr Valley. We could see the towers. We could see the sluices. We could see everything.

Spam the bomb-aimer, said, 'Good show. This is wizard.' He had been a bit worried, as all bomb-aimers are, in case they cannot see their aiming points, but as we came in over the tall fir trees his voice came up again rather quickly. 'You're going to hit them. You're going to hit those trees.'

'That's all right, Spam. I'm just getting my height.'

To Terry [navigator]: 'Check height, Terry.'
To Pulford [flight engineer]: 'Speed control, Flight-Engineer.'
To Trevor [rear gunner]: 'All guns ready, gunners,'
To Spam [bomb aimer]: 'Coming up, Spam.'

Terry turned on the spotlights and began giving directions – 'Down – down – down. Steady – steady.' We were then exactly sixty feet.

Pulford began working the speed; first he put a little flap to slow us down, then he opened the throttles to get the air speed indicator exactly against the red mark. Spam began lining up his sights against the towers. He had turned the fusing switch to the 'ON' position. I began flying.

The gunners had seen us coming. They could see us coming with our spotlights on for over two miles away. Now they opened up and their tracers began swirling towards us; some were even bouncing off the smooth surface of the lake. This was a horrible moment; we were being dragged along at four miles a minute, almost against our will, towards the things we were going to destroy. I think at that moment the boys did not want to go. I know I did not want to go. I thought to myself, 'In another minute we shall all be dead – so what?' I thought again, 'This is terrible – this feeling of fear – if it is fear.' By now we were a few hundred yards away and I said quickly to Pulford, under my breath, 'Better leave the throttles open now and stand by to pull me out of the seat if I get hit.' As I glanced at him I thought he looked a little glum on hearing this.

The Lancaster was really moving and I began looking through the special sight in my windscreen. Spam had his eyes glued to the bomb sight in front, his hand on his button; a special mechanism on board had already begun to work so that the mine would drop (we hoped) in the right spot. Terry was still checking the height.

Joe and Trev began to raise their guns. The flak could see us quite clearly now. It was not exactly an inferno. I have been through far worse flak than that; but we were very low. There was something sinister and slightly unnerving about the whole operation. My aircraft was so small and the dam was so large; it was thick and solid, and now it was angry. My aircraft was very small. We skimmed along the surface of the lake, and as we went my gunner was firing into the defences, and the defences were firing back with vigour, their shells whistling past us. For some reason, we were not being hit.

Spam said, 'Left – little more left – steady – steady – steady – coming up.' Of the next few seconds I remember only a series of kaleidoscopic incidents.

The chatter from Joe's front guns pushing out tracers which bounced off the left hand flak tower.
Pulford crouching beside me.
The smell of burnt cordite.
The cold sweat underneath my oxygen mask.

The tracers flashing past the windows – they all seemed the same colour now – and the inaccuracy of the gun positions near the power-station; they were all firing in the wrong direction.

The closeness of the dam wall.
Spam's exultant, 'Mine gone'.
    Hutch's [wireless operator] red Very lights to blind the flak-gunners.
    The speed of the whole thing.
    Someone saying over the R.T., 'Good show, Leader. Nice work.'

Then it was all over, and at last we were out of range, and there came over us all, I think, an immense feeling of relief and confidence.

    …

    As we circled round we could see a great 1,000-feet column of whiteness still hanging in the air where our mine had exploded. We could see with satisfaction that Spam had been good, and it had gone off in the right position. Then, as we came closer, we could see the explosion of the mine had caused a great disturbance upon the surface of the lake and the water had become broken and furious, as though it were being lashed by a gale. At first we thought that the dam itself had broken, because great sheets of water were slopping over the top of the wall like a gigantic basin.

In reality the Upkeep had skipped three times and sank after travelling 50yds, but short of the dam. Hutchison, the wireless operator, fired a red Very flare over the dam wall to indicate the Upkeep had been released and sent a message to No.5 Group HQ 'GONER68A' indicating they had released their Upkeep, it had exploded 5yds from the Möhne Dam with no apparent damage. Despite the personal brilliance of Gibson, his heroism, and his extraordinary efforts while in discomfort and pain, his personal effort had failed.

Five minutes later at 00:33 the water had subsided, and Gibson called Hopgood into attack. 'Hello M-Mother. You may attack now. Good luck.' Hopgood replied without any indication of his or his crew's injuries 'OK Leader. Attacking'. He made his run towards the dam, but the flak teams were prepared and ready. The Lancaster, already struggling with issues with the port outer engine, was hit several times. The port-inner engine was damaged, the large port-inner fuel tank was also hit which burst into flames, and the watching aircraft also noted hits to his starboard wing.

Hopgood continued his approach regardless. It is not known how badly injured he and his crew were, or how difficult it was to coordinate their attack with the depleted crew, but the circling Lancasters watched in horror as the Upkeep was released late, flew over the dam wall, and smashed into a power station on the air side of the dam.

Hopgood fought desperately to gain height so his crew could bale out; Minchin, the wireless operator, even managed to fire a red Very light in accordance with his instructions. Hopgood and Brennan, the flight engineer, desperately tried to sort the fires out. Hopgood fought hard with his dying Lancaster and managed to get to about 500ft when the Lancaster exploded, at which point he ordered the crew to bale out.

Fraser, the bomb aimer in the nose, managed to get out through the forward escape hatch. Burcher fought with his rear turret which was powered from one of the, by then useless, engines, but eventually managed to manually turn it; while grabbing his parachute he noticed the badly injured Minchin struggling back down towards the entrance hatch. Burcher pushed Minchin out of the door, pulling his D-Ring for him before being ejected through the door himself.

Sadly, Minchin didn't survive, but even though Burcher hit the tail fin and badly injured his back, he and Fraser both survived. The rest of the crew sadly died with the aircraft. It was the fourth Lancaster lost and only one Upkeep had been used.

As the shock of Hopgood's demise was playing out, Knight arrived at the Möhne Reservoir followed shortly afterwards by Jack's Lancaster. Though they may not have been able to see the horror of Hopgood's loss, they will certainly have heard the concerned chatter of the other crews over the R/T.

I can't imagine what their feelings and emotions would have been. Fear, horror, dread, trepidation? All, no doubt, and many more besides, but

Luftwaffe officer inspects the remains of Hopgood's AJ-M.

sentiment and anger aside, these were professional and experienced airmen and they had a job to do. Maudslay joined the Lancasters in their left-hand orbit and he and his crew began familiarising themselves with the features from the model, maps, and photos they had studied so hard several hours before.

With the death of Hopgood, Gibson had lost his closest friend in the squadron and the operation wasn't going well at all. They were six aircraft down and only one Upkeep used, albeit unsuccessfully. But Gibson was a leader and incredibly brave so, despite the losses and failures so far, he put his own fears to one side and prepared for the next aircraft.

At 00:36, as Martin was getting into position south-east of the Möhne Dam, Munro in AJ-W had arrived back at Scampton complete with his Upkeep. Without the use of radio, he wasn't able to contact the tower, so his approach took him straight in. What he didn't know was that Rice had also turned back and having completed his preparations for a difficult landing, was also on final approach. Munro flew directly beneath Rice without seeing him. Rice, already fighting with his damaged Lancaster, aborted his landing and took a long careful orbit before finally landing at 00:47, coming to a halt on the Lancaster's two tailfins. An unfortunate accident was avoided by the smallest of margins, but two of the crews were back home safe even if they hadn't managed to complete their mission.

Gibson called Martin at 00:38. He was an outstanding and skilful pilot considered to be one of the best in the squadron. There are various accounts of Gibson's R/T instruction from, 'Come in number three, you can go in now,' but more likely, 'Hello P-Popsie. Are you ready?' Martin replied 'OK, Leader. Going in.'

Gibson, as well as being an incredible leader, was exceptionally brave. Having already twice run the gauntlet of a low-level approach to the dam, he flew starboard alongside and slightly ahead of Martin. Risking the lives of himself and his crew he attempted to draw some of the flak away from Martin's Lancaster, as the front gunners in both Lancasters fired a stream of tracers at the dam's defenders.

The two Lancasters were soon down at low level, Martin exactly at 60ft, 217 mph, both front gunners firing furiously. Hay, Martin's bomb aimer and squadron bombing leader, watched intently as the two towers converged in his bombsight. Just as he was pressing the Upkeep release button, Martin's Lancaster was hit in the starboard wing.

Perhaps the Lancaster jolted slightly, or the Upkeep had sustained some damage when it fell from the Lancaster several hours earlier and was out of balance, or maybe it was just the way it was spinning, but instead of skipping towards the dam it veered off to the left, exploding over 20yds from the dam near the western shore of the reservoir. Another failure message was transmitted back to Grantham 'GONER58A' (Upkeep released, exploded 50yds from the Möhne Dam, with no apparent breach). Three top-class pilots and their elite crews had tried and not one had made a direct hit.

Gibson called in Young, the fourth attempt. This time Gibson flew around the northern (air) side of the dam with his gunners engaging the flak defences and flashing his navigation lights as a further distraction. Martin flew alongside Young on his port side to draw some of the remaining flak. At 00:43 Young's Upkeep skipped three times, hit the dam wall about centre and exploded at a depth of 30ft as planned.

It seems that the Upkeep had caused the dam to crumble but it wasn't actually noticed by any of the aircrew and a 'GONER78A' was sent to Grantham. Maltby was called in, and as he did so Gibson and Martin circled over the dam to draw fire from the flak gunners. As he approached Maltby thought he could already see the dam crumbling but released his Upkeep at 00:49; as with the previous attempt, it bounced accurately, sank in contact with the dam and exploded.

Spray from the attacks was hanging in the air, misting up the valley and, more importantly, restricting visibility; Gibson pressed on and called in Shannon. As Shannon ran from the southeast, Martin, banking over the dam, had seen the dam collapse sending a torrent of water down the valley and excitedly shouted over R/T 'Hell, it's gone! It's gone! Look at it for Christ's sake!' The Möhne Dam had at last been breached, but Maltby's wireless operator, Stone, transmitted the incorrect code of 'GONER78A'. Gibson, seconds after calling Shannon in, hurriedly instructed him to 'Skip it' while he flew closer to have a proper look.

Jack's Lancaster had been circling out of range of the German defences and he would probably have seen very little of the action of the other Lancasters, but would have been listening intently on excited R/T interactions. With little risk of flak all the Lancasters, amid continued excited chatter which died away as they looked down in awe, circled around the dam to review the historic spectacle. Little did any of them realise how significant a piece of British history they had just created.

In Gibson's Lancaster Hutchison sat back at his little desk and tapped in Morse the codeword, confirming the Möhne Dam had been breached. Five Upkeeps had been used, but in reality the dam had been breached by the first accurate attack. It was 00:49, though the message wasn't received in Grantham until 00:56. German sources later claimed that six attempts had been made, but the first attempt was actually Gibson's dummy run.

Gibson, concerned that time was running on, called for a halt to the excited R/T chatter and sent Martin and Maltby home. He instructed Young, who had already released his Upkeep, to accompany him to the Eder Dam to act as controller in the event he had any issues. The remaining three Lancasters with Upkeeps were ordered to make their way to the Eder Dam. Max Hastings in his book *Chastise* suggests (without any firm evidence) that taking Young as deputy controller at the Eder Dam 'was an odd decision by Gibson, which can only have reflected lack of confidence in Maudslay'.

As the five Wave 1 Lancasters departed for the fifteen-minute flight further southeast to the Eder Reservoir, Gibson had spent more than forty minutes of intense low-level, highly pressurised flying at the Möhne Reservoir.

Möhne Dam breached.

McCarthy's Sorpe Attack

While crossing Holland and Germany, McCarthy's two gunners, Batson and Rodger, requested and were given permission to fire on goods or military trains. As they did so one turned out to be a flak train which vigorously returned fire causing some, though at the time undetermined, damage to AJ-T.

Having struggled with navigation and hampered by mist, McCarthy arrived at the Sorpe Dam at 00:15. It was perfect visibility; he was surprised that there was no evidence of any previous attack. Having had no radio contact, he was unaware that of the five Wave 2 Lancasters detailed to attack the Sorpe Dam, two had crashed and the other two had returned to base; he was the only one to have made it.

The Sorpe Dam was an earthen bank rather than a brick-built gravity dam; the Upkeep would need to be dropped at 180 mph without spinning, on the water-side of the dam, as near to the centre as possible so that it would roll down the embankment and explode. This required the Lancaster to fly parallel to the dam as low as possible and needed absolute accuracy.

After a brief look during which he exclaimed 'Jeez! How do we get down there?' he came in steeply and low over the village of Langscheid, avoiding a church steeple on the north-western side of the dam. Despite being the longest dam at 2,250ft, it had densely wooded slopes on the opposite side; bomb aimer Johnson was unhappy and the drop was aborted. Fortunately, the dam was undefended as it took nine more attempts, much to the consternation of his crew members, before he was satisfied.

After more than half an hour over the Sorpe Reservoir, much to the relief of the rest of the crew, at 00:46 the Upkeep was finally released at a height of only 30ft. It exploded, sending a huge fountain of water up and over the dam. After circling for a few minutes McCarthy, despite an initial elation that he had been successful, could see only superficial damage to the parapet of the dam, but no breach. He banked round to port and set course for home. A 'GONER79C' message was immediately sent, though not received at Grantham until 03:00.

At around 01:00, just after the five Wave 1 Lancasters departed the Möhne for the Eder Dam, McCarthy overflew the rapidly emptying reservoir. He was amazed at the devastation down the valley. Maltby, flying slightly ahead of Martin, had passed the waypoint of Ahlen, heading west. The five Wave 3 Lancasters had crossed the English coast at Southwold and were heading for Holland.

By 01:15 Maltby, followed a few minutes later by Martin, had turned due north at Dülmen on their designated return route to home. McCarthy though, still struggling with his navigation equipment, had strayed into flak over the heavily defended city of Hamm, north of the Möhne Reservoir, having decided his best option was to simply retrace his outbound route.

Wave 3 were approaching the Dutch coast around Scheldt.

Attacking the Eder Dam

Though the Eder Dam was less than fifty miles to the southeast of the Möhne Dam, the five navigators found the navigation between the two difficult. Undulating hills, convoluted valleys, and small towns and villages proved difficult to distinguish between as early morning mist started to fill the valleys. Power lines strung between valleys was a continual fear. Despite the lack of any flak defences, flying in formation at low level was impossible so the five Lancasters proceeded individually.

Elsewhere, at 01:30, Maltby and Martin had reached the waypoint of Noordhorn without any notable incident and turned northwest. McCarthy had successfully negotiated his way around Hamm and was approaching Rees, while the five Wave 3 aircraft had passed over the Scheldt Estuary and were heading for Roosendaal.

At the same time Gibson, having flown at tree top height, had arrived at the western edge of the thin, long, steep-sided and snaking Eder Reservoir. As he flew eastwards towards the dam he had difficulty in determining between the waters of the reservoir and mist. It took several minutes, but eventually the dam was identified behind a sharp bend nestled in a deep-sided valley. He circled around the eastern end of the reservoir and then flew down the steep sided valley and the village of Waldeck to assess the topography before banking up and over the dam.

Other than difficulties in navigating from the Möhne to the Eder Reservoir there is no record of any hostilities and it is believed the flight for all five Lancasters was uneventful. Young arrived at the Eder Dam a few minutes after Gibson and began circling. Shannon, with his Upkeep still rotating from his aborted attack on the Möhne Dam, struggled with navigating, but at around 01:35 he was setting himself for a dummy run on what he believed was the Eder Dam. Gibson, obviously concerned by the lack of other Lancasters joining him, asked over R/T 'Hello Cooler aircraft. Can you see the target?'

Shannon immediately replied that he thought he could, but Gibson sent a red Very flare over the dam to confirm its location. It turned out that

Shannon was at the Rehbach Dam, located in a similar looking bend in the Eder Reservoir, but two miles west of the Eder Dam.

Presumably, Maudslay and Knight had also seen the flare because almost immediately they joined Gibson and Young and the five Lancasters flew in a left-hand orbit around the eastern end of the Eder Reservoir. The enormity of their task was immediately obvious. There had been no three-dimensional scale model of the Eder Reservoir. It was a serious omission as the maps and aerial photographs that had been provided did not show the real perspective, nor show the significant difficulties of approaching the dam at the required height, speed and distance; neither had the crews practiced such a difficult approach.

Steep banks and heavily wooded hills towered at over 400ft above the Eder Reservoir. The approach required a steep descent from about 1,000ft, which they decided was best achieved by descending down a valley, roughly parallel to the curved dam, south-west past the town of Waldeck and the Schloss Waldeck (castle) standing on a promontory at about 400ft. Then a steep, 90° descending turn to port, heading south-east over the Hammerbergspitze (a densely forested spit of land) and finally, with less than a mile to the dam, levelling off at 60ft, getting the speed correct, and releasing the Upkeep at 245ft from the Eder Dam. Once over the dam, full power and a steep climb to avoid the abrupt and heavily wooded Michelskopf, rising to over 1,000ft straight ahead, before pulling around to port and rejoining the left-handed circuit.

Fortunately, as reconnaissance flights had correctly reported, there were no German flak defences or barrage balloons. Once the Lancasters had reached the Eder Dam the difficulties were starkly obvious. Having said that, these were young, expertly skilled, highly trained pilots at the top of their abilities. All of

Eder Dam looking from the south-east. Hammerbergspitze on the left, Schloss Waldeck on the right.

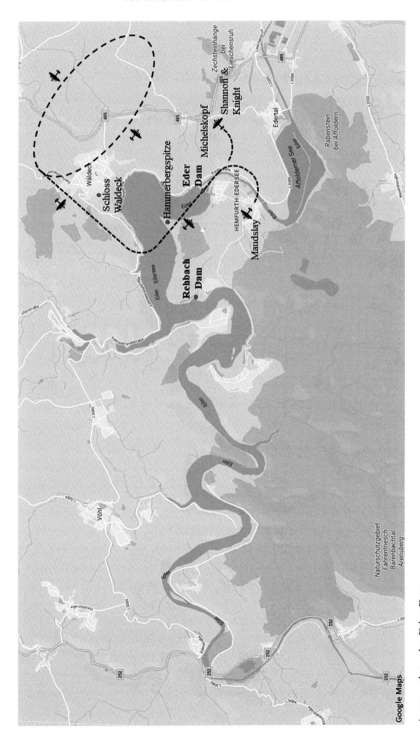

Approach to the Eder Dam.

137

the pilots but Knight had previous gallantry awards, and all were exceptionally brave. Gibson had just attacked and then flown as decoy several times at the Möhne Dam, risking his own and his crew's lives to draw fire away from the other attacking Lancasters. But the task at the Eder Dam was unprecedented. It would require the utmost skill, determination, concentration, complete coordination of all crew members, not to mention nerves of steel.

The faint glimmer of dawn was just starting to rise above the horizon, it was 01:39. Gibson contacted Shannon: 'O.K. Dave, Start your attack.' Shannon flew a wide circuit over the high ridges before diving down the valley past Schloss Waldeck. As he crossed the Hammerbergspitze his dive hadn't been steep enough, so as he levelled off he was too high. He hurriedly slammed the throttles wide open and hauled back the control column, just clearing the opposite ridge as described by Walker (Shannon's navigator),

> It was situated in a hole. It was very, very difficult to get low enough, quick enough, and have everything settled down – 240 miles per hour at 60 feet. So we did this dummy run, but right ahead of us was a hill. The pilot had to put on full power and go screaming over that hill.

Maudslay had probably instructed his wireless operator, Cottam, to start the spinning of the Upkeep. Cottam would have moved from his normal seated position and crouched over and turned the T-bar handle on the floor beneath his desk to the on position. He will have stayed there as he watch the rev-counter, mounted just beneath his desk, build up to and maintain the required 500 rpm.

As he pulled the aircraft round to make another attempt, Shannon was clearly showing the strain of his efforts and breathlessly reported, 'Sorry Leader. Made a mess of that. I'll try again.' After four more failed attempts, each time he was too close to the dam before he was at the correct height, he announced, 'I think I'd better circle and try to get to know this place.' Gibson responded 'O.K. Dave. You hang around a bit and let someone else have a crack.' With only three Upkeeps it was imperative none were wasted by an incorrect approach.

Gibson called up Maudslay. 'Hello Z Zebra. You can go in now.' It was finally time. All the training and preparation was all for this moment. The stress of the flight, the intense concentration and physical effort by all crew members were about to be put to the ultimate test. They had been airborne for almost four hours already and there is no way of knowing what terrors they had endured so far.

It was a difficult approach; Shannon had demonstrated that already and it wasn't an approach they had practiced. Time was pressing on; any misjudgement could be fatal.

Maudslay acknowledged. Urquhart, the navigator, switched the spotlights on and stood with his head firmly fixed in the Perspex blister on the right-hand side of the cockpit. Maudslay pulled the Lancaster out of its orbit, dived down the gorge, passed Schloss Waldeck, banked hard round to port and over Hammerbergspitze, then levelled out, but as with Shannon, it proved very difficult to get the height correct. Maudslay heaved back on the heavy Lancaster, Jack will have held the throttles firmly through the gate for maximum power, or maybe Maudslay had instinctively reached forward with his right hand and rammed the throttle levers forward himself. The Lancaster banked away and climbed almost vertically, before Maudslay circled round for his second attempt; as with the first, he was unable to obtain the correct height as he approached the dam and again aborted the attack.

There are several versions about what happened next. Gibson wrote in his book *Enemy Coast Ahead*:

> Henry [Maudslay] made two attempts. He said he found it very difficult, and gave the other boys some advice on the best way to go about it. Then he called up and told us that he was going in to make his final run. We could see him running in.
>
> Suddenly he pulled away; something seemed to be wrong, but he turned quickly, climbed up over the mountain and put his nose right down, literally flinging his machine into the valley. This time he was running straight and true for the middle of the wall. We saw his spotlights together, so he must have been at sixty feet. We saw the red ball of his Very light shooting out behind his tail, and we knew he had dropped his weapon.
>
> A split second later we saw something else: Henry Maudslay had dropped his mine too late. It had hit the top of the parapet and had exploded immediately on impact with a slow, yellow, vivid flame which lit up the whole valley like daylight for just a few seconds. We could see him quite clearly banking steeply a few feet above it.
>
> Perhaps the blast was doing that. It all seemed so sudden and vicious and the flame seemed so very cruel. Someone said, 'He has blown himself up.' Trevor [Trevor-Roper, Gibson's rear-gunner] said, 'Bomb-aimer must have been wounded.' It

looked as though Henry had been unlucky enough to do the thing we all might have done.

Paul Brickhill has much the same story in his book *The Dam Busters*, presumably based on Gibson's account. However, James Holland in *Dambusters: The race to smash the dams 1943*, Max Hastings in *Chastise* and John Sweetman in *The Dambusters Raid*, suggest that after Maudslay's two failed attempts he held off while Shannon made two further unsuccessful attempts before finally releasing the Upkeep on the third attempt, after which Maudslay made a third attempt. Rob Owen in *Henry Maudslay Dam Buster* and Max Arthur in *Dambusters*, both quote eyewitness accounts that describe both versions.

Whatever the actual sequence of events, Shannon's Upkeep skipped twice before hitting the water side of the dam wall, sinking and exploding to the right of centre. Although Shannon believed he saw a small breach, Gibson's and Knight's crews saw no perceptible damage. Shannon's wireless operator Goodale transmitted 'GONER79B'.

All accounts agree that Maudslay dropped his Upkeep at his third attempt. So, what went wrong? Although we will never know, we can speculate and look at possibilities.

Sweetman suggests that as Maudslay made his third attempt, Gibson noticed that something was hanging down from Maudslay's Lancaster which he believed was from damage occurred earlier between the Scheldt and the Rhine. Additionally, Trevor Roper, Gibson's rear gunner, commented that Maudslay's bomb aimer must have been wounded. There is no record of any conversation between the surviving crews in which Maudslay mentioned any injuries or damage to his aeroplane. Although it is possible, and may explain why Knight had taken the lead of the vic formation around Rees if Maudslay's bomb aimer, Fuller, had been injured and not able to assist with the navigation, which was his key secondary role.

If we assume Fuller had not been previously injured, it is pertinent to revisit the roles of the crew members during the attack on the Eder Dam and review what they would have been doing during the attack, and what would have been the consequences of them being injured and unable to perform their roles. As previously stated, it was a complete team effort requiring full cooperation and coordination from all the seven crew members.

Born in Leamington Spa on 21 July 1921 into a wealthy engineering family, he had attended Eton where he had excelled in sport. After being called up in 1940 he was sent to Canada for pilot training.

He was solely responsible for controlling the flight path of the heavy Lancaster. It would have taken the ultimate flying ability using both his hands and feet to control the 30-ton Lancaster. There were no power-assisted controls. The steep and precise manoeuvring required would have needed total strength and concentration. Maudslay was an experienced and competent pilot. He had already received the Distinguished Flying Cross (DFC) awarded for 'an act or acts of valour, courage or devotion to

Henry Maudslay – pilot.

duty while flying in active operations against the enemy'. He was at the peak of his flying abilities. He wasn't quite 22 years old, but his piloting credentials were impeccable. He had amassed almost thirty operations before being selected to test the then new Lancaster in preparation for its service introduction. He knew how to use the Lancaster and how to push it, and himself, to the extent of its, and his, flying envelope.

Although he was not known to Gibson before joining 617 Squadron his reputation would have preceded him, and he was selected as B-Flight commander. However, his professional pride may have been dented following the accident at Reculver when his Lancaster AJ-X was severely damaged after dropping a test Upkeep too low. It may have been compounded by the fact Hopgood and Young were selected to deputise for Gibson in the event of anything happening to Gibson.

It is difficult to believe these were contributory factors in his performance at the Eder Dam, although in his book Max Hastings states:

> 'B' Flight's commander cannot have been in a happy state of mind. Beyond the apprehension inseparable from what he was charged to do, Gibson had made explicit a lack of confidence in him, by appointing Hopgood and Young deputy leaders for the two dams' attacks. This decision was probably influenced by Maudslay's performance in training, and especially by his accident at Reculver. Now the pilot was called upon to make the fierce effort of concentration essential to survive an approach up the Eder lake.

As captain of his aircraft he would have been able to perform some of the crew's other activities in addition to his own if there had been a serious injury to any crew member. It would not have been easy but if Jack, for instance, had been injured, Maudslay would have been able, as difficult as it might have been, to control the engines and flaps to ensure the correct settings and speed for the descent and approach to the dam.

Maudslay would have also been able to release the Upkeep. He had a secondary release button to his left at the edge of the cockpit canopy and a manual release lever on his right-hand side near the flap select lever should Fuller the bomb aimer have been unable to release the Upkeep. He did not have the special bombsight to determine the distance from the dam, though he could have guessed if Fuller wasn't able to use the bombsight or to communicate with him.

Similarly, if the navigator, Urquhart, was incapacitated in any way, and nobody else was available to observe the spotlights, Maudslay could have guessed at the height. In the worst-case scenario, Maudslay might have been able to perform all four operations: fly the aeroplane, control its speed, guess the aeroplanes height and distance, and release the Upkeep.

If Maudslay had been incapacitated, none of the other crew members would have been able to take control of the Lancaster. There were no dual controls and Jack (as with many flight engineers) might have been able to fly a Lancaster straight and level under supervision from Maudslay, he certainly would not have been able to fly it with the skill and precision that was required for the attack at the Eder Dam.

Jack was born in the hamlet of New Smithy near Chinley in the Peak District. Before joining the RAF he had worked in a bleaching mill.

He was clearly a skilful, dedicated, and conscientious flight engineer. His main role during the attack at the dam was to ensure that the engines and flaps were managed to ensure the correct speed, attitude, and power settings required for the very difficult approach.

Jack has been detailed in the previous chapters. At the time of the raid, although he probably wasn't aware of it, he had been recommended for a Distinguished

Jack Marriott – flight engineer.

Flying Medal (DFM) from his previous squadron by Wing Commander W.M. Russell DFC, 50 Squadron CO. This is the non-commissioned officer version of the DFC and awarded for the same reasons.

In the case of injuries, it's possible that Jack may have been able to switch the spotlights on and the motor to rotate the Upkeep, though the latter would need him to have moved backwards down the fuselage. Possibly, if he performed the operation early enough, he may have been able to ensure it was up to 500 rpm. He

Robert Urquhart – navigator.

might have been able to observe the height through the blister, but not at the same time as managing the engines; it's also possible that in the absence of a bomb aimer, he could have used the manual Upkeep release lever on Maudslay's command.

Other than Maudslay himself, none of the other crew could have performed the significant flight engineer duties that were Jack's priority.

Urquhart was born in 1919 in Saskatchewan, Canada. Before joining the Royal Canadian Air Force (RCAF) and transferring to Britain he had worked as a jeweller. After first being selected for pilot training he eventually qualified as a navigator.

During the attack on the Eder Dam, Urquhart's main role was to switch on the spotlight altimeter and then, while standing, observe the lights on the water through the blister on the starboard side of the rear cockpit while directing Maudslay to the correct height by calling out UP – DOWN – STEADY commands for Maudslay as the circles of light came together.

Cottam was also a Canadian, born in 1912 in Edmonton where he had worked as a clerk and a driver before joining the RCAF.

At the Eder Dam, Cottam's role was to start the Upkeep spinning and ensure it was rotating at 500 rpm. This was perhaps

Alden Cottam – wireless operator.

Above left: Michael Fuller – bomb aimer.

Above middle: William Tytherleigh – front gunner.

Above right: Norman Burrows – rear gunner.

done quite a while before the attack was started and once up to speed, he may have been able to perform the height monitoring if Urquhart or Jack had not been unable to do so. Additionally, he would have fired the Very pistol to confirm the Upkeep had been released and transmit the 'GONER' message back to base.

Fuller was born in Reigate Surrey in 1920. Before the war he worked as a Post Office telephone engineer before joining the RAF in 1940.

Although during the flight Fuller worked closely with Urquhart, his sole role when attacking the dam was to ensure the Upkeep was dropped at the correct distance from the dam. This required him to instruct Maudslay to go LEFT or RIGHT and to use his bombsight to determine the correct distance before pressing the Upkeep release button. He would not have been able to undertake any of the other activities.

Born in Cambridge in 1921, Tytherleigh had moved to Sussex when he was young. After joining the RAF in 1940 he qualified as wireless operator/air gunner.

Since there were no flak defences at the Eder Dam, Tytherleigh's role would have been as an observer fastidiously looking out for danger.

Born in Liverpool in 1914 Burrows joined the RAF in 1941 but did not attend Air Gunnery School until the following year.

Similar to Tytherleigh, Burrows in the rear turret would have been alert looking out for danger throughout the whole of the flight.

With so much skill, experience, concentration, and technique honed by their intensive training, it's difficult to believe that the approach and release of the Upkeep that went so badly wrong was the result of ineptitude by one or more of the crew members.

As previously stated, there are no confirmed reports of previous damage to Maudslay's Lancaster, nor injury to any of his crew before arriving at the Eder Reservoir. It would seem then that the issue that caused the Upkeep to fail so badly must have been the result of something that happened once they had arrived.

I'm sure we can discount any misgivings Maudslay may have had about his own abilities, despite the fact that Max Hastings writes that Sutherland, the front gunner in Knight's Lancaster AJ-N, reported Gibson had openly criticised Maudslay over VHF radio saying, 'Henry, that's very nice flying, but you will have to do better than that.' So any concerns or doubts about his own or crew's abilities would have been far at the back of his mind with the intense concentration and physical effort needed.

So, what might have happened? It is conceivable that there could have been no injuries and the crew as a team got the approach disastrously wrong. But this was a highly qualified and extensively trained crew. I personally think that something must have happened just prior to the release of the Upkeep.

If we review the five crew members with actions at the dam – the pilot, flight engineer, navigator, wireless operator, and bomb aimer – it may be possible to determine a scenario that could offer a possible explanation.

In a Lancaster the only crew member to have a harness was the pilot. The navigator and wireless operator had fixed seats, while the flight engineer had a fold-away 'dickey' seat with a hook-on back strap, which by all accounts most flight engineers did not use, preferring to stand beside the pilot during operations with the seat in its stowage position.

From Gibson's account it is obvious that his crew clearly saw Maudslay making his third and disastrous approach. He states, 'We saw his spotlights together, so he must have been at sixty feet.' Perhaps the spotlight altimeter was inaccurate, and the two lights had come together when the Lancaster was higher than 60ft. As with all the Dambuster Lancasters, Maudslay also had a second altimeter at eye level at the top on his instrument console marked in red chinagraph at 60ft, which would have given him some indication of his height. So, I think we can assume that on the final run Maudslay was at the correct height. Prior to that Gibson stated, 'We could see him running in. Suddenly he pulled away;

something seemed to be wrong, but he turned quickly, climbed up over the mountain and put his nose right down, literally flinging his machine into the valley.' With the lack of any other information, it's difficult to know what may have occurred. I see two possible scenarios that could loosely fit this description.

The first: 'We could see him running in.' Perhaps Maudslay was over the reservoir having cleared the spit of land, the Hammerbergspitze, and was approaching the dam, but he wasn't happy with the approach. So he pulled up before the dam climbed up and circled round and made another approach. I can't imagine this is what happened as it would have been on his fourth attempt that he released the Upkeep. None of the existing reports suggest Maudslay made four attempts, all are quite specific that he released the Upkeep on the third approach.

A more likely second scenario is that on the third attempt Maudslay had descended down the valley adjacent to Schloss Waldeck. Maybe he was going too fast and 'Suddenly he pulled away; something seemed to be wrong.' Maybe he was adjusting his approach or just trying to lose excess airspeed. Then he 'turned quickly, climbed up over the mountain and put his nose right down, literally flinging his machine into the valley'. This, I believe, was the steep turn to port before the Hammerbergspitze. I suspect that Gibson or his ghost writer had misunderstood that the Hammerbergspitze was a steep-sided spit of land rather than a mountain. Then Maudslay rapidly adjusted his height, 'put his nose right down, literally flinging his machine into the valley'. Again, I suspect ghost-writer misinterpretation and that 'the valley' was the portion of the Eder Reservoir between the Hammerbergspitze and the dam, as Gibson then goes on to state 'this time he was running straight and true for the middle of the wall. We saw his spotlights together, so he must have been at sixty feet.'

Whatever, the sequence events, and there are conflicting accounts of what happened, I believe that something occurred on the third approach which caused problems for the Maudslay crew. Both Sweetman and Owen (from unattributed 617 Squadron archives) report that something had been observed hanging down from Maudslay's Lancaster AJ-Z as it made its final approach. Although Owen suggests that may have been 'indicative of damage sustained on the flight to the target – between the Scheldt and the Rhine', I think it may have been the result of damage sustained at the Eder Reservoir itself, even though there is no indication from aircrew who survived the attack on the Eder that Maudslay was in any difficulty other than from the challenging approach.

We will never know what actually happened, we can only surmise. As previously stated, the Lancasters used on the raid were very heavy; carrying a 4½ ton Upkeep the Lancaster was almost 30 tons. Though often described in contemporary reports as easy to handle, the Lancaster had no power assisted controls. It required strength in both hands and legs and utmost concentration to control the precise low-level flying and manoeuvring required for the attack on the Eder Dam.

Some pilots found that once the Upkeep was rotating it introduced a vibration or juddering; some reports state that this was so bad it made the instruments unreadable. Perhaps it also made the Lancaster more difficult to handle.

The dive down the valley past Schloss Waldeck would require cautious flying, and with Jack carefully managing the airspeed using throttles and flaps. If the airspeed wasn't controlled, the inertia at the end of the dive would have been too great and would have made it difficult to reduce in time to release the Upkeep. This happened several times with Shannon, on Maudslay's two previous attempts, and with Knight's first attempt.

Grayston, the flight engineer on AJ-N which dropped their Upkeep after Maudslay, described how he managed to control the speed. Jack presumably had the same or a similar method,

> we carried out our first run and we were above the speed permitted, so we aborted the first run but we learned a lot from it, so I discovered that you had to get the power up to get 240 [mph], so on the second run I choked the throttles right back to engine idle and let it glide down to the right height. There were only a few seconds involved here before you get level and then release – five or seven seconds.
>
> ….
>
> I was responsible for airspeed, so I shut the engines right back and let them idle down to 60 feet, with my fingers crossed that they'd open up when I slammed the throttles forward.

On Maudslay's third and final attempt, both Brickhill and Owen suggest that the approach to the dam was too fast, while Gibson, Hastings and Sweetman suggest that the Upkeep was released too late. Flying the Lancaster so low, the speed in relation to objects on the ground would have appeared so much faster so there was less reaction time – only adding to the incredible stress they were already under.

Perhaps releasing the Upkeep too late was a consequence of approaching too fast, but maybe something happened on the final approach. If we review Gibson's observation that:

> We could see him running in. Suddenly he pulled away; something seemed to be wrong, but he turned quickly, climbed up over the mountain and put his nose right down, literally flinging his machine into the valley. This time he was running straight and true for the middle of the wall. We saw his spotlights together, so he must have been at sixty feet.

My possible explanation for this is that having descended down the valley past Schloss Waldeck, Maudslay made a steep turn to port, but then as he flew over the Hammerbergspitze, which I think was incorrectly described as a mountain, he was too low and struck some of the trees, causing him to pull up and away: 'Suddenly he pulled away; something seemed to be wrong.' Maudslay then corrected himself, 'put his nose right down, literally flinging his machine into the valley'. Perhaps the steep turn to port was even over Hammerbergspitze. The wingspan of a Lancaster is 102ft. If a steep turn was attempted as he approached the required height of 60ft, there was a mere 10ft between wing tip and either the reservoir or the Hammerbergspitze, which had steep sides and was heavily wooded. But damage had been done to the Lancaster as evidenced by the fact there were reports of something hanging from the aircraft. Maybe the spotlight altimeters were incorrectly set, which might have explained why they were reported as flying so low over the English Channel when they were testing them earlier.

Additionally, for me it is inconceivable that both Jack, the flight engineer responsible for the aircraft's speed, and Fuller, the bomb aimer, got their responsibilities so wrong. Had the Lancaster struck trees as suggested, even just a glancing blow, it would have been a significant impact on the aircraft and on the crew who were probably not braced or anticipating it. As previously stated, only the pilot had a seat belt. Jack would have been standing at the side of the seated Maudslay with his head down inside the cockpit, intensely watching the airspeed indicator and the engine rev counters, while his left hand would probably have been on the flap lever and his right hand on the throttle levers. Fuller would have been lying prone, holding and watching intently through his hand-held bombsight with one hand, while holding the Upkeep release button in the other. Urquhart, the navigator will have been stood behind Jack with his head in the starboard cockpit blister looking down watching the spotlights. Cottam the wireless operator was probably kneeling, ensuring the Upkeep was spinning at 500 rpm, or he might have returned to his seat.

If the Lancaster had made impact with trees, initially Jack would have been flung violently forward into the instrument panel and probably smashed into from behind by Cottam. Similarly, Fuller would have been thrust further into the nose of the aircraft. Second World War Lancaster pilots did not wear hard helmets ('bonedomes'), only their leather flying helmets which offered no protection against impact. Jack may have been concussed or worse, or so shaken he couldn't see clearly, he may also have been crashed into by Cottam, who would also have been thrust forward. But whatever happened, I think he wasn't able to control the speed of the aircraft, which Maudslay would have had to do himself. Similarly, if Fuller the bomb aimer had been injured, as had been suggested by Gibson's rear-gunner ('Bomb-aimer must have been wounded'), Maudslay would have been required to release the Upkeep as well as fly the Lancaster and control the speed. My feeling is that Jack was more likely to have been injured because it would have been more difficult to control the Lancaster's speed without his vital input, and as a consequence of flying too fast, Fuller would have had less reaction time and the Upkeep would have been much harder to release at the correct distance – even if he was uninjured.

Regardless of reasons, whether the approach was too fast, too high, or the Upkeep released too near the dam, and despite whatever (if anything) had happened, the result was that the Upkeep did not even make a single skip on the surface of the Eder Reservoir. Cottam must have avoided serious injury and fired the Very flare from behind the astrodome at the back of the cockpit canopy to signal release the Upkeep.

The Upkeep struck the parapet of the dam a split second after Maudslay's Lancaster had flown over it. The ferocity of the impact caused the Upkeep to explode like a traditional bomb. There was a blinding flash that illuminated the whole valley. Observers saw AJ-Z banking steeply beyond and away in the fiery glow, Gibson surmised that 'perhaps the blast was doing that'.

Perhaps there had been no issues with Maudslay crew and/or Lancaster and it was just a badly released Upkeep, and the subsequent damage to AJ-Z was the result of the exploding Upkeep. Whatever the reasons, the damage to the dam was superficial, with rubble and debris from a wall strewn along the parapet and road running along the top of the dam. Part of the blinding flash was actually caused by debris falling onto power cables around the powerhouse at the base of the dam.

Gibson contacted Maudslay over R/T immediately:

> I spoke to him quickly, 'Henry – Henry. Z Zebra – Z Zebra.
> Are you O.K.?' No answer. I called again. Then we all thought
> we heard a very faint, tired voice say, 'I think so – stand by.' It
> seemed as though he was dazed, and his voice did not sound
> natural. But Henry had disappeared. There was no burning
> wreckage on the ground; there was no aircraft on fire in the air.
> There was nothing. Henry had disappeared.

Knight's front gunner Sutherland thought he heard a faint, barely
recognisable 'returning to base' message, while O'Brien the rear gunner
suggested Maudslay's voice sounded 'unnatural almost dehumanised'.

It was the last the four remaining Lancaster crews at the Eder Reservoir
heard or saw of the seven members of the crew of AJ-Z. They waited,
momentarily, expectant for an explosion and flash of AJ-Z as it crashed
into the ground. There was no further explosion. There was no further R/T
communication with Maudslay. AJ-Z had vanished into the advancing
dawn. The time was about 01:45.

As the smoke from Maudslay's Upkeep began to clear, Gibson called up
Astell not realising that not only was he not there, but had been shot down
and killed about an hour-and-a-half earlier. Gibson then called up Knight,
who was still orbiting over the hills.

As Knight made his approach, he encountered the same difficulties as both
Shannon and Maudslay had before him. Shannon and Gibson gave advice
over the R/T but it was of no use. Knight's first approach was aborted. As he
pulled up sharply and circled around for his second approach, the advice and
chatter over the R/T became too much of a distraction so he told the wireless
operator Kellow to turn the VHF radio off so his crew could all concentrate.

Gibson took the opportunity to call Astell again, but there was still no
reply. It was now clear that Knight was the last aircraft, the last Upkeep, and
the last chance to breach the Eder Dam.

Knight's flight engineer, Grayston, described how he controlled his
Lancaster for their second approach earlier. Knight was a meticulous pilot,
his second attempt was much better, he approached at 60ft and 222 mph,
just to the left of Shannon's approach line. At 450yds from the dam the
Upkeep was released.

Gibson wrote that he crossed his fingers. The Upkeep skipped three times
and struck the dam just to the right of centre. As they flew over the dam,

Knight's rear gunner O'Brien recalled that he dreaded that the explosion would occur under the Lancaster as had happened with Maudslay. But it didn't. As they pulled away to safety the Upkeep detonated with a brilliant flash and huge plume of water being sent high above the dam.

Gibson, flying above and to starboard of him, moments later saw 'the tremendous earthquake which shook the base of the dam, and then, as if a gigantic hand had punched a hole through cardboard, the whole thing collapsed'. Knight's wireless-operator Kellow gave a similar description, 'I could look back and down at the dam wall. It was still intact for a short while, then, as if some huge fist had been jabbed at the wall, a large, almost round black hole appeared and water gushed as from a large hose.' Water flooded through the hole for a few moments and before long, a length of the parapet crumbled leaving a huge breach in the Eder Dam.

It seems that Barnes Wallis had been correct that a single Upkeep detonating in the correct place was enough to breach the dams, even though it had taken five Upkeeps at the Möhne and three at the Eder Dam to get an Upkeep to the right place.

As the maelstrom flooded down the Eder Valley the banter over the R/T was excited and raucous. At 01:54 Gibson's wireless operator, Hutchison, transmitted the code 'DINGHY' back to base, who responded with a request for confirmation and a question as to whether there were any aircraft available to go to the Sorpe Dam. Hutchison transmitted 'NONE'.

The four Lancasters followed the torrent of water gushing from the breach in the Eder Dam downstream for a while. Gibson interrupted the jubilant chatter with the instruction to 'Good show boys. Let's all go home and get pie.' As the four Wave 1 Lancasters of Gibson, Young, Shannon and Knight swung round on a bearing back towards the Möhne Dam they must have considered that Maudslay had been lost. But it wasn't the case….

Around the time the Eder Dam was breached, the five Lancasters of Wave 3 were en route between Roosendaal and Rees. There is no doubt that defences along the route had been alerted by the previous Wave 1 Lancasters. Ottley, Brown, Townsend and Anderson all took evasive action and managed to negotiate the narrow gap between the German night-fighter airfields at Eindhoven and Gilze-Rijen. Unfortunately, Burpee was not so lucky. While it was believed that he strayed off track and was shot down over Gilze-Rijen airfield, Max Hastings suggests that,

> The Germans believed that this Lancaster, rather than being
> hit by flak, fell victim to a searchlight positioned on a tower

Eder Dam breached. Schloss Waldeck in the distance.

at Gilze-Rijen airfield. Its beam caught the cockpit of S-Sugar almost head-on, dazzling Burpee as he approached at sixty feet, and apparently causing him to hit a tree, plough through a plantation and finally crash into a disused garage on the airfield.

As the Lancaster came to a halt the Upkeep exploded with the death of all seven crew members. Burpee and AJ-S was the seventh Lancaster unable to complete their mission and the fifth Lancaster lost.

Elsewhere, Maltby and Martin had made it back over Holland and almost reached the safety of the North Sea.

Jack's Return Flight

Maudslay's Lancaster, AJ-Z, had not crashed during the attempt on the Eder Dam. We have no way of knowing how badly damaged the aircraft was or how injured the crew were. But at 01:57, Cottam the wireless operator, who clearly had been able to fire the Very signal over the Eder Dam, was also able to transmit a 'GONER28B' message. It seems probable that there was either some injury to the crew, damage to the aircraft, or both, as Maudslay immediately disappeared from the vicinity of the Eder Reservoir in an attempt to make his way home rather than either looking for a location to crash-land the Lancaster, or gain enough height for the crew to bale out. If there had been no damage or injuries, he would surely have joined the other Lancasters circling around admiring the destruction of the Eder Dam, and joined in with the mutual congratulations.

By that time, even if the aircraft had been damaged and Maudslay was flying his designated return route, which in the early stages was basically a reciprocal of the outbound route, they would have been roughly back in the area of the Möhne Reservoir. Under normal operations flight engineers would carefully manage fuel consumption and use the designated cruise power on all four engines. Jack, having nearly a full Tour of Operations under his belt, would have been an expert at doing this. It's likely that all returning Lancasters on Operation Chastise ignored this, all four engines would have been 'fire-walled' – throttles pushed all the way forward to give maximum power and speed disregarding fuel consumption.

> Gibson (AJ-G): 'I turned to Pulford [flight engineer]. 'Put her into maximum cruising. Don't worry about petrol consumption.' … 'more revs'. The needle crept round. It got very noisy inside … Terry smiled and watched the air-speed needle creep round. We were now doing a smooth 240 indicated, and the exhaust stubs glowed red hot with the power she was throwing out.'

Shannon (AJ-L): 'We went back individually, not in formation. I just got down on the deck and opened the throttles and went.'

Sumpter (AJ-L): 'We did maximum speed until we were clear of the coast, and stayed low level all the way back to England.'

Johnson (AJ-N): 'We put everything through the throttle and went back to the Möhne Dam, because that was the approved route for going home. … We set route from there to go home with full throttle, which the engineer, Ray Grayston, said we could use because we'd got petrol and didn't mind wasting it.'

At around 02:20 Gibson, Shannon, and Knight had individually flown back over the Möhne Dam and turned at Ahlen, heading west towards Holland. Knight, though, had to take evasive action over the Möhne Dam as there was a flak gun still active around the dam. The four remaining Wave 3 Lancasters had passed over the Rhine at Rees and would have been heading east towards them. McCarthy was back over the North Sea on course for home.

At 02:22 Townsend was instructed to attack the Ennepe Dam. Six minutes later Anderson was instructed to attack the Sorpe Dam, as was Burpee at 02:30 who, unbeknown to Grantham, had already been shot down. At the same time, Ottley acknowledged a command from Grantham to attack the Lister Dam.

Two minutes later, at 02:32, Ottley's instruction was changed to attack the Sorpe Dam instead. No acknowledgement was issued from Ottley's Lancaster. He had strayed off course and his crew were no doubt too busy trying to save their lives. It seems that Ottley had turned south before reaching Ahlen and flown over Hamm, whose air defences had no doubt been alerted by the returning McCarthy about an hour-and-a-half earlier.

At 02:35, Ottley's Lancaster AJ-C took a direct hit in a main fuel tank which caused a fierce fire. It seems that Ottley steered his Lancaster away from Hamm, perhaps to avoid crashing into an outlying village but more likely trying to crash-land his stricken Lancaster. Unfortunately, the fuel tank exploded, ripping the wing off and causing the Lancaster to smash into the edge of a wood. The rear gunner, Tees, was thrown clear still in his turret and though badly burned and injured, survived and was taken prisoner. Sadly, all other six crew members were killed in the impact. AJ-C was the sixth Lancaster lost.

The three remaining Wave 3 Lancasters had banked round to the south at Ahlen. Brown and Anderson were heading for the Sorpe Reservoir and Townsend the Ennepe Reservoir. Elsewhere Maltby, Martin, and McCarthy were over the North Sea heading for the Lincolnshire coast. Gibson and

Young were flying back towards Rees while Shannon was taking a different return route home having turned north between Ahlen and Rees at Dülmen heading for Nordhorn.

Maudslay's Lancaster AJ-Z was still airborne, more than likely limping back the same route that Gibson and Young were following some way behind. The lack of radio communication with Maudslay was perhaps caused by blast damage sustained at the Eder Dam, or purely from being out of range. Just after 02:30 AJ-Z had reached the vicinity of the waypoint at Rees. It was either tracking too far north or had turned to starboard too late, but it was slightly off track as it approached the German town of Emmerich on the Rhine near to the Dutch border. It is unlikely that Maudslay would have intended to fly over Emmerich as it was known to have significant oil storage facilities and to be heavily defended.

The distance from the Eder Dam is 140 miles and if the aircraft had not been damaged and was being flown at full throttle, without the Upkeep and with less fuel, it should have been able to achieve an airspeed of about 230 mph and taken around thirty-five to forty minutes. It had taken Maudslay fifty, an airspeed of only 170 mph. Maybe the aircraft had been damaged, but not so badly that the crew needed to bale out. Maybe Jack was injured and couldn't manage the engines efficiently (unlikely, as Maudslay should have been able to), or maybe Fuller, the bomb aimer, was injured and couldn't help with navigating, which was a crucial responsibility flying at such a low level.

Whatever the reason, we know that Emmerich's flak teams heard the Lancaster approaching from the south-east. Like Hamm, the air defences around Emmerich's oil refineries had been alerted earlier by the outbound Lancasters. Even before they had visual contact they had trained their guns ready. Within a short space of time AJ-Z appeared, flying low and heading in a direction that would take it over the centre of the city of Emmerich.

There were two flak batteries on the eastern side of Emmerich: The Keep with two flak teams, and Home flak which had positions in Nierenberger Strasse and another in the industrial harbour, each with three 20mm anti-aircraft guns. The flak team from The Keep flak team opened fire first. They engaged the Lancaster at a distance of about half a mile, causing Maudslay to bank sharply starboard to the north, with rear gunner Burrows frantically firing back towards the flak emplacements around the harbour area. All twelve of the 20mm flak guns then engaged Maudslay's low-flying Lancaster, many of which fired almost horizontally, taking the tops off nearby trees. The plight of AJ-Z was hopeless. At 02:36 AJ-Z, with all seven crew members, crashed into the ground.

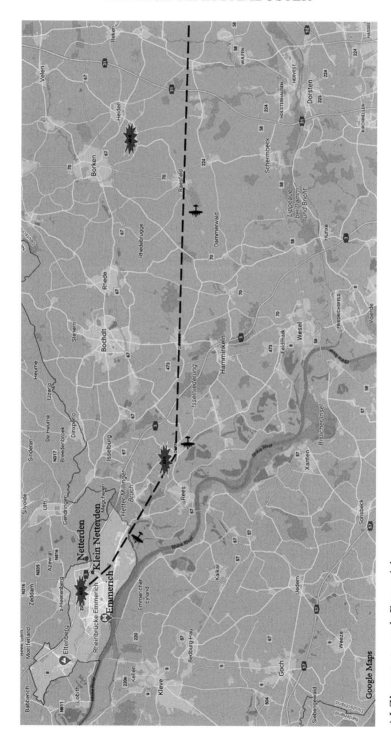

AJ-Z's route towards Emmerich.

AJ-Z's route around Emmerich.

Wreckage purported to be that of AJ-Z on the morning of 17 May.

There are two eye-witness reports given a short time after the event. They both came from gunners of the Home flak team stationed in the harbour area beside the Rhine. Both Johannes Doerwald and Herr Feldman have similar accounts of the incident, though Doerwald gave a different account of the event several years later. Doerwald, who was 16 years old at the time, was credited with, and later awarded a medal for, a direct hit that caused an engine or fuel tank to explode. At such low level, even if Maudslay had not been injured in the explosion, the Lancaster would have been totally uncontrollable.

Some years after his original testimony, Doerwald suggested that a shell had hit the cockpit area of the Lancaster which he presumed had killed the pilot instantly. He further stated that there had been no fire in the engine, but the Lancaster had rolled onto its back before crashing into a field alongside a brickworks near the village of Klein Netterden just to the north-east of Emmerich.

There were no survivors from the seven crew members. Jack was just 23 years old, Maudslay only 21. It was the seventh Dambuster to have been lost.

Brown's Sorpe Attack

As the time approached 03:00, Maltby and Martin were almost back across the North Sea approaching the safety of the Lincolnshire mainland. McCarthy was not far behind approaching from further to the north. Shannon was nearing the North Sea around Petten, north of Alkmaar, and Knight was over the north of the Zuiderzee heading west. Brown, Townsend and Anderson had all turned south and were heading for their designated targets.

Gibson and Young had followed a similar route to Maudslay, they must have passed quite near his crash site and possibly saw the burning wreckage. They continued through Holland in a north-westerly direction, turned west-west-north over Harderwijk, flown over the Zuiderzee, and were flying west over the Helder Peninsula north of Amsterdam.

It was the most southerly of the return routes. Gibson

> called up Melvyn [Young, AJ-A] on the R/T. He had been with me all the way round as deputy-leader when Mickey [Martin, AJ-P] had gone home with his leaking petrol tank. He was quite all right at the Eder. Now there was no reply. We wondered what had happened.

Young had been flying slightly ahead of Gibson. He only had limited experience of low flying and it has been said that he was uncomfortable with the practice. On the outward leg, as leader of his three-ship vic formation, he had been chastised by both Maltby and Shannon for not staying very low. It seems that as he approached the Dutch coastline at Castricum aan Zee he was once again flying far too high. He was almost in sight of safety but provided an easy target for the very last flak teams in enemy territory.

He was shot down as he overflew the coast, crashing into a sandbar about 100yds from the beach. Again, there were no survivors. It was the eighth and last Lancaster crew lost on Operation Chastise. It was 02:58. At the same time, about twenty-five miles further north, Knight had safely crossed the coast and was flying over the North Sea on his way home.

Gibson successfully overflew the same area less than fifteen minutes later. He had only just shaken-off a night fighter. He too had climbed slightly and then pushed his Lancaster nose down as low as he could to get maximum speed.

> Down went the Lanc. Until we were a few feet off the ground, for this was the only way to survive. And we wanted to survive. ... We flew low along that canal, as low as we had flown that day. Our belly nearly scraped the water, our wings would have knocked horses off the towpath.

He made it; he was over the sea heading home.

Around the same time, Maltby and Martin were back over the English countryside almost home. Back over Germany, Brown was approaching the Sorpe Dam but Anderson, having taken evasive action to avoid flak and searchlights, had been forced off track between Rees and Ahlen. With the coming of dawn and gathering mist in the valleys he was unable to identify any landmarks. To make matters worse, the four guns in the rear turret had also given problems. At 03:10 he appeared to be hopelessly lost and decided to abort the mission and return to base, complete with his Upkeep, by the same route he had come, rather than one of the designated return routes.

Brown, though, had struggled on. He had seen Burpee shot down in AJ-S and flying so low had, at one point, only avoided flak by flying down a woodland road and narrowly missed crashing into a castle by doing a steep turn so that his wing missed two towers. Despite increasing mist he managed to locate the Sorpe Dam. Unaware that McCarthy had already released his Upkeep and unable to see the rubble that littered the ramparts of the dam, they made their preparations. Just as McCarthy had several

The wreckage of Young's AJ-A.

160

hours earlier, Brown struggled to find the correct approach. Three times they dropped down over the village of Langscheid running parallel to the dam, and three times they were unsatisfied and aborted. Brown then decided to mark their approach by dropping incendiary flares alongside the dam. On a dummy run Oancia, the bomb aimer, released the flares through the flare chute. Finally, on their seventh run, the Upkeep was accurately released, more or less at the centre of the dam. As the Lancaster pulled away the crew observed the explosion which did little more than to add more rubble to that created by McCarthy. It was at 03:14. 'GONER78C' was transmitted back to base as McDonald, the rear gunner, yelled over the intercom to Brown, 'Get out of here! Go on, get moving.'

The Sorpe Dam remained intact though in later reconnaissance photographs some superficial damage can be seen.

It was the final Upkeep dropped on the Sorpe Dam that night. It wasn't, however, the last attempt to bomb it. On 15 October 1944, eighteen Lancasters of 9 Squadron attacked using another Barnes Wallis design, the 5 ton 'Tallboy' bomb, dropped from a height of 15,000ft. No aircraft were lost, but the dam, which had received several hits, did not collapse and there was no leakage. The reservoir was drained in 1958 for repair work and several unexploded Tallboys had to be removed and defused.

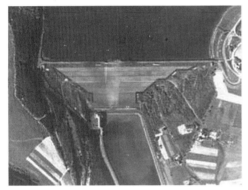 

Above left: Upkeep damage to the parapet of the Sorpe Dam.

Above right: Tallboy damage to the Sorpe Dam in 1944.

Townsend's Ennepe Attack

As Brown was enduring the perils of bombing the Sorpe Dam, Maltby arrived back at RAF Scampton followed five minutes later at 03:15 by Martin.

At 03:25 McCarthy landed awkwardly but safely, the flak that had hit them on their return over Hamm had, unbeknown to the crew, punctured the starboard tyre. The first three crews to have completed their mission were back safely.

By 03:30 Brown was back over the empty Möhne Reservoir heading home. Gibson, Shannon and Knight were over the North Sea, almost in sight of the Lincolnshire coast. Anderson was heading back over Holland towards the Scheldt, but Townsend in AJ-O had arrived at the Ennepe Dam.

In some accounts it is suggested that it was the Bever Dam (an earthwork dam like the Sorpe) a little further south (and post-war records, including Jack's RAF Service Record, indicate the Schwelme Dam – which doesn't even exist). Even his wireless operator, Chalmers, seemed unsure:

Ennepe Dam.

As we approached our target, we did quite a lot of steaming around to find out just which dam was which – there was more than one in that area. Finally we decided we had got the one we had as our target. There were a lot of dams around, so it was very difficult to identify our one – but as far as our skipper was concerned we found the one we briefed to attack so whether it was the right one or not it was the one we were briefed to do. The navigator was quite convinced it was the right one so I took his word for it.

AJ-O's flight had already been harrowing. Having run the gauntlet of flak and searchlights increasing mist had made their navigation difficult. To make matters worse, when they arrived at the Ennepe Reservoir and Chalmers, the wireless operator, set their Upkeep revolving, the vibration (which all the Lancasters had experienced) was so bad that the juddering unnerved the crew. Nevertheless, they stuck steadfastly to their task, making three unsuccessful approaches before finally releasing the Upkeep on their fourth attempt.

The badly balanced Upkeep which had caused difficulties in controlling the Lancaster skipped twice before sinking 50yds short of the dam wall. The huge explosion did no more than create an enormous splash and soak the ramparts. At 03:37 another failed message 'GONER58E' was transmitted back to base.

The last ever 'Bouncing Bomb' had been dropped in anger.

The End of Operation Chastise

Brown, flying AJ-F, had strayed over Hamm and was targeted by flak. Fortunately, though being hit, the Lancaster flew on with no injuries or apparent damage.

Shannon landed back at Scampton at 04:06 and at 04:15, after six hours and thirty-six minutes, Gibson landed safely. Though not as long as some Second World War Bomber Command flights, it was an incredible achievement for all the crews; Gibson, with lack of sleep the previous night, pain with his gout, and having the least actual flying training of any of the pilots, had spent the longest time airborne. He had attacked the Möhne Dam, then controlled subsequent attacks at both the Möhne and Eder Dams.

Knight landed back at 04:20 and Anderson, having negotiated his way eastwards through Holland and back along his outbound route, arrived at 05:30 complete with his unused Upkeep.

Brown had taken the northerly route through Germany and encountered more flak as he overflew the Helder Peninsula. The fuselage was peppered with bullet holes and a direct hit had caused a gaping hole in the fuselage side of AJ-F. Fortunately, there were no injuries and no real damage to the control of the aircraft. Once Brown had flown clear of the coast and was flying over the North Sea back towards the English coast he handed over control of the Lancaster to his flight engineer Feneron (no mean feat as there was only single controls in the Lancaster), and went back and had a look at the damage for himself. He landed back three minutes after Anderson at 05:33.

Townsend had also returned by a northerly route that had taken him through Germany and Holland towards Stavoren, then westerly across the Zuiderzee back to England. Although he had encountered flak at the Ennepe Dam he flew back without encountering any more until he was over the Helder Peninsula. Avoiding any damage, he had instructed Powell, his flight engineer, to feather an engine that had started to give oil warnings. Oil from

164

the front guns had also smeared the cockpit windscreen restricting forward visibility, so Townsend, who was known to dislike grass runways, made his final approach on three engines, downwind into the rising sun, with his head through the quarterlight. It was not his best landing. Before a gathered throng of onlookers, well-wishers and signatories he bounced the Lancaster down the runway. At least the last bounce was successful. He was the last of the Operation Chastise Lancasters to land, and like Brown and Anderson before him it was in daylight. The time was 06:15.

Operation Chastise was over. From the first take-off to the last landing it had taken a total of eight hours and forty-seven minutes. Though shorter than some Second World War bomber ops, for those team members that had remained in the UK it had been a long, stressful wait.

By then the airfield was quiet with a bizarre atmosphere of sadness and euphoria. Sadness at the loss of eight whole crews, fifty-six members of their squadron. Elation that such as secretive, difficult, and important operation had resulted in the destruction of two of their main objectives. Many of the crews went away to celebrate. Others went to bed. Some hung around hoping for the missing Lancasters to return, or at least get notification they had landed safely elsewhere. It wasn't to happen.

Byers, Barlow, Astell, Hopgood, Burpee, and Ottley were known to have crashed. Maudslay's and Young's fate was at that time unknown. Everybody feared the worst but hoped for the best.

Munro and Rice were both disappointed they had to return without completing their mission. Anderson's return without having made an attempt wasn't well received. At least one of the other pilot's accused him of being 'in a hurry to get to bed'. Gibson, renowned for his forthrightness and the never-give-in attitude demonstrated so visibly on the operation, was less impressed. He immediately removed Anderson from 617 Squadron and posted him back to 49 Squadron with his complete crew, which included navigator John Nugent whose home in Stoney Middleton was not far from Jack's and Astell's in the Peak District.

In summary there were:

> Twenty-three Avro Lancaster B.III converted to Type 464 Provisioning specifically for Operation Chastise. Two were test and training aircraft only. One (AJ-X) was badly damaged four days before the raid and could not be repaired in time. One had an engine problem on the day of the raid (AJ-Q) and the crew switched to the only available spare aircraft (AJ-T).

Twenty-three different crews were assigned to 617 Squadron. Two left the squadron before Operation Chastise and two did not take part in the raid, leaving nineteen crews.

Three crews returned without reaching their target.

Five Lancasters crashed. Three were shot down.

Eleven Upkeeps were used in anger.

Eight crews reached their target, released their Upkeep and returned.

Three crews reached their target, released their Upkeep but failed to return.

In total 133 aircrew took part.

> Ninety from the UK
> Twenty-seven from Canada
> Thirteen from Australia
> Two from New Zealand
> One from the USA.

Fifty-three aircrew were killed on the raid.

Three were taken prisoners of war.

Thirty-two were later killed in action after Operation Chastise.

Forty-eight survived the Second World War.

The Morning After and the
Following Weeks

Though Gibson had not known Maudslay before the formation of 617 Squadron, and probably barely got to know him during training, he would have been aware of his strengths and weakness as evidenced by Maudslay having the position of B-Flight commander. However, several authors state that Gibson may have been disappointed, not only with the incident at Reculver but also with Maudslay's general performance in training. This may have been the reason that Hopgood, rather than Maudslay, was selected as backup commander for the attack on the Eder Dam and for the curt response from Gibson after Maudslay had aborted his first approaches at the Eder Reservoir: 'Henry, that's very nice flying, but you will have to do better than that.'

Nobody knew what had happened to Maudslay and his crew. For Gibson, Shannon and Knight, who had witnessed the explosion beneath his Lancaster at the Eder Dam, they assumed that his aircraft had crashed soon after. They hoped that AJ-Z had force landed or at least the crew had baled out.

In Gibson's book, written sometime after the event, by which time he would have known the fate of the crew of AJ-Z, there is no indication about any concerns over Maudslay. In fact, he makes a special mention of him

> Bill [Astell], Hoppy [Hopgood], Henry [Maudslay], Barlow, Byers and Ottley had all gone. They had all got the hammer. The light flak had given it to most of them, as it always will to low flying aircraft – that is, the unlucky ones. They had all gone quickly, except perhaps for Henry. Henry, the born leader. A great loss, but he gave his life for a cause for which men should be proud. Boys like Henry are the cream of our youth. They die bravely and they die young.

As Gibson and the other survivors of 617 Squadron made their way back to Scampton the wreckage of Lancaster AJ-Z lay smouldering in an agricultural field north-east of Emmerich. It contained the bodies of the seven crew members, more than likely all killed on impact.

Though local defence forces and possibly medical teams may have attended the crash site immediately, it wasn't until the first light of Monday 17 May that German officials inspected the site. They identified the aircraft as a British Lancaster bomber and from the wreckage recovered all seven dead crew members. It seems that because of the ferocity of the impact only Jack and wireless operator Cottam could be identified. Once the inspection had been completed the seven corpses were all removed in coffins.

At Scampton, Gibson having arrived back after more than six-and-half hours strenuous flying and an operation debriefing, all on little sleep the previous night, did not stay long at the celebrations. He was the squadron commander and still had work to do, as depicted in the very last sequence of the 1955 film which shows Barnes Wallis asking: 'Aren't you going to turn in, Gibby?' to which he replied, 'No – I have to write some letters first'.

As messages of congratulations started to arrive, Gibson had already left the party and went over to No.2 Hangar where, together with Flight

Final scene from The Dambusters film showing Wallis (Michael Redgrave) and Gibson (Richard Todd) leaving to write letters.

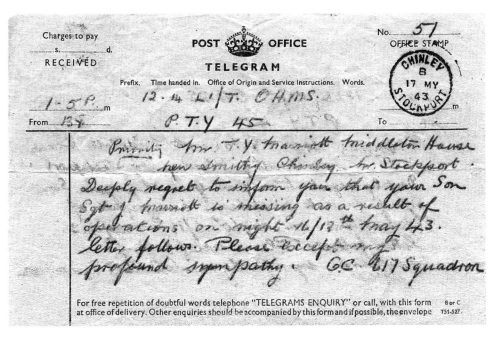

Gibson's telegram to Jack's father 17 May. (Transcript on p.289)

Lieutenant Humphries (617 Squadron Adjutant), he prepared casualty telegrams for the next of kin of the fifty-six crew members who had failed to return.

All were a standard format and contained the same text (apart from names and addresses):

All the completed telegrams were despatched via Post Office telegram. The telegram destined for Jack's father was received at the GPO transmitting office at 12:14.

The secrecy of Operation Chastise had ensured that in Chinley, Jack's family were completely oblivious to the activities of the previous twenty-four hours. In Chinley, Monday 17 May had started like any other working week. Jack's father, Thomas, had gone off to work repairing a local road; his sister, Floss, had taken Norma the short distance to school and returned home and was busying around the house.

When Jack was on operations his family would always attentively listen to the BBC news at 08:00 for information about bomber operations the previous night. They hoped and prayed that Jack's squadron was not listed in those that had aircraft which had failed to return. But Jack had told them he was non-operational, they had nothing to worry about – so they thought.

The news, though interesting, had less importance as they believed Jack was not implicated.

On Monday afternoon at 13:05, less than twelve hours after Jack was shot down, the GPO in Chinley received the telegram from Gibson marked 'O.H.M.S.' – On His Majesty's Service. The telegram messenger was dispatched on his motorbike the short distance to New Smithy. It probably went past Norma as she was playing in the school playground adjacent to the road. It arrived at Middleton House. Only Floss was in. She signed receipt of the telegram for her father. She didn't have to open it. She had been dreading receiving a telegram since Jack had signed up. She feared it was the worst news possible.

Devastated, distraught and tearful, she rushed out of the house to find her father. As she passed the school, Norma saw her mother and immediately knew, even at 10 years of age, that it was something serious. Something must have happened to Jack. Even though the telegram stated missing, it didn't ease the pain. If anything, the not knowing made it worse.

Back at Scampton, following a day of drinking and celebrating, most of the crews went on leave. The surviving aircrew were stood down, each given seven days, and their ground crews three. Gibson, though, stayed on a few days to write the follow-up letters he had promised on the initial telegram.

Two days later, on 19 May, as the Marriott family nervously waited for news, Jack's body, together with the six crew members with whom he had spent the last few hours of his short life, had been taken to the Nord Friedhof (Northern Military Cemetery) in Düsseldorf. They were laid to rest at 11:00 in seven plots 35–41. Jack was buried in 37 and Cottam in 38, the others simply identified as 'Unbekannt Eng. Flieger' (unknown English aviator).

Gibson completed his letter to Jack's father on 20 May. Though it was based on an accepted format it contained Gibson's personal observations of the events as he witnessed them, and the hope that Jack with his crew may still be alive. Though the majority of the letter is typed, the salutation and close is handwritten by Gibson.

After completing the fifty-six letters, Gibson then departed on leave which he spent with his wife Eve.

When the letter arrived at the Marriotts' it would have been of little comfort. On the same day a letter from his colleagues and friends at The Forge Bleach works also arrived. It was comforting that he was so well thought of, but the Marriott family anguish continued.

Reference :-
DO/2/43.

No. 617
Squadron, RAF. Station,
Scampton, Lincs.

20th. May, 1943.

My Dear Mr Marriot,

It is with deep regret that I write to confirm my telegram advising you that your son, Sergeant J. Marriott, is missing as a result of operations on the night of 16/17th. May, 1943.

Sergeant Marriott was Flight Engineer of an aircraft detailed to carry out an attack against the Eder Dam. The aircraft was seen to drop its load, and when the captain, Squadron Leader Maudslay, was called by radio, he seemed to be in extreme difficulty. It is possible, however, that the crew were able to abandon the aircraft and land safely in enemy territory, and if this is the case, news should reach you direct from the International Red Cross Committee within the next six weeks. Squadron Leader Maudslay would, I am sure, do everything possible to ensure the safety of his crew.

Please accept my sincere sympathy during this anxious period of waiting.

I have arranged for your son's personal effects to be taken care of by the Committee of Adjustment Officer at this Station, and will be forwarded to you through normal channels in due course.

If there is any way in which I can help you, please let me know.

Yours Very Sincerely,
P. Gibson

Wing Commander,
Commanding, 617 Squadron, RAF.

T.H. Marriott Esq.,
Middleton House,
New Smithy,
Chinley,
nr. Stockport,
Cheshire.

Gibson's letter to Jack's father 20 May. (Transcript on p.290)

The "FORGE" Social & Athletic Union

Founded 1923		President: CHARLES HADFIELD, Esq.
For the welfare of employees of Messrs. J. J. Hadfield, Ltd. Forge Bleach Works, CHINLEY.	20/5/43 193....	Hon. Treasurer: G. NADEN. Hon. Secretary: A. MARTIN.

Mr. Marriott,

    Middleton House,

      New Smithy,

        CHINLEY.

Dear Mr. Marriott,

    It is with very deep regret that the members of the "Union" learned that Jack was missing, and may we extend to you our hope, that you will receive more reassuring news in the near future.

    We all realise what a great debt we owe to the lads who are carrying out these operations, without any thought of self, and yet so ready to see that every atom of themselves is put to the job on hand.

    It is such thoughts that make us proud we knew Jack, and trust that there will be some good news of him soon.

                    Yours sincerely,

                  for The "Forge" Social & Athletic Union

                  W. H. Markham

Letter from the sports club of Jack's previous employer 20 May. (Transcript on p.291)

MISSING AIRMAN.—Mr. Thomas Marriott, of New Smithy, received an official telegram on Monday stating that his son, Sergt. F/Engineer Jack Marriott, of the R.A.F., was missing after an operational flight. Sergt. Marriott has been in the R.A.F. for about two years and has done a great deal of operational flying. Before joining up he was engaged at Forge Bleachworks. It is hoped that news may soon be heard of him.

Before the end of the week the local Chinley newspaper had reported that Jack was missing, while back at Scampton the Committee of Adjustment were already collecting, processing and moving the possessions of those 'missing as a result of air operations' so their rooms could be quickly reallocated to the replacement aircrews which started arriving the same day. Everything Jack owned was added to an inventory and removed for storage.

On Thursday 27 May, King George VI and Queen Elizabeth visited Scampton while on a tour of RAF stations. The surviving aircrew were all presented before them, together with a recommendation for thirty-four decorations. The King also reviewed options for the 617 Squadron badge in a competition from all ranks of the squadron. From a shortlist of two he selected the now famous image of a broken dam with three lightning bolts and the motto *'Apres Moi Le Deluge'* (After Me The Flood).

While this was in process Jack's family continued to wait in the agonising hope of some positive news. On 30 May Jack's father received a letter from the Air Ministry Casualty Branch expressing their regret and confirming that they continued to make enquiries through the International Red Cross.

Less than a week later on 6 June, several replacement standard Lancaster B.IIIs started to arrive direct from the production line at Woodford for acceptance trials. EE150 became the new AJ-Z. Munro managed to crash EE145, the new AJ-T on landing at Scampton after a training flight. Fortunately, there were no casualties.

Gibson introduces King George VI to Martin and his crew of AJ-P at RAF Scampton 17 May.

GERrard 9234
XXXXXXXX

AIR MINISTRY

XXXXXXXXXXXXXXXX

XXXXXXXXXXXXXXXX

P. 404210/2/43/P.4.A.2.

Casualty Branch,
77, OXFORD STREET,
LONDON, W. 1.

30th May, 1943.

Sir,

I am commanded by the Air Council to express to you their great regret on learning that your son, Sergeant John Marriott, Royal Air Force, is missing as the result of air operations on the night of 16th May, 1943, when a Lancaster aircraft in which he was flying as flight engineer set out for action during moonlight and was not heard from again. This does not necessarily mean that he is killed or wounded, and if he is a prisoner of war he should be able to communicate with you in due course. Meanwhile enquiries are being made through the International Red Cross Committee and as soon as any definite news is received you will be at once informed.

If any information regarding your son is received by you from any source you are requested to be kind enough to communicate it immediately to the Air Ministry.

The Air Council desire me to convey to you their sympathy in your present anxiety.

I am, Sir,

Your obedient Servant,

J. A. Smith

T. H. Marriott Esq.,
Middleton House,
Chinley,
Nr. Stockport. Cheshire.

Letter from the Air Ministry Casualty Branch 30 May. (Transcript on p.291)

As the Marriott, Maudslay, Urquhart, Cottam, Fuller, Tytherleigh, and Burrows families waited and hoped for positive news, adulation and praise continued to be directed to the surviving 617 Squadron members. On Tuesday 22 June, those to be decorated were in London for their investiture at Buckingham Palace followed by a lavish party hosted by the Avro Company at the Hungaria Restaurant, Regent Street. Of the thirty-four

WON D.F.M.—The Distinguished Flying Medal has been awarded to Sergt. Flight - Engineer Jack Marriott, R.A.F., who has been missing since the raid on the Eder dam in Germany, in May. His relatives do not know what act of gallantry won him the decoration, but it was for something before the raid on the dam, as the citation mentions a squadron to which he was attached before the raid on which he was reported missing. Sergt. Marriott took part in many raids over Germany and Italy and with twenty more hours flying would have become entitled to six months ground duty. He is the son of Mr. Thomas Marriott and the late Mrs. Marriott, of Middleton House, New Smithy, and was employed at Forge Bleachworks before he joined the R.A.F. Relatives and friends are anxiously awaiting news of the gallant airman.

decorations awarded for those who participated in Operation Chastise, none were awarded posthumously, and only a single flight engineer (Pulford of Gibson's crew) received a medal. However, when Jack left 50 Squadron he had been recommended for a Distinguished Flying Medal (DFM). His citation stating his 'efficiency and enthusiasm for operational flying and his determination in helping to hit the targets'.

Replacement crews continued to arrive at Scampton and flight training resumed. On 2 July Maltby was promoted to Squadron Leader and took the role of A-Flight commander. The same day saw the arrival of Squadron Leader George Holden from 102 Squadron. Not universally liked, he was

Telephone No:-
COLNBROOK 231-232-233.

In reply please
quote reference:-
CD/100374/F28598.

Central Depository,
Royal Air Force,
Colnbrook,
Slough, Bucks.

3rd July, 1943

100374 Sgt. Marriott J.

Dear *Sir*,

The personal effects of your *Son* as listed on the attached inventory have now reached this office from the Unit and will be held in safe custody pending the receipt of further evidence which will enable a conclusive classification of the casualty to be made.

In the case of casualties reported as "missing" unless definite evidence comes to light in the meantime, authority to release the effects is not normally received from the Air Ministry until at least six months from the date of the casualty, since official action to presume death is rarely taken before the expiration of this period.

In the case of casualties ultimately reported "Prisoner of War", the Air Ministry will as a general rule, only authorise the release of effects on the written request of the officer or airman concerned. In these circumstances, in order to expedite release, any original letter received from a Prisoner of War in this connection should be forwarded to this office for perusal and early return.

In the meantime, may I be permitted to express my sympathy with you in this period of anxiety.

Yours faithfully,

Squadron Leader, Commanding,
R.A.F. Central Depository.

T.H. Marriott Esq,
Middleton House,
Chinley. NR. STOCKPORT, Cheshire.

Letter from the RAF Central Depository 3 July. (Transcript on p.292)

hugely experienced, decorated, and took over Maudslay's role as B-Flight commander.

On 5 July the Royal Air Force Central Depository at RAF Colnbrook notified Jack's father that all his personal effects had been received and would be held safely until confirmation of his fate was received.

617 Squadron were back in action on 15 July when they were detailed to attack targets in northern Italy. Despite receiving new aircraft, they were still

not up to full strength and borrowed several Lancasters from neighbouring 57 Squadron. Twelve aircraft were involved. Six attacked Arquata Scrivia (sixty miles southeast of Turin) and six attacked San Polo d'Enza without loss before continuing to fly south to RAF Blida in Algeria. Poor weather prevented their return to Scampton until 24 July, bombing Leghorn in Italy on their way back. A further operation dropping leaflets over the northern Italian cities of Milan, Turin, Genoa and Bologna on 29 July also saw them flying on to RAF Blida. Though there were no casualties and most crews returned on 1 August, McCarthy and Munro had technical issues preventing their return until 3 and 5 July respectively.

As the days passed with no further news on Jack's fate, the thoughts of all his crewmate's relatives will have become more and more desperate with hope fading, just waiting for the inevitable bad news. On 21 July *The Times* printed an official Air Ministry Casualty Communiqué (Number 259) listing the aircraft and crew as missing. The same communiqué was also published in *Flight* on 29 July and *The Aeroplane* on 30 July.

After Operation Chastise Gibson never flew again operationally for 617 Squadron. He had been told at the beginning of the operation he would fly just one more mission and the RAF hierarchy kept to their word. He was a celebrity in demand and called upon to undertake many official and publicity duties.

Gibson and Holden air and groundcrew next to ED933 (AJ-X) 2 August 1943 (Left to right – Leading aircraftman Harding, Leading aircraftman Twigg, Pilot Officer Taerum, ??, Flight Lieutenant Trevor-Roper, Flight Lieutenant Hutchison, Wing Commander Gibson, Corporal Wood, Squadron Leader Holden, Sergeant Elliot, Pilot Officer Spafford, aircraftman Vivian).

On 2 August Gibson, complete with his Operation Chastise crew and using ED933 (AJ-X), the aircraft Jack had used for some of the initial dams training before the accident at Reculver, undertook a low-level cross-country training flight. Also, on board was Holden, who was to become the next 617 Squadron Commander.

As stated earlier, Holden wasn't well liked; he was considered by many to be a show-off and too flash. He upset several of the squadron when they were at RAF Blida where he terrorised a local goat herder by driving a jeep directly at the flock. Pulford, the flight engineer, refused to fly back with him and never flew with him again. Anyway, checkout for Holden complete, it was Gibson's last flight for 617 Squadron. The following day, 3 August, Holden was confirmed as the new 617 Squadron commander and Gibson departed Scampton for London and then on to a publicity tour of the USA.

Confirmation of Death

On 4 August, five of the original Lancaster Type 464s, including Jack's old Lancaster ED933 (AJ-X), flew down to Farnborough in preparation for Upkeep trials at the Ashley Walk bombing range in the New Forest. They were there for trials with forward rotating Upkeeps for potential use against canals, beach fortifications, and submarine pens.

On 5 August, the second day of the trials, Lancaster ED765, by then recoded AJ-M, made its run as the fifth Lancaster. As the pilot, Flying Officer Kellaway, made his approach he was too close to the preceding Lancaster and was caught in its slipstream. This caused ED765 to become very difficult to control and Kellaway, while trying to avoid a row of pylons, clipped his port wingtip causing the ED765 to belly flop onto the ground and slide across the ground before bursting into flames.

Kellaway suffered a broken leg and the rest of the crew minor injuries. ED765 had been the first prototype Lancaster Type 464. It hadn't been used on the Dambuster raid but was used extensively for trials before being delivered to 617 Squadron on 8 July.

This all went unnoticed at the Marriott household where the long wait for news continued.

On 11 August, the International Red Cross received a notification from the German Authorities citing their 'Totenliste #153', in which several of the 617 Squadron crews were listed as having been killed during the night of 16/17 May. It confirmed that a Lancaster had crashed with seven dead, of which two were identified as Sergeant Marriott and Flying Officer Urquhart, the other five were listed as unidentified.

The information was passed to the Air Ministry Casualty Branch who, at 08:45 on 12 August, sent a further telegram to Jack's father. It was received at Chinley GPO at 09:05 and in a standard short message simply stated: 'J Marriott is believed to have lost his life as a result of air operations on the night of 16th/17th/5/43. Stop. The air Council express their profound sympathy. Stop'.

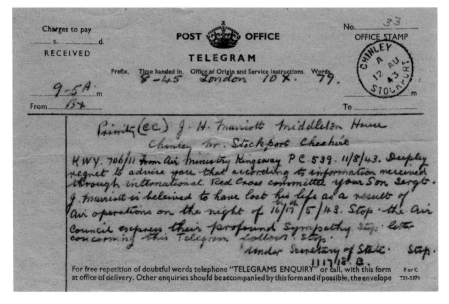

Air Ministry telegram to Jack's father 12 August. (Transcript on p.292)

It had been eighty-seven long and worrying days since the shocking news that Jack was missing. It wasn't the news the Marriotts wanted to hear, but sadly it was what they had feared and expected. Jack had given his life and his family could now mourn his passing and celebrate his short life. Several local newspapers carried a brief obituary.

The same day another five Lancasters set off for further trials. Holden, the new squadron commander, stayed back at Scampton however. Less than two weeks after taking over the squadron, he sat down to write his own personal letters of sympathy to Jack's and his crewmates' families.

Though the Ashley Walk Upkeep trials were completed without further incident and were considered to have been a success, no Upkeeps were ever used in anger again.

A week later a further official confirmatory letter from the Casualty Branch of the Air Ministry, dated 17 August 1943, was received by Jack's father.

Naval and Military

MARRIOTT. — In ever-loving memory of Flight Eng. Sergt. Jack Marriott, D.F.M., missing on night of May 16-17th, 1943, on Ruhr Dam operations, interred at Dusseldorf with his comrades on May 19th, 1943, aged 23. Never forgotten.

It basically confirmed the previous telegram and Holden's letter, but stated that although there was no reason to doubt the validity of the information received via the International Red

CONFIRMATION OF DEATH

No. 617 Squadron,
R.A.F., Station, Scampton,
Lincoln.

13th August 1943.

My dear *Mr. Marriott,*

It is with deepest regret that I now have to write to confirm the telegram you have received that your son Sgt. J.Marriott was killed in action on the night of 16/17th May 1943.

Please accept my sincere and heartfelt sympathy and that of all members of this Squadron in the sad loss which you have sustained.

Yours *Sincerely*

Geo Holden

SQUADRON LEADER,
COMMANDING NO. 617 SQUADRON R.A.F.,

Letter from Squadron Leader George Holden to Jack's father 13 August 1943. (Transcript on p.293)

Cross Committee, Jack's status would be recorded as 'missing believed killed'.

Even though the letter hinted at a slim hope that Jack might still be alive, it really confirmed the previous communications. It was not the news the Marriott family wanted, but now there was some closure.

Jack's details were added to his mother's gravestone in the Chinley Independent Chapel at Chapel Milton, less than a mile from the family home at New Smithy. A space was left for Jack's father and the engraved inscription at the bottom simply stated. 'Also Flt. Eng. Sergeant John Marriott/Missing night of 16th-17th May on Ruhr Dam Operations. Interred at Dusseldorf 19th May 1943, aged 23 years. One of the best.'

Errard 9234

P.404210/2/43/P.4.A.2.

Casualty Branch,
77, Oxford Street,
London, W.1.

Sir,   17 August, 1943.

I am commanded by the Air Council to inform you that they have with great regret to confirm the telegram in which you were notified that, in view of information now received from the International Red Cross Committee, your son, Sergeant John Marriott, Royal Air Force, is believed to have lost his life as the result of the air operations on the night of 16th May, 1943.

The Committee's telegram, quoting official German information, states that your son and the six other occupants of the aircraft in which he was flying on that night were killed on 17th May. It contains no information regarding the place of their burial nor any other details.

Although there is unhappily little reason to doubt the accuracy of this report, the casualty will be recorded as "missing believed killed" until confirmed by further evidence, or until, in the absence of such evidence, it becomes necessary, owing to lapse of time, to presume for official purposes that death has occurred. In the absence of confirmatory evidence death would not be presumed until at least six months from the date when your son was reported missing.

The Air Council desire me to express their deep sympathy with you in your grave anxiety.

I am, Sir,

Your obedient Servant,

Charles Evans

Letter from Casualty Branch of the Air Ministry to Jack's father 17 August 1943. (Transcript on p.293)

182

Marriott family grave in the Chinley Independent Chapel at Chapel Milton.

Thomas Marriott put a notification in the local Chinley paper, while at the same time Gwen Maudslay, the mother of Jack's pilot, issued a notification in the Deaths section of *The Times*. Before she contacted the newspapers, however, it seems that she took the time to personally send a handwritten letter to each of the families of the crew members that had died that night with her son Henry.

A poignant and moving letter. I'm sure it will have given some comfort to the Marriott family, knowing that he had not only been awarded for his work as a flight engineer with the award of the DFM, but more importantly the recognition from his pilot and captain, with whom he had spent so much time in the months preceding their deaths and beside whom he had sat for the last few hours of both their lives.

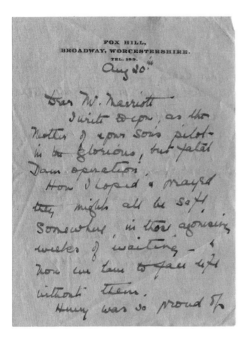
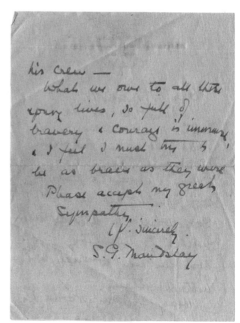

Letter from Gwen Maudslay (mother of Jack's pilot) to Jack's father, 20 August. (Transcript on p.294)

Robert Owen, whose book *Henry Maudslay: Dambuster* details the close relationship with Henry and his mother, wrote about the contents of the letter:

Very much what I would have imagined from Gwen Maudslay. Short and positive, with a stoicism – life must go on. It echoes the mood and tone of some of Henry's own letters to her. Very much 'get to grips and carry on'. There is a sense of duty and acceptance, and pride. Yet beneath this and the sentiments expressed I feel Mrs Maudslay always carried the loss. She kept so many of Henry's effects – toys from boyhood, mementoes from his schooldays, books and his letters to her – he would always be with her; yet from this letter one may imagine that signs of him may have been a reassurance and comforting reminder, rather than a troublesome spectre.

Jack's RAF Service Record was simply updated. In the section 'Next of Kin', or person to be notified of casualties, Jack's father was listed. In the Miscellaneous section: 'On the night of the 16th/17th May 1943 this airman took part in the extremely hazardous and highly successful raid on the Moehne, Eder, Sorpe and Schwelme dams, from which he failed to return.' In the 'Discharge' section: 'Killed in Action, 17-5-43 with 2 years and 345 days service.'

617 Squadron had continued training both at low and high altitudes, but Scampton, their home since their inception on 21 March, still had grass runways which were unsuitable for heavy bombers. On 30 August the squadron moved to RAF Coningsby which had long bitumen runways more suitable for aircraft with heavy bomb loads. The squadron's short stay at Scampton, less than six months, was over. They were never to return, but the association between 617 Squadron, The Dambusters, and Scampton is fixed indelibly into history. The newly arriving Lancasters were also allocated a new squadron code of KC, while the original Lancaster Type 464s retained their AJ code.

Two weeks after moving to RAF Coningsby, 617 Squadron prepared for another significant raid. On 14 September, Holden prepared a Battle Order for an attack on the heavily defended Dortmund-Ems Canal. It was to be another low-level mission. A plan to use the Upkeep was dropped in favour of each Lancaster carrying a single 12,000lb High Capacity (HC) light case 'Blockbuster' bomb (not the 12,000lb Tallboy bomb as designed by Barnes Wallis).

Eight Lancasters, led by Holden, escorted by six Mosquitos departed from RAF Coningsby in Operation Garlic. The Lancaster crews included the two new crews of Holden and Allsebrook; four crews that had taken part on Operation Chastise: Maltby, Shannon, Knight and Rice; and the two crews who had been stood down from Operation Chastise: Wilson and Divall. The weather had deteriorated over the target and the mission was aborted at 00:38 while the Lancasters were still over the North Sea.

As they turned back to home Maltby's aircraft JA981 (KC-J), crashed into the sea. There are several versions of what happened; Brickhill describes his Lancaster being caught in the slipstream of one of the other aircraft. Just as Kellaway had struggled with an uncontrollable aircraft in a similar situation at Ashley Walk, so too had Maltby fought with his heavy Lancaster. Brickhill continues that as his wing flicked downwards it caused the nose to drop and before it could be corrected, the wingtip hit the water causing the Lancaster to cartwheel and disappear below the surface. Alternatively, it has been suggested there was a collision with a Mosquito returning from another mission over Germany that also went missing that night.

Whatever happened, Shannon circled around the spot for two hours desperately looking for survivors and sending radio fixes to an Air Sea

Rescue team. Unfortunately, they only found an oil slick. The ninth Dambuster had died.

The weather was better the following day and Martin, who had returned from leave that morning, insisted on making up the eighth place – much to the dismay of his crew. It was a day described by many writing about 617 Squadron as their 'Blackest Hour'.

The eight Lancasters made their way, low level, in loose formation, in two groups of four. They traversed the North Sea and Holland without incident flying at around 50ft in radio silence. Having crossed the German border, they approached the small town of Nordhorn. Holden, less experienced at low flying than the other crews, flew straight across the town and climbed to about 300ft to avoid factory chimneys and a church spire. Martin, Knight and Wilson simply banked around the town and maintained their low level. Silhouetted against the moonlight, Holden presented an ideal target for the only light flak gun in Nordhorn.

Holden's Lancaster EE144 (KC-S) was hit in the large port-inner fuel tank causing a long stream of flame. As he struggled with the stricken Lancaster it lurched to the left beneath the Lancasters of Knight and Wilson. Martin, watching on, broke radio silence and shouted over R/T for them to 'Break outwards!' Wilson was just banking away as Holden's Lancaster crashed and exploded beneath him. Fortunately for Wilson, though shaky, his Lancaster was not damaged. Holden's 12,000lb HC bomb exploded fifteen minutes later. Along with Holden, four crewmembers of Gibson's Dambuster team were killed: navigator Taerum, wireless operator Hutchison, bomb aimer Spafford, and front gunner Deering. The flight engineer, Powell, was also an ex-Dambuster, previously with Townsend's crew.

Martin immediately assumed control of the mission but as they approached, the target was covered in mist. They climbed up to 150ft to be clear of the mist, which then suddenly dispersed as they were over the heavily protected target. All seven aircraft struggled to maintain contact with the target, and new squadron pilot Allsebrook was the next to be lost. Wilson announced over R/T he was going into attack. It's not known what happened, but it appears the bomb was still aboard his aircraft when it hit the ground. Similarly, Divall made a short announcement before unsuccessfully releasing his bomb and crashing.

Knight had been flying one-minute box circuits waiting for his turn to bomb when he hit some treetops. The tail plane was badly damaged, and branches filled the radiators of both port engines, which then stopped working. He struggled to gain height and, unable to continue, Knight asked for permission to jettison his bomb. Having done so he gradually gained height, but was unable to gain speed and found controlling the aircraft impossible. He held the aircraft steady while the crew baled out and then attempted a belly landing. Sadly, he was killed when his aircraft hit a ditch and bank crossing the field in which he was attempting to execute his forced landing.

Rice was badly hit by flak and had to jettison his bomb. Shannon managed to drop his bomb but only on the tow path, and although Martin's landed in the canal it failed to cause serious damage. Operation Garlic was a disaster. Over the two days six crews were lost, including two of the original Dambusters and the two Dambuster crews who were stood down on the night of Operation Chastise. Ten of the original pilots that took part on the Dambuster Raid had been killed, together with the two reserve pilots.

Shannon, Rice and Martin landed safely back at RAF Coningsby. Martin was immediately promoted and became temporary Squadron Commander. Holden had been in charge for a mere forty-five days; it was just over a month after he had written to Jack's father, and had been to break the news to Maltby's widow only the previous day. Martin then had the awful task of writing not only to Holden's family, but to those of his colleagues that had trained and flown with him on Operation Chastise: Knight, Wilson and Divall.

Less than two weeks later, on 23 September, Anderson and his crew – who had all taken part in Operation Chastise only to return with their Upkeep and were immediately banished back to 49 Squadron – were killed on a bombing mission to Mannheim. Another seven Dambusters lost.

Back at the Air Ministry Casualty Branch, authorisation for the release of Jack's belongings had been signed. His effects were packed and sent to his home in New Smithy. On 30 September, Casualty Branch confirmed in writing the location of the graves of Jack Marriot and Alden Cottam, but 'with bitter regret' added that it was not possible to state which of the other five were in each grave. At least for the Marriott and Cottam families there was some closure and they could now complete their mourning process. Sadly, for the other five families, their anguish continued.

Towards the end of October, Martin was informed that a permanent replacement commander had been appointed. On 25 October the highly decorated and charismatic Leonard Cheshire joined 617 Squadron, taking charge as their new Commanding Officer on 10 November.

A few days later the Marriotts received a letter from the Air Ministry who, following up their letter of 30 September, rather bluntly, confirmed that Jack had been killed.

TELEPHONE: GERRARD 9234

Extn............

Any communications on the
subject of this letter should
be addressed to :—

THE
UNDER SECRETARY
OF STATE,

and the following number
quoted :—

Your Ref. P.404210/2/43/P.4.B.8.

chapel

AIR MINISTRY

(Casualty Branch),

73-77, OXFORD STREET,

W.I.

1 2 NOV 1943

Sir,

    With reference to the letter from this
Department of 30th September, 1943, I am directed
to inform you that action has now been taken to
presume, for official purposes, that your son,
1003474 Sergeant J. Marriott lost his life on
17th May, 1943.

    I am to express the sympathy of the
Department with you in your great loss.

        I am, Sir,
           Your obedient Servant,

           D. Bent

        for Director of Personal Services.

T.H. Marriott, Esq.,
   Middleton House,
      Chinley,
         near STOCKPORT,
           Cheshire.

Letter from the Air Ministry to Jack's father 12 November 1943. (Transcript on p.294)

The very same day a standard royal sympathy letter arrived from King George VI. It simply read:

BUCKINGHAM PALACE

The Queen and I offer you our heartfelt sympathy in your great sorrow.

We pray that your country's gratitude for a life so nobly given in its service may bring you some measure of consolation.

George R.I.

T. H. Marriott, Esq.

Letter from Buckingham Palace 12 November 1943. (Transcript on p.295)

More 617 Squadron Activity and Losses

617 Squadron continued their specialised training interspersed with occasional operations. By 7 December, six of the Lancaster Type 464s had been converted back to near standard. Many had considerable battle damage to repair and the Merlin engines on some had paid a heavy price and needed to be replaced. On some of the Lancasters, the Dambuster modifications were removed and bulging bomb bay doors attached to accommodate the 12,000lb HC bombs. They were also all given new KC squadron codes.

On 18 November, one of the original ten standard Lancasters that had remained with the squadron (ED735 by then recoded as KC-R) was lost returning from a mission to bomb the Antheor Viaduct in southern France. After the mission on 11 November the eight 617 Squadron Lancasters had flown to Blida in Algeria. ED735, though, had diverted to Rabat in Morocco and was lost without trace on the return journey over the Bay of Biscay.

Sadly, two more of the original Lancaster Type 464s, although converted back to near standard Lancaster configuration, were lost on 10 December. ED825 (KC-E) formally McCarthy's AJ-T and ED886 (KC-O), Townsend's AJ-O from Operation Chastise, were both shot down while flying out of RAF Tempsford on SOE (Special Operations Executive) supply drops over Doullens in northern France.

Ten days later, Rice was on an operation to bomb an armaments factory in the Belgium city of Liege. Though Pathfinders had marked the target, they were not visible to the eight Lancasters and so, with heavy flak and reports of night fighters, Cheshire in the lead aborted the mission. As Rice turned for home he was engaged by a fighter. The Lancaster was badly damaged and broke up as it plummeted earthwards.

Only Rice managed to escape by parachute. The other six crew members, all of whom had set off on Operation Chastise only to return early after they lost their Upkeep, died with the aircraft. Rice evaded capture for a while but was eventually taken prisoner.

MORE 617 SQUADRON ACTIVITY AND LOSSES

On 9 January 1944, 617 Squadron moved their base from RAF Coningsby a few miles north to RAF Woodhall Spa. A few days later, on 13 January, Jack's original Lancaster ED933 (AJ-X) was involved in another incident. Piloted by Cheshire, the aircraft hit a flock of birds on take-off, fortunately causing no injuries or serious damage to the aircraft.

It wasn't long before another Dambuster Lancaster Type 464 was lost. On 20 January ED918 (AJ-F), used by Brown to attack the Sorpe Dam, was undertaking low-level bombing exercises in The Wash. The pilot, O'Shaughnessy, descended too low and clipped the sea causing the Lancaster to become uncontrollable. The aircraft crashed into the beach, smashed into a seawall, and then burst into flames, killing the pilot and one of the four crew members on board.

Early in February Bob Hay, bomb aimer for Martin and 617 Squadron bombing leader for Operation Chastise, lost his life in an attempt to destroy the Antheor Viaduct near Cannes. Martin's Lancaster was badly damaged in the very low-level attack, but he managed to land in Sardinia. His flight engineer, Whittaker, had been injured but unfortunately Hay, his long-time bomb aimer, had been killed instantly. The attack had been a complete failure.

Pulford, who had been Gibson's flight engineer and who had avoided being killed with Holden when he swapped to the crew piloted by Squadron Leader Suggitt, was on the same attack. While Martin had made an emergency landing in Sardinia, the other Lancasters had landed back at RAF Ford near the English south coast.

The following morning, 13 February, there was heavy rain and patchy fog. Most of the crews decided to wait until it cleared before returning to RAF Woodhall Spa. Suggitt, however, thought he would be able to make the short journey. By the time he came to depart the weather had deteriorated. As he took off, he appeared to clip a tree causing the Lancaster to crash, killing all onboard, near the village of Upwaltham.

The last surviving member of Gibson's team, Richard Trevor-Roper, the rear gunner, had transferred out of 617 Squadron by the time the rest of the Operation Chastise crew were joined by Holden. He was killed flying with 97 Squadron on a disastrous raid on Nuremburg on 31 March. Gibson was then the only surviving member of his Dambuster crew. He had arrived back from America at the end of 1943. He was desperate to get back on operational flying but was prevented from doing so. He had various staff roles and for a while considered politics, even being selected as the prospective parliamentary candidate for Macclesfield before turning down the opportunity in August.

THE HIGH PEAK DAMBUSTER

By mid-April 1944 the remaining Dambuster Lancaster Type 464s were seldom used. They were flown to nearby RAF Metheringham for storage, but maintained in near operational readiness just in case they were needed.

On 30 April yet another Dambuster was lost in a flying incident. Brian Jagger, who had been Shannon's front gunner for Operation Chastise, was killed when the 49 Squadron Lancaster he was in crashed during a Fighter Affiliation Exercise.

A year on from Operation Chastise celebrations were held in the officers' mess at RAF Woodhall Spa to mark the anniversary. In that year another thirty-one of the participating crews had been lost and apart from the Non-Commissioned Officers, Gibson was also a significant absentee as he was away on holiday.

Three days later, however, on Friday 19 May 1944, a further party was held for all ranks, notable for Gibson accidently standing on a huge celebratory cake as he climbed on a table to give a speech.

Gibson, though, still hadn't flown since the Dambusters raid and on 5 July finally flew, albeit as a second pilot, in a Lancaster again. The pilot was none other than Jack's original 50 Squadron pilot, Drew Wyness. About a week later ex-Dambuster Martin took Gibson for a flight in a Mosquito. He was desperate to get back on operations. On 19 July he finally joined a Lancaster crew from RAF East Kirkby for an attack on a V-1 flying bomb launch site at Criel-sur-Mer in France.

On 4 August he arrived at RAF Coningsby, home of the elite No.54 Base Flight as Air Staff Officer and although it was a predominately desk job, he still managed to fly occasionally and flew operationally on at least three occasions in marker aircraft; twice in a Lockheed P-38 Lightning and once in a Mosquito.

Extract from Gibson's Flying Logbook.

More 617 Squadron Deaths

On 25 August, Jack's original 50 Squadron pilot Drew Wyness, with whom he had completed twenty-five operations, transferred from 57 Squadron to 617 Squadron. By then he had been promoted to squadron leader.

Bad weather restricted his flying to training and bombing exercises. Wyness's first mission was not until 11 September, against the dreaded battleship *Tirpitz*, which was anchored out of range of British bombers in Kaafjord in Norway.

Twenty Lancasters from 617 Squadron departed RAF Woodhall Spa for RAF Lossiemouth in Scotland to refuel and then continue to the remote Russian airfield at Yagodnik, about fifteen miles south of Arkhangelsk.

Yagodnik Airfield showing one of the Lancasters, the two 511 Squadron Liberators and the 540 Squadron Mosquito.

They were accompanied by eighteen Lancasters from 9 Squadron from RAF Bardney, two 511 Squadron Liberators (with spares and ground crew), and a single 540 Squadron Mosquito.

The flight towards Arkhangelsk went well except that one of the 9 Squadron Lancasters had to return home when its 12,000lb Tallboy bomb became loose. Avoiding being targeted by Swedish, Finnish and Russian anti-aircraft defences, the remaining aircraft continued without incident. By the time they approached Yagodnik, however, the weather had deteriorated, thick clouds made navigation difficult.

Only twenty-six of the Lancasters were able to find and land at Yagodnik safely, the others either landed at different airfields or crash-landed. Incredibly, none of the crews were injured but six Lancasters were written off and another two of those that eventually found their way to Yagodnik were also too badly damaged to be used. Wyness was piloting Lancaster ME559 (KC-Y), which made a forced landing near the settlement of Kegostrov nearer to Arkhangelsk. It was so badly damaged that it could not be repaired and used in the raid.

On 15 September, the remaining airworthy Lancasters made their attack before returning to Yagodnik to refuel. Though some damage had been inflicted on the *Tirpitz* the operation was unsuccessful in sinking the battleship.

Wyness's Lancaster ME559 (KC-Y) had to be left in Russia with the five other damaged Lancasters. The Russian Air Force eventually managed to repair ME559 and one other using the others for spares. They were operated for a while on patrol, reconnaissance, and naval escort duties.

Wyness's Lancaster ME559 (KC-Y) after crash landing at Kegostrov

Wyness and his crew flew back to the UK as passengers in separate Lancasters on 17 September. Sadly, two of his crew, flight engineer Flying Officer Naylor and wireless operator Flying Officer Shea, were both killed when the Lancaster in which they were travelling home crashed into high ground at Nesbyen, about 100 miles northwest of Oslo in Norway.

During this time Gibson had done little flying, but on 19 September it was announced he would be controller for a difficult and untested tactic of Dispersed Marking at Rheydt near Mönchengladbach. There is uncertainty and some controversy about what happened, but having selected a navigator he had to travel from Coningsby to Woodhall Spa, where there was a spare Mosquito. He rejected the spare aircraft and commandeered another Mosquito KB267. He took off and arrived over the target, but marking of the area proved difficult and the attack was confused. It has been suggested that Gibson remained over the area for a while, possibly to assess the success of the raid or to check anti-aircraft gun locations. Having left the area, possibly with a damaged engine, Gibson's Mosquito crashed at Steenbergen in Holland. There are various theories as to the cause of the crash, but whatever the reason Guy Gibson, the charismatic leader of the Dambusters, was killed.

Despite the loss of two of his crew, Wyness too had continued flying on operations. On 23 September, just over a year since Holden had lost his life there, he was on another operation at the Dortmund-Ems Canal. After losing sight of the Target Indicator in cloud at 14,000ft, he was ordered to try again at 12,000ft. Unable to locate the target, he returned home without using his Tallboy. On 3 October, he was piloting one of eight Lancasters with 12,000lb Tallboy bombs which took off to support an operation against the seawall at Westkapelle. The main attack, using conventional bombs, breached the sea wall, so 617 Squadron who were still en route were ordered to abort their mission and returned to RAF Woodhall Spa with their unused bombs.

Lancaster ME559 (KC-Y) with a modified nose section in use by the Soviet Air Force after being repaired.

His next mission was sadly to be his last. On 7 October, Wyness was flying Lancaster NG180 (KC-S), one of thirteen Lancasters with Tallboys detailed to attack the Kembs Barrage on the River Rhine on the French-German border near Basel. The plan was for seven Lancasters to release their bombs from 8,000ft, the other six to bomb from 1,000ft. A fighter escort of North American Mustangs from 315 Polish Squadron led by the enigmatic Jan Zumbach, 129 Squadron and 306 Polish Squadron attacked flak positions with guns and rockets. Wyness was in the group of six Lancasters at low level. Despite some success from the Mustangs he was subjected to heavy flak as he made his approach. With his two port engines badly damaged he jettisoned his Tallboy but was unable to gain any height as he departed northwards along the Rhine. Some reports suggest that he first collided with power cables, but whatever happened he managed to ditch the Lancaster in the Rhine at low speed.

The crew members were uninjured and managed to inflate the dinghy from its stowage compartment in the starboard wing. Witnesses saw all seven crew get in and start paddling towards the French side of the river. As German soldiers prepared a boat on the opposite bank, three of the crew were seen to jump out of the dinghy and swim to the French bank of the river. As the German patrol boat approached it fired warning shots and then made Wyness and the three other crew members paddle to the German side of the river, where they were arrested by a German Pioneer unit and taken to the Town Hall of nearby Rheinweiler. Before long, Herr Gruenner the local Gestapo Kreisleiter of Loerrach and Muelheim arrived. After a cursory interrogation, Wyness and his three crew members were taken back to the Rhine, shot in the back of the head, and their bodies thrown into the river.

A few days later the bodies of Wyness and his wireless operator, Flying Officer Hosie, were recovered from the river on the French bank near the town of Chalampe. The bodies of navigator Flight Lieutenant Williams and wireless operator Flying Officer Honig were recovered several weeks later further downstream. The other three crew members were never heard of again. It is presumed they had been captured and also executed.

Gruenner was captured by French troops in 1945. After a trial he was sentenced to death and handed over to American forces. While awaiting a further trial he managed to escape and made his way to Argentina where he died in 1971.

Jack's Decoration, but not for Operation Chastise

The war in Europe ended in early May 1945, and in Japan four months later in September. The Second World War had lasted six years. By late 1945, military administration was starting to clear the backlog of awards and decorations. Jack's brother Bill had been in touch about the flying decoration for which Jack had been recommended before joining 617 Squadron. His citation simply made a recommendation for him to receive an award due to his 'efficiency and enthusiasm for operational flying and his determination in helping to hit the targets'.

Sadly, for Jack there was no decoration for Operation Chastise. There were no awards for any of the crews that had been killed. Of the thirty-four awards made to the aircrews that survived the dams raid, only a single award went to a flight engineer – Gibson's Sergeant Pulford.

At the end of November 1945, Bill received a letter from the Secretary of the Central Chancery of The Orders of Knighthood at St James's Palace inviting him to Buckingham Palace to receive Jack's posthumous DFM on behalf of his father. The letter outlined dress code, guests and travel arrangements.

Bill and brother Joe dutifully attended the ceremony. They arrived at the gates to Buckingham Palace where their invitation letter was inspected. They were then escorted across the Palace courtyard by two guards and met at the door of the Palace by Beefeaters. Guards then led Bill to the recipients' waiting area and Joe was led to the visitors' seating area in a luxurious room decorated in red and gold and adorned with paintings.

King George entered the room followed by the Lord Chamberlain and then, through a separate door, those who were receiving their awards. Each walked up in single file to the platform where the King was standing. Bill gratefully and proudly walked up to receive a Memorial Scroll and the DFM, presented on a velvet cushion.

CENTRAL CHANCERY OF
THE ORDERS OF KNIGHTHOOD,
ST JAMES'S PALACE, S.W.1.

22nd November 1945.

Sir,

I have the honour to inform you that your attendance
is required at Buckingham Palace at 10.15 o'clock a.m.
(doors open at 9.45 o'clock a.m.) on Tuesday, the 18th
December, 1945, in order that you, ~~as next of kin~~, may
receive from The King ~~this~~ on behalf of your father, the Distinguished
Flying Medal awarded to his son, the late Sergeant John Marriott, Royal
Air Force.

DRESS: Service Dress, Civil Defence Uniform, Morning Dress
        or dark Lounge Suit.

You may be accompanied by one relation only, who must
be a blood relation of the deceased (children under seven
years of age may not attend) and I shall be glad if you will
complete the enclosed form and return it to me immediately.
Two third class return railway vouchers will be forwarded to
you if you so desire, and I shall be glad if you will give
the details required on the form enclosed.

This letter should be produced on entering the
Palace as no further cards of admission will be issued.

I am, Sir,
Your obedient Servant,

Mr. Marriott, Junr.   Secretary

Letter from the Central Chancery 22 November 1945. (Transcript on p.295)

198

This scroll commemorates

Sergeant J. Marriott, D.F.M.
Royal Air Force

held in honour as one who
served King and Country in
the world war of 1939-1945
and gave his life to save
mankind from tyranny. May
his sacrifice help to bring
the peace and freedom for
which he died.

Jack's memorial scroll

What Became of the Dambuster Lancasters and Upkeeps?

By the middle of 1944 only eleven of the twenty-three purpose-modified Avro Lancaster B.III Special Type 464 remained. Six of those had already been flown to storage at RAF Metheringham.

The last operational use of any of them was 8 June 1944 when ED909, by then recoded as KC-P, and Jack's original Dambuster ED933 recoded as KC-N, took part in attack on the Saumur railway tunnel and a nearby bridge in the Loire region of France. Both Lancasters had been converted back to near normal configuration but with bulging bomb doors to accommodate the Tallboy bombs, though for this mission they carried standard 1,000lb bombs. Both returned from the raid unscathed.

Although trials had been undertaken and consideration had been given to the further use of Upkeeps, it was clear that by the end of 1944, none were going to be used. By the beginning of January 1945, most of the Lancaster Type 464s were transferred to 46 Maintenance Unit (46 MU) at RAF Lossiemouth in north-east Scotland for storage. They were to be maintained in a state whereby they could be available at seven days' notice, but this was later extended to twenty-one days.

The unused Upkeeps were held in storage at Scampton. During routine inspections in March 1945, one was found to have deteriorated so badly it was deemed to be unsafe. As no standard Lancaster was able to carry an Upkeep, Jack's old ED933 was flown down from RAF Lossiemouth in April 1945. The Upkeep was flown out over the North Sea and dropped from 1,000ft. After disposing of it, ED933 was returned to RAF Lossiemouth.

Once the war was over there was no need to store the special and historic Lancaster Type 464s that had been used for Operation Chastise. Like most military aircraft they were surplus to requirements and costly to keep. Despite their historic legacy they were all struck off charge.

WHAT BECAME OF THE DAMBUSTER LANCASTERS?

Following the end of the war there was no requirement to maintain a stockpile of weapons and the RAF had been disposing their surplus munitions at sea. By early 1946 the stored Upkeeps were displaying signs of deterioration, so instructions were prepared to include the disposal of the remaining unused thirty-seven in what was known as Operation Guzzle.

As no other aircraft were capable of carrying the Upkeep, three of the Lancaster Type 464s, ED906, ED909 and Guy Gibson's ED932 were refurbished at RAF Lossiemouth and delivered to Scampton. ED909 arrived on 13 August 1946 and was allocated the Station Flight code YF-B. The other two arrived on 27 August, ED906 allocated YF-A and ED932 YF-C. Despite the refurbishment at Lossiemouth, they all still required considerable maintenance to get them ready. ED932 needed to have its four Merlin engines replaced.

Operation Guzzle started on 22 August. The Lancasters flew with the Upkeeps out over the Atlantic Ocean to a position about 300 miles west of Glasgow. The Upkeeps were released from 10,000ft and without spinning or fusing. Flights continued through to December 1946 but Lancaster serviceability issues frequently disrupted operations. On one occasion, ED932 suffered a bird strike on take-off that resulted in a crash-landing on return to Scampton nearly six hours later. Though the aircraft was eventually repaired, Operation Guzzle was completed by the other two Lancaster Type 464s. The last flight for Operation Guzzle was on 21 December.

During that time the eight other Lancaster Type 464s at Lossiemouth had all been unceremoniously scrapped. Jack's ED933 was broken up on 2 October. The three at Scampton were used by the Station Flight for a while but were struck off charge again in July 1947 and, without any consideration for their historic value, were scrapped on 29 July.

Lancaster ED906 (YF-A) as used on Operation Guzzle

Lancaster ED909 (YF-B) being scrapped at RAF Scampton.

After just over four years, the Dambuster Lancasters Type 464, with comparatively few photographs or detailed records, were consigned to the history books. Little was retained for posterity, only a few small artefacts survive to this day.

Fortunately, when ED932 was being scrapped, the Avro Chief Inspector instructed his team to retain the control column and the throttle quadrant. After passing through several hands these two precious items remain and are on display at the Lincolnshire Aviation Heritage Centre in East Kirkby.

ED932 control column and the throttle quadrant.

Reburial

As time passed by, the memories of Jack did not diminish for the Marriott family. They had lost a very special member of their family. But nor had the authorities forgotten.

Almost five years after Jack had lost his life, and three years after the end of the war, a letter dated 16 April 1948 from a G. Haslam at the Air Ministry arrived with Jack's father. It stated that, in accordance with government policy, those 'fallen in Germany should not be left in isolated cemeteries, but should rest together in special military cemeteries which have been selected for the natural beauty and peace of their surroundings'.

The letter confirmed that Jack had been exhumed (3 October 1946) from his grave at the Nord Friedhof cemetery in Düsseldorf and reburied in Grave 18, Row B, Plot 5 at Reichswald Forest Military Cemetery south-west of Kleve, and only about ten miles from where he had been shot down at Emmerich. He was laid to rest with a temporary grave marker alongside the rest of his crew, though only Maudslay, Cottam, and Burrows had been identified by nametags on their tunics. Tytherleigh, Urquhart, and Fuller shared the same grave.

The letter went on to say that the grave 'will be maintained in perpetuity by the Imperial War Graves Commission[32] who will consult you, later on, regarding the inscription upon the headstone they will erect to his memory'.

A follow-up letter dated 26 October from S. Baker at the Air Ministry reported that owing to a replotting at Reichswald Forest Military Cemetery, Jack's actual location was Grave 4, Row C, Plot V. Also buried nearby was Astell, who had taken off in Jack's three-ship vic formation and was killed on the outbound journey. He was one of Maudslay's best friends and his home in the Peak District was less than three miles from Jack's home at New Smithy.

Tel. No.
SLOANE 3467 Ext...........

AIR MINISTRY,
2, SEVILLE STREET,
LONDON, S.W.1.

P.404210/43/S.14.Cas.C.7.

16 April, 1948

Dear Mr. Marriott,

I am deeply sorry to renew your grief in the sad loss of
your son, Sergeant J. Marriott, but I am sure you will wish
to know of the removal of his grave from Dusseldorf Cemetery,
to Reichswald Forest Military Cemetery, Cleve, where he now
rests in Grave 18, Row B, Plot 5. You will be glad to know
that the comrades who lost their lives with him rest in
graves nearby.

I must explain that this reburial is in accordance
with the policy agreed upon by His Majesty's and the Commonwealth Governments that our fallen in Germany should not be
left in isolated cemeteries, but should rest together in
special military cemeteries which have been selected for the
natural beauty and peace of their surroundings. The graves
there will be maintained in perpetuity by the Imperial War
Graves Commission who will consult you, later on, regarding
the inscription upon the headstone they will erect to his
memory. A photograph of the grave will be sent to you
although this may not be for some considerable time.

I do hope the thought that his last resting place will
always be reverently tended may be of some slight comfort to
you in the great loss you have sustained.

Yours sincerely,

T.H. Marriott, Esq.,
Middleton House,
Chinley,
Near Stockport,
Cheshire.

Gm.Haslam

Letter from the Air Ministry 16 April 1948. (Transcript on p.296)

Having had to deal with the management of a considerable number of
graves, the Imperial War Graves Commission were eventually in a position
to administer the graves of Jack and his crew members. In a standard-
format letter dated 10 October 1949, the Under Secretary of State for Air
confirmed to Jack's father that the Imperial War Graves Commission were
able to replace Jack's temporary cross with a permanent headstone. The
letter also contained details of a specimen of the standard RAF headstone,
together with a photo of Jack's temporary headstone.

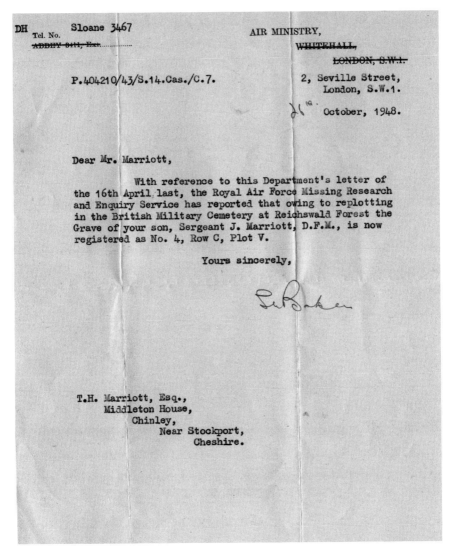

DH Tel. No. Sloane 3467
ABBEY 8111, Ext.

AIR MINISTRY,
WHITEHALL,
LONDON, S.W.1.

P.404210/43/S.14.Cas./C.7.

2, Seville Street,
London, S.W.1.

26th October, 1948.

Dear Mr. Marriott,

With reference to this Department's letter of the 16th April last, the Royal Air Force Missing Research and Enquiry Service has reported that owing to replotting in the British Military Cemetery at Reichswald Forest the Grave of your son, Sergeant J. Marriott, D.F.M., is now registered as No. 4, Row C, Plot V.

Yours sincerely,

T.H. Marriott, Esq.,
    Middleton House,
        Chinley,
            Near Stockport,
                Cheshire.

Letter from the Air Ministry 26 October 1948. (Transcript on p.297)

A further letter from the Imperial War Graves Commission, dated 6 December 1950, notified that a headstone, in Portland Stone with a carved RAF logo and inscription of Jack's service number, rank, name, crew position, service (RAF), date of birth and age will mark all the graves 'thus every man, rich or poor, General or Private, will be honoured in the same way'. The letter also confirmed that there would be space at the bottom of the headstone for a personal inscription but that the cost to the Marriott family for this had risen from 7s 6d to £1.

GW

Ref. No. P.404210/43/S.14
Gas(a).3.

The *Under Secretary of State for Air* presents his compliments to

......T.H. Marriott, Esq.,................and begs to forward herewith photographs

of cross marking the grave of No....1003474. Sergeant........................(rank)

John MARRIOTT D.F.M.,
....(full name).

These have been received from the Army Graves Service, who are responsible for the temporary marking of war graves.

Temporary crosses will be replaced in due course by permanent headstones to be erected by the Imperial War Graves Commission. Details of the inscription on the temporary cross will be carefully checked at that stage and any errors rectified before the permanent headstone is erected.

Air Ministry, London, S.W.1   Date......10 October, 1949.

Letter from The Under Secretary of State for Air 10 October 1949.

Temporary crosses at Reichswald Forest Military Cemetery

By this time Jack's father was a very ill man. There was no reply to the request for any personal inscription on Jack's headstone. Of the seven crew members that died with Jack, Maudslay, Tytherleigh, Cottam, and Fuller have a personalised inscription. The headstone was eventually replaced and a photograph sent to the Marriott family.

206

Tel.: Bourne End 594.

IMPERIAL WAR GRAVES COMMISSION,

WOOBURN HOUSE, WOOBURN GREEN,

HIGH WYCOMBE, BUCKS.

6 DEC 1950

Dear Sir or Madam,

I venture to ask for your assistance in completing the attached form.

The Imperial War Graves Commission have been entrusted, for this war as for the last, with the duty of permanently commemorating those members of His Majesty's Naval, Military and Air Forces from all parts of the British Empire who die in the service of the Allied cause. The Commission will consequently be responsible for marking and caring for the graves, or, in the case of those who have no known grave, for making provision for other suitable form of commemoration and also for recording all names in permanent Registers. This work will be carried out at the cost of the Commission, whose funds are provided by all the Governments of the Empire.

A headstone of the same simple pattern will, as before, mark each grave; thus every man, rich or poor, General or Private, will be honoured in the same way.

In order to carry out these duties, and to complete the permanent Registers, the Commission desire certain additional information which they hope you will be so good as to supply on the attached form, which should then be returned to the Commission.

You will notice that a space has been left on the form for a personal inscription to be selected by the relatives, if they so desire, for engraving on the headstone. Where, owing to the course of military operations, it has so far been impossible to find or identify a grave, no personal inscription should be inserted on the form. Should the grave eventually be discovered, I shall, of course, write to you again, and you will then have a further opportunity to choose an inscription.

Some relatives have expressed the wish to pay for this personal inscription, and an opportunity will be given to them later on of meeting the cost. Should they not wish to do so, the cost will be borne by the Commission.

Owing to increase in the cost of engraving Personal Inscriptions since the attached form was printed, the amount which may be paid by relatives has been raised from 7s. 6d. to £1.

Yours faithfully,

F. HIGGINSON,

Secretary.

(5141/3188) Wt. P.0082/3575 30m. 4/49 T. & B. Gp. 468

Above and overleaf: Letter from the Imperial War Graves Commission 6 December 1950.

Jack's elder sister May had moved to the family home in New Smithy to help look after his father. Sadly, Thomas passed away on 22 March 1951 and is buried at Chinley Independent Chapel in Chapel Milton, in the same plot as Jack's mother Lois who had died ten years earlier, beneath the same gravestone that had been engraved with Jack's details.

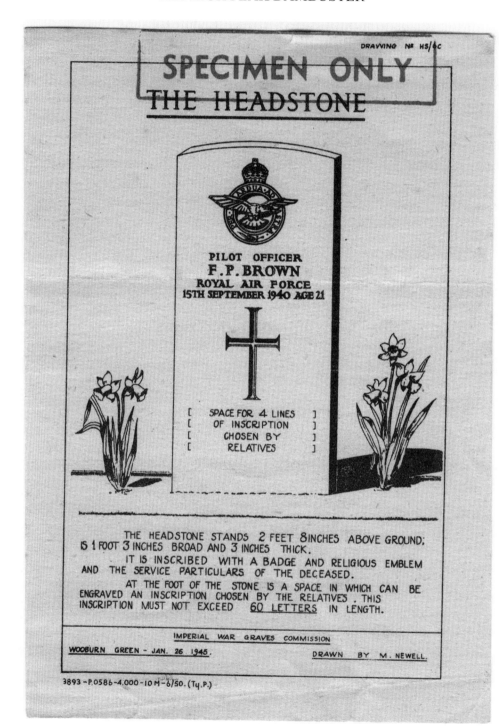

Jack's grave at
Reichswald Forest
Military Cemetery.

Jack's CWGC
memorial certificate.

The Story Continues and the Legend Grows

Despite censorship and military restrictions around the detail of Operation Chastise, it was promoted with propaganda and government publicity. The realisation of the monumental effort it had taken to achieve it was, and still is, a subject of national pride. Newspapers were full of the story. The surviving crews were feted and treated like celebrity heroes.

Guy Gibson was an instant superstar, which was only enhanced during his tour of America. While there, he wrote a series of articles for the *North Atlantic Weekly* magazine. The style and quality of the writing suggest that it was probably written by Gibson, though there are some that believe they were ghost-written by the serving RAF officer and author Roald Dahl. It's also believed that an approach to Hollywood for a film based on the writings was rejected.

When he returned to England the articles were expanded and incorporated into his book *Enemy Coast Ahead*, which was completed during early 1944 but only published after his death in 1946. The book details much of his RAF career before 617 Squadron with only the last few pages dedicated, without too much detail, to Operation Chastise.

What it did, however, was to introduce and remind the public of some of the main characters and describe the difficulties of the operation. It did, however, serve to stoke the fire of public imagination.

It is not surprising then that in 1951, Australian ex-fighter pilot author Paul Brickhill was commissioned to write the wartime history of 617 Squadron. It relied heavily on Gibson's earlier work but was expanded using the recollection of some of the survivors and giving a little more information on the Upkeep, Operation Chastise, and the later operations of the squadron.

The book, simply entitled *The Dam Busters*, became an instant classic. Many of 617 Squadron crew were referred to by name, but as with Gibson's book it mainly concentrated on the pilots; though Maudslay gets several mentions as he did in Gibson's book, very few of the lower ranks did. Jack was no exception, he did not get a mention personally, his and his crewmates involvement is inferred by their association with Maudslay.

Brickhill's book remains to this day, even among some other stunning works on this topic, as the pre-eminent piece of work on the Dambusters and 617 Squadron. It wasn't long before the head of production at Associated British Picture Corporation (ABPC) approached Brickhill and acquired the screen rights to the book.

Work on the script started in 1952 but the complete story was considered to be too much for a film, so the script was condensed into a film about solely Operation Chastise and the successful attacks on the Möhne and Eder Dams.

While bound by the confines of secrecy that still surrounded much of the raid, the script paid significant attention to historical accuracy. Many of the survivors that had taken part were contacted and copies of the script sent to some of the relatives of those who had been killed in the raid to ensure they were happy with the way that their relatives were depicted in the film.

In a letter dated 13 January 1954, ABPC's Elstree Studios Production Supervisor Bill (W.A.) Whitaker contacted Jack's late father via the Air Ministry. The letter, together with a copy of the script, confirmed that a film was being made of the Dambusters and he wanted to ensure that the scenes in which Jack was represented were portrayed accurately and sympathetically.

How proud the Marriott family were. Jack was always a hero to them, and now he was, though not named specifically, going to be immortalised forever for his small, but not insignificant, part in the greatest war story ever told. The letter arrived with Jack's younger sister May, by then Mrs Hawksley, still living at Middleton House.

Having read the script with sister Floss, she passed it on to Jack's brothers Bill, Joe, and Charlie for their perusal. After they had all read and confirmed that, although they could not comment on the historical aspects of the film, they were happy with the portrayal of Jack in the scenes that featured his character. On 12 February she responded, returning the script.

211

Letter from Associated British Picture Corporation 13 January 1954. (Transcript on p.297)

```
                                    Middleton House,
                                       New Smithy,
                                          CHINLEY.
                                             Derbys.


                                    12th. February, 1954.


W. A. Whittaker, Esq.,
Associated British Picture Corporation Ltd.,
Elstree Studios,
BOREHAM WOOD.
Herts.


Dear Sir,

            Your letter of the 13th. January last has been
handed to me due to the death, some two years ago, of my father -
Mr. T.H. Marriott, to whom it was actually addressed.

            I have to say that I have carefully read, with
much interest, the script of the proposed film, and return same to
you herewith.    I would apologise for the delay which has ensued in
letting you have this script back but this has been due to the fact
that my brothers were anxious to read it and as they live away from
here it has taken a little time.

                     Yours faithfully,

                     (MRS. M. HAWKSLEY)
```

Letter to Associated British Picture Corporation 12 February 1954. (Transcript on p.298)

The film was completed and despite some historical inaccuracies, restrictions with continuing secrecy over some aspects of the raid and in particular the Upkeep, and the limits of special effects of the time, it was – and still is – one of the best British films and the number one war film ever made.

The failed attack by Maudslay on the Eder Dam is clearly and accurately presented in accordance with Gibson's and Brickhill's books. However, the scene in the film clearly shows Maudslay flying in from the left of the Eder Dam with Waldeck Castle on their right, when they actually flew down the valley to the right of the dam with Waldeck Castle on their left.

A further inaccuracy, and probably using artistic licence for cinematic reasons, was ED937 being shown to crash just after flying over the Eder Dam, even though by the time the script was being written the actual location of the crash of ED937 in Emmerich was known.

G.R. Boak, the General Secretary of The Royal Air Forces Association, who were managing the event in a letter to May Hawksley on 21 March 1955 confirmed the date, location, the attendance of Princess Margaret, and asked if May would like one or two tickets.

Above: Still from the 1955 *The Dam Busters* film showing an un-named actor as Jack (left) and Richard Thorp as Henry Maudslay over the Eder Reservoir.

Left: The premiere for the film was at the Empire Theatre, Leicester Square in London on 16 May 1955, the twelfth anniversary of the raid.

The Royal Air Forces Association

(Incorporated by Royal Charter)

(Registered under the War Charities Act, 1940)

Please quote in reply:— RAFA/NHQ/1092.2.

21st March, 1955.

Dear Mrs. H~~~~~~~~

    We have now finalised plans for the Premiere of the film "The Dam Busters". This is to take place at the Empire Theatre, Leicester Square, London W. 1., at 7.45 p.m. for 8.15 p.m. on the 16th May, the Anniversary of the actual raid.

    Her Royal Highness The Princess Margaret has graciously consented to attend, and the proceeds of this World Premiere are to be equally divided between this Association, the R.A.F. Benevolent Fund, the R.A.F. Escaping Society, and the Pathfinder Association.

    If you would like to have an invitation to attend the Premiere, I should be most grateful if you would let me know so that I can make sure that some very special seats are booked for you. When you write perhaps you will tell me if you would like one or two seats.

Yours sincerely,

(G.R.BOAK)
General Secretary.

Letter from Royal Air Forces Association 21 March 1955. (Transcript on p.299)

Clearly a difficult decision to make, May contacted Boak via telephone to discuss the possibility of having three tickets and of meeting Princess Margaret. It wasn't a subject to which Boak could immediately reply, but before a decision had been made May confirmed she was not in a position to attend and wrote a letter to confirm that two tickets would be required for her brothers Joe and Charlie.

Letter to Royal Air Force Association 5 April 1955. (Transcript on p.299)

THE STORY CONTINUES AND THE LEGEND GROWS

Boak replied to May's letter on 19 April advising that only one of the brothers would be able to meet Princess Margaret and asked for confirmation which one it was to be. In a further telephone call May confirmed that it would be Charlie, the younger brother of the two, who had enjoyed a close but short relationship with Jack.

The film premiere was on a very wet Monday evening. Along with Charlie Marriott, fourteen of the original crew members were introduced to Princess Margaret. Other dignitaries included Barnes Wallis, Richard Todd, Gibson's

Honorary Vice-Presidents:
Marshal of the R.A.F.
The LORD TEDDER,
G.C.B., D.C.L., LL.D.
Dame HELEN C.I. GWYNNE-VAUGHAN,
G.B.E., LL.D., D.SC., F.I.S.
Marshal of the R.A.F.
Sir JOHN C. SLESSOR
G.C.B., D.S.O., M.C.
Vice-Presidents:
Air Vice-Marshal
Sir GEOFFREY BROMET,
K.B.E., C.B., D.S.O.
Air Chief Marshal
Sir FREDERICK BOWHILL,
G.B.E., K.C.B., C.M.G., D.S.O.
Air Chief Commandant
Dame KATHERINE TREFUSIS FORBES,
D.B.E.

Patron:
HER MAJESTY THE QUEEN
Vice-Patron:
Air Chief Commandant
H.R.H. THE DUCHESS OF GLOUCESTER,
C.I., G.C.V.O., G.B.E.
President:
Marshal of the R.A.F.
H.R.H. THE DUKE OF EDINBURGH
K.G., KT., G.B.E.

Chairman of the Council:
Air Marshal
Sir ROBERT H. M. S. SAUNDBY,
K.B.E., C.B., M.C., D.F.C., A.F.C.
Vice-Chairman:
Mr. K. T. JAGO, M.B.E.
Chairman of the Executive Committee:
Group Captain R. C. VAUGHAN,
O.B.E., M.C., Q.C., J.P.,
Hon. Treasurer:
Air Commodore J. SWIRE GRIFFITHS,
C.B., C.B.E.
General Secretary:
Mr. G. R. BOAK

All Communications to be addressed to:
The General Secretary, R.A.F.A.,
83, Portland Place,
London, W.1.
Telephone & Telegrams: LANgham 8181

Please quote in reply:— RAFA/NHQ/GRB/1092

19th April, 1955

Dear Mrs. Hawkesley,

Thank you so much for your letter.

We would very much like to present one of your brothers to Her Royal Highness Princess Margaret. Unfortunately, owing to the numbers, it will not be possible to present them both.

I wonder if you would like to enquire from them if they would like me to arrange for one of them to be presented and if so, whose name would they like me to submit to the Palace.

Kindest regards,

Yours sincerely,

(G. R. BOAK)
General Secretary

Letter from Royal Air Forces Association 19 April 1955. (Transcript on p.300)

father Alexander and former wife Eve Hyman. The film was premiered again the following evening and after release the reviews were positive; its reputation and the public's fascination in the film, the story, and the characters behind it has not diminished since. In fact, it is quite the opposite; even now, more than seventy-five years after the event, there is continued and growing interest.

Left: Film premiere at the Empire Theatre, Leicester Square 16 May 1955.

Below: Princess Margaret being introduced to attendees of the film premiere 16 May 1955.

Norma's Pride

The interest in the Dambusters from the general public has never waned, neither has the memory and affection of Jack's niece Norma. Now Mrs Bagshaw, she has maintained the memory of Jack since his ill-fated raid on the Eder Dam. The town of Chinley too, on its War Memorial with a backdrop of the beautiful Cracken Edge and Chinley Churn, proudly displays Jack's name in the sections, 'Persons known to have lost their lives while on Active Service 1939-1945'.

Chinley Roll of
Honour memorial.

Plans for a permanent 617 Squadron memorial had been discussed for some time. It eventually came to fruition in Woodhall Spa on a rainy Sunday 17 May 1987. A large crowd of over 1,500 people, including many ex-Dambusters and RAF dignitaries. A stunning stone representation of a breached dam with was unveiled. The memorial is 10ft high, buff York stone represents the dam wall with recessed water slipways inlaid with slate carrying the names of all 617 Squadron members who lost their life during the Second World War. The breach in the middle has Westmorland grey slate simulating the breached water which is engraved with the 617 Squadron crest and the operations in which 617 Squadron took part. Jack's name significantly and appropriately is close to that of Henry Maudslay.

In 1993 Norma, together with her cousins Brian Marriott (son of Jack's brother Bill) and Keith Marriott (son of Joe), attended the 50th anniversary commemoration of Operation Chastise at RAF Marham. During the commemoration Jack's DFM was presented to 617 Squadron representatives. The medal was put on display, initially in the RAF Marham, and later the RAF Lossiemouth, 617 Squadron crew room, together with memorabilia from other notable Second World War 617 Squadron members. As a fitting tribute to the Dambusters, the last airworthy Lancaster in the UK, operated by the Royal Air Force's Battle of Britain Memorial Flight (BBMF), flew low over the Derwent Dam in Derbyshire.

Woodhall Spa 617 Squadron memorial.

NORMA'S PRIDE

Right: Jack's DFM presented to 617 Squadron

Below: Letter from Royal Air Forces Association 31 March 2011. (Transcript on p.300)

ROYAL AIR FORCES
Association
Friendship | Help | Support

From: Liz Fredericks
Legacy, Trusts and In-Memoriam
Royal Air Forces Association
Central Headquarters
117½ Loughborough Road
Leicester LE4 5ND
Tel: 0116 268 8766
Fax: 0116 266 5012
Email: liz.fredericks@rafa.org.uk

Mr and Mrs N Bagshaw
59 Clement Road
Marple Bridge
STOCKPORT
SK6 5AG

31 March 2011

RAFA/RemGard/RemStones/106

RAF REMEMBRANCE GARDEN.

Dear Mr and Mrs Bagshaw

I do hope you are both keeping well.

Your unwavering patience has paid off at last – I am pleased to let you know that the remembrance stone commemorating the life of Jack Marriott has now been laid in the RAF Association Remembrance Garden.

We are currently arranging a service to be held at the National Memorial Arboretum on Friday 20 May 2011 to bless the remembrance crosses and stones. The service, which will take place in the remembrance garden itself, will start at 1130 hours and finish at approximately 1150 hours.

This will be a private service for those people and RAFA branches who have placed a commemoration in the garden and we would therefore like to invite you to attend.

Do let me know if you would like any further details about the service – my direct line number is 0116 268 8766 and my email address is liz.fredericks@rafa.org.uk. I would be grateful to hear by Thursday 28 April if you wish to attend.

With very best wishes

Yours sincerely

Liz Fredericks

National Memorial Arboretum
Alrewas   ALREWAS.

Following a long period of discussion and pressure from Norma, a letter from the Royal Air Forces Association, dated 31 March 2011, confirmed that a remembrance stone commemorating Jack had been laid in their remembrance garden at the National Memorial Arboretum in Staffordshire. Norma was delighted to attend the private service on Friday 20 May 2011 to pay her respect.

Commemorations also took place in 2013 for the 70th anniversary of the raid at RAF Coningsby. Several of their then current 617 Squadron Panavia Tornado GR4s were adorned with a commemorative fin to mark the occasion, and two Tornados, together with the BBMF Lancaster, made spectacular low-level passes at both the Dambuster training locations of Derwent Dam and Eyebrook Dam on the border of Leicestershire and Rutland.

Norma was again invited to the Royal Air Forces Association Service of Remembrance on Friday 20 June 2014.

Soon afterwards 617 Squadron was once again disbanded as their Tornado aircraft were retired from service. Norma, concerned at what may happen to Jack's precious DFM, contacted 617 Squadron.

In a polite letter the 617 Squadron Commanding Officer Wing Commander David Arthurton confirmed that it had been catalogued by the RAF Historical Branch and transferred to the RAF Museum at Hendon for storage. He confirmed his understanding that it would be returned to 617 Squadron, who reformed at RAF Marham in April 2018 with Lockheed F-35B Lightnings.

Norma at the RAF Remembrance Garden.

NORMA'S PRIDE

Right:
617 Squadron
Tornado with
commemorative fin.

Below: Letter from
617 Squadron
Commanding
Officer 15 October
2013. (Transcript
on p.301)

From Wing Commander D S Arthurton MA RAF

Officer Commanding
No 617 Squadron
'The Dambusters'

Royal Air Force
Lossiemouth
Elgin
Moray
IV31 4JH

Tel: 01343 817617

Mrs N Bagshaw
59 Clement Road
Marple Bridge
STOCKPORT
SK6 5AG

15 October 2013

Dear Mrs Bagshaw

DISTINGUISHED FLYING MEDAL BELONGING TO SERGEANT JOHN MARRIOTT

Thank you for your letter of 4 October, in which you asked what would be done with your uncle's Distinguished Flying Medal, which you kindly presented to the Squadron on the 50th Anniversary of the Dams Raid. You may wish to know that it is currently on display in the Squadron's crewroom, alongside medals belonging to other notable members of the Squadron from the Second World War.

All the Squadron's memorabilia has recently been catalogued by the RAF Air Historical Branch in preparation for the Squadron's disbandment in March 2014. They have decided that your uncle's medal will be transferred to the RAF Museum at Hendon for safekeeping. Unfortunately, I cannot say whether the Museum intends to put it on public display. However, it will be returned to 617 Squadron when it reforms with the new Lightning II aircraft, which is currently planned to take place in 2016.

Kind regards,

David Arthurton

223

THE HIGH PEAK DAMBUSTER

Sunday 21 September 2014 was an historic occasion when the only two surviving flying Lancasters in the world made an emotional and epic low flypast of the Derwent Dam. The Canadian Warplane Heritage Museum's aircraft had flown across the Atlantic and made several dazzling displays together with the BBMF Lancaster. The sight of two Lancasters in close formation over the Derwent had not seen since the training of the Dambusters in early 1943.

Derwent Reservoir 21 September 2014.

Memorials and Mysterious Memorials

As previously stated, Jack is remembered with an inscription on the Chinley War Memorial, on the family gravestone in the cemetery of Chinley Independent Chapel, Woodhall Spa 617 Squadron Memorial, Royal Air Forces Association Remembrance Garden at the National Memorial Arboretum, and there is a large wall plaque with a list of all Operation Chastise crew members at RAF Scampton's Heritage Centre, located in the historic No.2 Hangar.

For a long time there was no memorial at the actual ED937 (AJ-Z) crash site near Emmerich. However, during June 2018, seventy-five years after the crash, a mysterious memorial cross appeared near the site. The memorial was a simple white cross, fixed with the shape of a Lancaster carrying the registration ED937 on the left wing, the squadron code AJ-Z on the right, and the date, May 17 1943, down the shaft. Seven artificial poppies representing each member of the crew adorned the shaft and crossbar.

By the time it was erected there were plans and a campaign to raise money for a permanent memorial but neither local residents nor the campaign organisers were aware of who had installed the cross. There were no clues, except perhaps that the month of May was written in English rather than Mai in German.

The local newspaper, *NRZ Emmerich*, became involved and eventually a Dutch pilot named Jens van Gessel made contact by phone. He was originally from the town of s-Heerenberg just north of Emmerich across the border in Holland. He had spent many years living in Scotland flying helicopters for the oil industry, which may explain why he had written the month as the English May rather than German Mai, or Dutch Mei. He had also previously been a member of the Emmerich Flugsportverein (Flying Club), where he became interested in the crash of ED937. He concluded that had the Lancaster not crashed where it had it would have flown over, possibly crashing into, his town of s-Heerenberg. He further speculated that perhaps Maudslay had purposely crashed in the field to prevent any civilian casualties in s-Heerenberg.

RAF Scampton's Heritage Centre.

Emmerich's mysterious commemorative cross.

By the time the mystery of the cross was resolved, plans for a permanent memorial were well advanced. German war historian, researcher and Lancaster enthusiast Marcel Hahn, with help from British aviation enthusiast Mark Welch, both of whom had long been fascinated by the fate of AJ-Z, arranged for a permanent memorial to be installed on the spot where ED937 had crashed. It was the last Dambuster crash site on land to have a permanent memorial.

The stone memorial with all the crew names engraved was unveiled in Emmerich am Rhein, Germany, on Friday 17 May 2019, seventy-six years from the day the aircraft was shot down.

The Burgomeister of Emmerich, Peter Hinze, welcomed the guests before a speech by RAF representative Wing Commander Paul Withers from the NATO Combined Air Operations Centre in Uedem who stated:

> Henry Maudslay and his crew gave their lives attempting a difficult and dangerous mission in the hope that it would contribute to bringing to an end one of the darkest periods in European history. Since the end of the war, Europe has enjoyed relative peace and stability. It has done so because post-war reconciliation led to strong bonds of friendship between former enemies, aided by a strong NATO alliance. That this memorial stone has been created is evidence of the strength of those bonds of friendship and it is a fantastic tribute to the crew of AJ-Z.

Norma lays a white rose at the Emmerich memorial.

Norma travelled from her home near Stockport with her daughter Claire to attend, and among the other guests were Maudslay's nieces Victoria Trevelyan, Susan Maudslay-Maguire, Angela Gardiner, and nephew Nigel Maudslay.

Marcel Hahn addresses the attendees.

Norma at the site of the AJ-Z crash site.

Also in attendance was Johannes Doerwald, the 16-year-old gun-layer who was credited with bringing down the Lancaster. In a speech he said:

> I still remember well the moonlit night of 16-17 May 1943, when the catastrophe at the dams happened. A four-engined bomber flew past us at low altitude towards the Möhnesee. I cannot forget the sight of this colossus.
>
> When the gunner released 'fire' I was so excited that I had forgotten to put the safety lever around. The machine flew so low that it collided 20 km from here with a high voltage line. Then on the return flight came Lancaster ED937. I still recall today how it was hit by the tracer ammunition.

The unveiling was completed with Marcel and Mark paying tribute to each of the individual crew members before a minute's silence as the memorial stone was unveiled.

Marcel Hahn presented Norma with several fragments of aluminium from Jack's crashed Lancaster, black, twisted, and corroded and a little piece of Perspex. Small items but hugely significant and nostalgic. Maybe the Perspex was part of the cockpit that Jack had looked out from.

Marcel Hahn, Johannes Doerwald, Mark Welch, Wing Commander Paul Withers, and Burgomeister of Emmerich Peter Hinze.

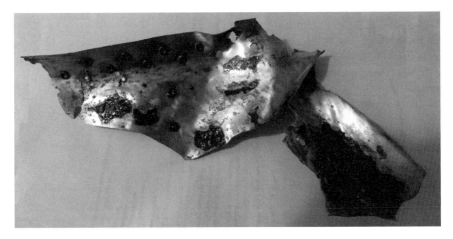

Fragment of Avro Lancaster ED937 (AJ-Z) presented to Norma.

Norma lays a white rose at Jack's grave in Reichswald Military Cemetery.

Following the ceremony, Norma travelled the short distance to Reichswald Military Cemetery to visit the last resting place of her beloved Uncle Jack. It was her first visit and very emotional.

There is also a mysterious unofficial 'Blue Plaque' memorial on the front wall of Jack's former home of Middleton House in New Smithy. Norma didn't know who had erected it and neither did Dambuster experts Rob Owen or Charles Foster. I managed to speak to the present owner and it seems that after Jack's father died, Middleton House continued to be occupied by Jack's sister May Hawksley. By the early 1960s the house had become unsuitable and she wanted to be nearer to the centre of Chinley and its services. She arranged for a house swap with Chinley resident Graham Hadfield who, once in occupation, modernised the house including the removal of the rear staircase, replacing it with an upstairs bathroom. Graham eventually sold the house to the present owner, Raymond Ball, in 1978. Sometime after moving in Raymond was in discussion with his neighbours and the topic of the previous occupants of Middleton House and of Jack's involvement in the Dambusters was raised. Raymond realised the significance of the house and felt that a fitting memorial should commemorate the short life of the Dambuster that had spent his early life there. So, in 2012 and at his own expense, he had a local blacksmith create the plaque which he duly erected by his front door.

Above and left: Jack's former home of Middleton House in New Smithy.

Appendix 1

Abbreviations

RAF rank abbreviations listed in Appendix 2.

A&AEE	Aeroplane and Armament Experimental Establishment
AOC	Air Officer Commanding
ASI	Air Speed Indicator
CO	Commanding Officer
Erk	RAF nickname for groundcrew originating in the First World War derived from Airk (short for aircraftman)
ft	feet (12 inches)
flak	Flugabwehrkanone (also referred to as Fliegerabwehrkanone) meaning aircraft-defence cannon
HCU	Heavy Conversion Unit
hp	Horse power
HQ	Headquarters
ILS	Instrument Landing System
lb(s)	Pound(s) (weight)
m	metre
m^3	cubic metres
mm	millimetre
MU	Maintenance Unit
mph	miles per hour
Op	Operational mission
RAE	Royal Aircraft Establishment
RAF	Royal Air Force
RAFVR	Royal Air Force Volunteer Reserve
RCAF	Royal Canadian Air Force

RNZAF	Royal New Zealand Air Force
rpm	revolutions per minute
R/T	Radio Telephone (or Radio Telephony)
SASO	Senior Air Staff Officer
Sqn.	Squadron
WAAF	Women's Auxiliary Air Force
yd(s)	yard(s) (3ft)

Appendix 2

RAF Ranks, Wings and Brevets

RAF ranks including abbreviations (abbrv.) as used in the text.

Commissioned Officer ranks

Rank	Abbrv.	Lower arm insignia
Marshal of the RAF	MRAF	
Air Chief Marshal	ACM	
Air Marshal	AM	
Air Vice Marshal	AVM	
Air Commodore	ACom	
Group Captain	Gp Capt	
Wing Commander	Wg Cdr	
Squadron Leader	Sqn Ldr	
Flight Lieutenant	Flt Lt	
Flying Officer	Fg Off	
Pilot Officer	Plt Off	

Non-Commissioned Officer ranks

Rank	Abbrv.	Lower arm insignia
Flight Sergeant (aircrew)	Flt Sgt	
Sergeant (aircrew)	Sgt	
Corporal	Cpl	

Enlisted ranks

Senior Aircraftman	SAC	
Leading Aircraftman	LAC	
Aircraftman 1st Class	AC1	
Aircraftman 2nd Class	AC2	

RAF wings and aircrew brevets (flying badges)

	Pilot	
	Flight Engineer	
	Navigator	

	Bomb Aimer	
	Wireless Operator	
	Air Gunner	

Appendix 3

Operation Chastise Aircrew Names

Aircrew with rank at the time of Operation Chastise of the 19 Lancasters used.

KIA = Killed In Action, KAS = Killed on Active Service
FE = Flight Engineer, Nav = Navigator, WO = Wireless Operator
BA = Bomb Aimer, FG = Front Gunner, RG = Rear Gunner

WAVE 1

Avro Lancaster B.III Type 464 - ED932 (AJ-G)					
Role	Rank	Name	From	Fate	
Pilot	Wg Cdr	Guy Gibson	106 Sqn.	KIA 19/09/1944	UK
FE	Sgt	John Pulford	97 Sqn.	KAS 13/02/1944	UK
Nav	Plt Off	Harlo 'Terry' Taerum	1654 HCU	KIA 16/09/1943	CAN
WO	Flt Lt	Robert 'Hutch' Hutchison	1654 HCU	KIA 16/09/1943	UK
BA	Plt Off	Frederick 'Spam' Spafford	50 Sqn.	KIA 16/09/1943	AUS
FG	Flt Sgt	George Deering	103 Sqn.	KIA 16/09/1943	UK
RG	Flt Lt	Richard Trevor-Roper	50 Sqn.	KIA 31/03/1944	UK
Take off: 21:39 Landing: 04:15		Dropped Upkeep at Möhne Dam. Continued to Eder Dam. Returned safely.		Duration:	6:36

Avro Lancaster B.III Type 464 - ED925 (AJ-M)

Role	Rank	Name	From	Fate	
Pilot	Flt Lt	John 'Hoppy' Hopgood	106 Sqn.	KIA 17/05/1943	UK
FE	Sgt	Charles Brennan	1660 HCU	KIA 17/05/1943	CAN
Nav	Fg Off	Kenneth Earnshaw	50 Sqn.	KIA 17/05/1943	UK
WO	Sgt	John Minchin	49 Sqn.	KIA 17/05/1943	UK
BA	Flt Sgt	John Fraser	50 Sqn.	Died 02/06/1962	CAN
FG	Plt Off	George Gregory	44 Sqn.	KIA 17/05/1943	UK
RG	Plt Off	Anthony Burcher	1654 HCU	Died 09/08/1995	AUS
Take off: 21:39 Shotdown: 00:33		Shot down at Möhne Dam. All crew killed except Fraser and Burcher.		Duration:	2:54

Avro Lancaster B.III Type 464 - ED909 (AJ-P)

Role	Rank	Name	From	Fate	
Pilot	Flt Lt	Harold 'Mick' Martin	1654 HCU	Died 03/11/1988	AUS
FE	Plt Off	Ivan Whittaker	50 Sqn.	Died 22/08/1979	UK
Nav	Flt Lt	Jack Leggo	50 Sqn.	Died 14/11/1983	AUS
WO	Fg Off	Len Chambers	50 Sqn.	Died 01/03/1985	NZ
BA	Flt Lt	Robert 'Bob' Hay	50 Sqn.	KIA 12/02/1944	AUS
FG	Plt Off	Bertie 'Toby' Foxlee	50 Sqn.	Died 06/03/1985	AUS
RG	Flt Sgt	Thomas Simpson	50 Sqn.	Died 02/04/1998	AUS
Take off: 21:39 Landing: 03:19		Dropped Upkeep at Möhne Dam. Returned safely.		Duration:	5:40

Avro Lancaster B.III Type 464 – ED887 (AJ-A)

Role	Rank	Name	From	Fate	
Pilot	Sqn Ldr	Henry 'Dinghy' Young	57 Sqn.	KIA 17/05/1943	UK
FE	Sgt	David Horsfall	57 Sqn.	KIA 17/05/1943	UK
Nav	Flt Sgt	Charles Roberts	57 Sqn.	KIA 17/05/1943	UK

Avro Lancaster B.III Type 464 – ED887 (AJ-A)					
Role	**Rank**	**Name**	**From**	**Fate**	
WO	Sgt	Lawrence Nichols	57 Sqn.	KIA 17/05/1943	UK
BA	Fg Off	Vincent MacCausland	57 Sqn.	KIA 17/05/1943	CAN
FG	Sgt	Gordon Yeo	57 Sqn.	KIA 17/05/1943	UK
RG	Sgt	Wilfred Ibbotson	57 Sqn.	KIA 17/05/1943	UK
Take off: 21:47 Shotdown: 02:58		Dropped Upkeep at Möhne. Continued to Eder Dam. Shot down inbound over Dutch coast.		Duration:	5:11

Avro Lancaster B.III Type 464 - ED906 (AJ-J)					
Role	**Rank**	**Name**	**From**	**Fate**	
Pilot	Flt Lt	David Maltby	97 Sqn.	KIA 15/09/1943	UK
FE	Sgt	William Hatton	97 Sqn.	KIA 15/09/1943	UK
Nav	Sgt	Vivian Nicholson	97 Sqn.	KIA 15/09/1943	UK
WO	Sgt	Anthony Stone	97 Sqn.	KIA 15/09/1943	UK
BA	Plt Off	John Fort	97 Sqn.	KIA 15/09/1943	UK
FG	Sgt	Victor Hill	97 Sqn.	KIA 15/09/1943	UK
RG	Sgt	Harold Simmons	97 Sqn.	KIA 15/09/1943	UK
Take off: 21:47 Landing: 03:14		Dropped Upkeep at Möhne Dam. Returned safely.		Duration:	5:27

Avro Lancaster B.III Type 464 - ED929 (AJ-L)					
Role	**Rank**	**Name**	**From**	**Fate**	
Pilot	Flt Lt	David Shannon	83 Sqn.	Died 08/04/1993	AUS
FE	Sgt	Robert Henderson	57 Sqn.	Died 18/02/1961	UK
Nav	Fg Off	Daniel 'Danny' Walker	22 OTU[33]	Died 17/11/2001	CAN
WO	Fg Off	Brian Goodale	51 Sqn.	Died 16/12/1977	UK
BA	Flt Sgt	Leonard Sumpter	57 Sqn.	Died 30/09/1993	UK
FG	Sgt	Brian Jagger	50 Sqn.	KAS 30/04/1944	UK
RG	Fg Off	Jack Buckley	75 Sqn.	Died 06/05/1990	UK
Take off: 21:47 Landing: 04:06		Arrived at Möhne Dam. Dropped Upkeep at Eder Dam. Returned safely.		Duration:	6:19

Avro Lancaster B.III Type 464 - ED937 (AJ-Z)

Role	Rank	Name	From	Fate	
Pilot	Sqn Ldr	Henry Maudslay	50 Sqn.	KIA 17/05/1943	UK
FE	Sgt	Jack Marriott	50 Sqn.	KIA 17/05/1943	UK
Nav	Fg Off	Robert Urquhart	50 Sqn.	KIA 17/05/1943	CAN
WO	Sgt	Alden Cottam	50 Sqn.	KIA 17/05/1943	CAN
BA	Plt Off	Michael Fuller	50 Sqn.	KIA 17/05/1943	UK
FG	Fg Off	William 'Johnny' Tytherleigh	50 Sqn.	KIA 17/05/1943	UK
RG	Sgt	Norman 'Bunny' Burrows	50 Sqn.	KIA 17/05/1943	UK
Take off: 21:59 Shotdown: 02:36		Arrived at Möhne Dam. Dropped Upkeep at Eder Dam. Shot down on return.		Duration:	4:37

Avro Lancaster B.III Type 464 – ED864 (AJ-B)

Role	Rank	Name	From	Fate	
Pilot	Flt Lt	William 'Bill' Astell	57 Sqn.	KIA 17/05/1943	UK
FE	Sgt	John Kinnear	57 Sqn.	KIA 17/05/1943	UK
Nav	Plt off	Floyd Wile	57 Sqn.	KIA 17/05/1943	CAN
WO	Sgt	Abram Garshowitz	57 Sqn.	KIA 17/05/1943	CAN
BA	Fg Off	Donald Hopkinson	57 Sqn.	KIA 17/05/1943	UK
FG	Flt Sgt	Francis 'Frank' Garbas	57 Sqn.	KIA 17/05/1943	UK
RG	Sgt	Richard Bolitho	57 Sqn.	KIA 17/05/1943	UK
Take off: 21:59 Crashed: 00:15		Shot down outbound.		Duration:	2:16

Avro Lancaster B.III Type 464 - ED912 (AJ-N)

Role	Rank	Name	From	Fate	
Pilot	Plt Off	Leslie Knight	50 Sqn.	KIA 16/09/1943	AUS
FE	Sgt	Raymond Grayston	50 Sqn.	Died 15/04/2010	UK
Nav	Fg Off	Harold 'Sydney' Hobday	50 Sqn.	Died 24/02/2000	UK
WO	Flt Sgt	Robert Kellow	50 Sqn.	Died 12/02/1988	AUS

Avro Lancaster B.III Type 464 - ED912 (AJ-N)					
Role	Rank	Name	From	Fate	
BA	Fg Off	Edward Johnson	50 Sqn.	Died 01/10/2002	UK
FG	Sgt	Frederick Sutherland	50 Sqn.	Died 21/01/2019	CAN
RG	Sgt	Henry O'Brien	50 Sqn.	Died 12/09/1985	CAN
Take off: 21:59 Landing: 04:20		Arrived at Möhne Dam. Dropped Upkeep at Eder Dam. Returned safely.		Duration:	6:21

WAVE 2

Avro Lancaster B.III Type 464 – ED825 (AJ-T)					
Role	Rank	Name	From	Fate	
Pilot	Flt Lt	Joseph McCarthy	97 Sqn.	Died 06/09/1998	US
FE	Sgt	William Radcliffe	97 Sqn.	Died 05/07/1952	CAN
Nav	Flt Sgt	Donald MacLean	97 Sqn.	Died 16/07/1992	CAN
WO	Flt Sgt	Leonard Eaton	97 Sqn.	Died 22/03/1974	UK
BA	Sgt	George 'Johnny' Johnson	97 Sqn.		UK
FG	Sgt	Ronald Batson	97 Sqn.	Died 06/09/1998	UK
RG	Fg Off	David Rodger	97 Sqn.	Died 06/09/1998	CAN
Take off: 22:01 Landing: 03:25		Dropped Upkeep at Sorpe Dam. Returned safely.		Duration:	5:24

Avro Lancaster B.III Type 464 – ED927 (AJ-E)					
Role	Rank	Name	From	Fate	
Pilot	Flt Lt	Robert 'Norm' Barlow	61 Sqn.	KIA 16/05/1943	AUS
FE	Plt Off	Samuel 'Leslie' Whillis	61 Sqn.	KIA 16/05/1943	UK
Nav	Fg Off	Philip Burgess	61 Sqn.	KIA 16/05/1943	UK
WO	Fg Off	Charles Williams	61 Sqn.	KIA 16/05/1943	AUS
BA	Plt Off	Alan Gillespie	61 Sqn.	KIA 16/05/1943	UK

Avro Lancaster B.III Type 464 – ED927 (AJ-E)

Role	Rank	Name	From	Fate	
FG	Fg Off	Harvey Glinz	61 Sqn.	KIA 16/05/1943	CAN
RG	Sgt	Jack Liddell	61 Sqn.	KIA 16/05/1943	UK
Take off: 21:28 Crashed: 23:50		Crashed outbound.		Duration:	2:23

Avro Lancaster B.III Type 464 – ED921 (AJ-W)

Role	Rank	Name	From	Fate	
Pilot	Flt Lt	John 'Les' Munro	97 Sqn.	Died 02/08/2015	NZ
FE	Sqt	Frank Appleby	97 Sqn.	Died 15/09/1996	UK
Nav	Fg Off	Francis 'Jock' Rumbles	97 Sqn.	Died 26/02/1988	UK
WO	Sgt	Percy Pigeon	97 Sqn.	Died 23/03/1967	CAN
BA	Sgt	James 'Jimmy' Clay	97 Sqn.	Died 06/08/1995	UK
FG	Sgt	William 'Bill' Howarth	97 Sqn.	Died 12/01/1990	UK
RG	Flt Sgt	Harvey Weeks	97 Sqn.	Died 22/03/1992	CAN
Take off: 21:29 Landing: 00:36		Damaged by Flak outbound. Returned to base.		Duration:	3:07

Avro Lancaster B.III Type 464 – ED934 (AJ-K)

Role	Rank	Name	From	Fate	
Pilot	Plt Off	Vernon Byers	467 Sqn.	KIA 16/05/1943	CAN
FE	Sgt	Alastair Taylor	467 Sqn.	KIA 16/05/1943	UK
Nav	Fg Off	James Warner	467 Sqn.	KIA 16/05/1943	UK
WO	Sgt	John Wilkinson	467 Sqn.	KIA 16/05/1943	UK
BA	Plt Off	Arthur 'Neville' Whitaker	467 Sqn.	KIA 16/05/1943	UK
FG	Sgt	Charles Jarvie	467 Sqn.	KIA 16/05/1943	UK
RG	Flt Sgt	James McDowell	467 Sqn.	KIA 16/05/1943	UK
Take off: 21:30 Crashed: 22:57		Crashed outbound.		Duration:	1:28

Avro Lancaster B.III Type 464 – ED936 (AJ-H)					
Role	Rank	Name	From	Fate	
Pilot	Plt Off	Geoffrey Rice	57 Sqn.	Died 24/11/1981	UK
FE	Sgt	Edward Smith	57 Sqn.	KIA 20/12/1943	UK
Nav	Fg Off	Richard Macfarlane	57 Sqn.	KIA 20/12/1943	UK
WO	Sgt	Chester 'Bruce' Gowrie	57 Sqn.	KIA 20/12/1943	CAN
BA	Sgt	John Thrasher	57 Sqn.	KIA 20/12/1943	CAN
FG	Sgt	Thomas 'Bill' Maynard	57 Sqn.	KIA 20/12/1943	UK
RG	Sgt	Stephen Burns	57 Sqn.	KIA 20/12/1943	UK
Take off: 21:31 Landing: 00:47		Lost Upkeep after flying too low. Returned to base.		Duration:	3:16

WAVE 3

Avro Lancaster B.III Type 464 – ED910 (AJ-C)					
Role	Rank	Name	From	Fate	
Pilot	Plt Off	Warner 'Bill' Ottley	207 Sqn.	KIA 17/05/1943	UK
FE	Sgt	Ronald Marsden	207 Sqn.	KIA 17/05/1943	UK
Nav	Fg Off	Jack Barrett	207 Sqn.	KIA 17/05/1943	UK
WO	Sgt	Jack Guterman	207 Sqn.	KIA 17/05/1943	UK
BA	Sgt	Thomas Johnston	207 Sqn.	KIA 17/05/1943	UK
FG	Sgt	Harry Strange	207 Sqn.	KIA 17/05/1943	UK
RG	Sgt	Frederick Tees	207 Sqn.	Died 15/03/1982	UK
Take off: 00:09 Crashed: 02:35		Crashed outbound.		Duration:	2:26

Avro Lancaster B.III Type 464 – ED865 (AJ-S)					
Role	Rank	Name	From	Fate	
Pilot	Plt Off	Lewis Burpee	106 Sqn.	KIA 17/05/1943	CAN
FE	Sgt	Guy Pegler	106 Sqn.	KIA 17/05/1943	UK

Avro Lancaster B.III Type 464 – ED865 (AJ-S)

Role	Rank	Name	From	Fate	
Nav	Sgt	Thomas Jaye	106 Sqn.	KIA 17/05/1943	UK
WO	Plt Off	Leonard Weller	106 Sqn.	KIA 17/05/1943	UK
BA	Flt Sgt	James Arthur	106 Sqn.	KIA 17/05/1943	CAN
FG	Sgt	William Long	106 Sqn.	KIA 17/05/1943	UK
RG	Sgt	Joseph Brady	106 Sqn.	KIA 17/05/1943	CAN
Take off: 00:09 Crashed: 02:35		Crashed outbound.		Duration:	2:26

Avro Lancaster B.III Type 464 – ED918 (AJ-F)

Role	Rank	Name	From	Fate	
Pilot	Flt Sgt	Kenneth Brown	44 Sqn.	Died 23/12/2002	CAN
FE	Sgt	Harry Feneron	44 Sqn.	Died 18/11/1993	UK
Nav	Sgt	Dudley Heal	44 Sqn.	Died 07/02/1999	UK
WO	Sgt	Herbert Hewstone	44 Sqn.	Died 28/05/1980	UK
BA	Sgt	Stefan Oancia	44 Sqn.	Died 06/05/1999	CAN
FG	Sgt	Daniel Allatson	57 Sqn.	KIA 16/09/1943	UK
RG	Flt Sgt	Grant McDonald	44 Sqn.	Died 13/05/2012	CAN
Take off: 00:12 Landing: 05:33		Dropped Upkeep at Sorpe Dam. Returned safely.		Duration:	5:21

Avro Lancaster B.III Type 464 – ED886 (AJ-O)

Role	Rank	Name	From	Fate	
Pilot	Flt Sgt	William Townsend	49 Sqn.	Died 09/04/1991	UK
FE	Sgt	Dennis Powell	49 Sqn.	KIA 16/09/1943	UK
Nav	Plt Off	Cecil 'Lance' Howard	49 Sqn.	Died 26/12/1989	AUS
WO	Flt Sgt	George 'Jock' Chalmers	49 Sqn.	Died 06/08/2002	UK
BA	Sgt	Charles Franklin	49 Sqn.	Died 25/01/1975	UK
FG	Sgt	Douglas Webb	49 Sqn.	Died 08/12/1996	UK
RG	Sgt	Raymond Wilkinson	49 Sqn.	Died 27/07/1980	UK
Take off: 00:14 Landing: 06:15		Dropped Upkeep at Ennepe (or Bever) Dam. Returned safely.		Duration:	6:01

245

Avro Lancaster B.III Type 464 – ED924 (AJ-Y)					
Role	Rank	Name	From	Fate	
Pilot	Flt Sgt	Cyril Anderson	49 Sqn.	KIA 23/09/1943	UK
FE	Sgt	Robert Paterson	49 Sqn.	KIA 23/09/1943	UK
Nav	Sgt	John Nugent	49 Sqn.	KIA 23/09/1943	UK
WO	Sgt	William 'Douglas' Bickle	49 Sqn.	KIA 23/09/1943	UK
BA	Sgt	Gilbert Green	49 Sqn.	KIA 23/09/1943	UK
FG	Sgt	Eric Ewan	49 Sqn.	KIA 23/09/1943	UK
RG	Sgt	Arthur Buck	49 Sqn.	KIA 23/09/1943	UK
Take off: 00:15 Landing: 05:30		Unable to find Sorpe Dam. Returned safely.		Duration:	5:15

Summary of nationalities of the aircrew of the 19 Lancasters used on Operation Chastise

	Pilot	FE	Nav	WO	BA	FG	RG	Total
UK	10	17	12	12	12	15	12	90
Canada	3	2	5	4	5	3	5	27
Australia	4	0	2	2	2	1	2	13
USA	1	0	0	0	0	0	0	1
New Zealand	1	0	0	1	0	0	0	2
Total	19	19	19	19	19	19	19	133

Key: FE=Flight Engineer, Nav=Navigator, WO=Wireless Operator, BA=Bomb-Aimer, FG=Front Gunner, RG=Rear Gunner.

Fate of the aircrew who took part in Operation Chastise

Total Aircrew who participated	133
Killed on Operation Chastise	53
Prisoner of War	3
Killed in Action after Operation Chastise	32
Survived the Second World War	48

Appendix 4

Avro 693 Lancaster B.III

Specifications

Role	Heavy Bomber
Engines	4 x Packard Merlin 28 1,300 hp
Crew 7	Pilot Flight Engineer / co-Pilot Navigator Wireless Operator Bomb Aimer / Front Gunner Mid-upper Gunner Rear Gunner
Wingspan	102ft
Length Overall	69ft 6 in
Height Overall	20ft 6 in
Empty Weight	31,642lb
Max. Loaded Weight	65,000lb
Speed	287 mph @ 11,500ft 234 mph @ 21,000ft
Service Ceiling	24,500ft
Range	with 14,000lb bomb load: 1,660 miles

Armament

Front turret	Frazer Nash FN-5A with two .303 Brownings
Mid-upper Turret	Frazer Nash FN-50 with two .303 Brownings
Rear Turret	Frazer Nash FN-20 with four .303 Brownings

Avro 693 Lancaster B.III TYPE 464 Provisioning

Specifications

Role	Operation Chastise low level bomber
Engines	4 x Packard Merlin 28 1,300 hp
Crew 7	Pilot Flight Engineer / co-Pilot Navigator / height monitor Wireless Operator / spinning & monitoring Upkeep Bomb Aimer / co-Navigator Front Gunner Rear Gunner
Wingspan	102ft
Length Overall	69ft 6 in
Height Overall	20ft 6 in
Empty Weight	31,642lb
Max. Loaded Weight	42,000lb (with a single Upkeep)
Speed	240 mph
Service Ceiling	Flew at less than 100ft
Range	1,4000 miles plus

Armament

Front turret	Frazer Nash FN-5A with two .303 Brownings
Mid-upper Turret	Not present
Rear Turret	Frazer Nash FN-20 with four .303 Brownings

Appendix 5

Avro 693 Lancaster B.III
Flight Engineer's Panel

Standard Lancaster Instrument panel (from Lancaster Pilot's and Flight Engineer's Notes)

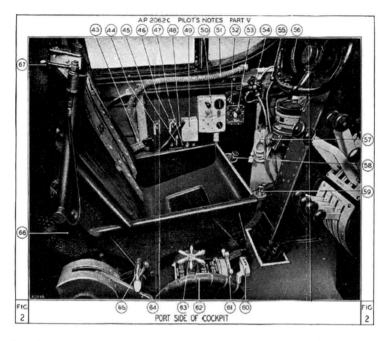

Standard Lancaster pilot's position (from Lancaster Pilot's and Flight Engineer's Notes).

Standard Lancaster Flight Engineer's panel (from Lancaster Pilot's and Flight Engineer's Notes).

Key

1	Instrument flying panel	32	Boost control cut-out
2	D.F. indicator	33	Signalling switch box (recognition lights)
3	Landing light switches	34	ID lights colour selector switches
4	Undercarriage indicator switch	35	DR compass switches
5	DR compass repeater	36	Auto controls steering lever
6	DR comp. deviation card holder	37	P.4. comp. deviation card holder
7	Ignition switches	38	P.4. compass
8	Boost gauges	39	Undercarriage position indicator
9	Rpm indicators	40	ASI correction card holder
10	Booster coil switch	41	Beam approach indicator
11	Slow-running cut-out switches	42	Watch holder
12	I.F.F. detonator buttons	43	Bomb door control
13	I.F.F. switch	44	Navigation light switch
14	Engine starter switches	45	D switch
15	Bomb containers jettison button	46	Auto controls main switch
16	Bomb jettison control	47	Pushbutton unit for T.R. 1196
17	Vacuum change-over cock	48	Seat raising lever
18	Oxygen regulator	49	Mixer box
19	Feathering buttons	50	Beam approach control unit
20	Triple pressure gauge	51	Oxygen connection
21	Signalling switchbox (ID lamps)	52	Pilot's call light
22	Fire-extinguisher buttons	53	Auto controls attitude control
23	Suction gauge	54	Auto controls cock
24	Starboard master engine cocks	55	Auto controls clutch
25	Supercharger gear change control panel	56	Brake lever
26	Flaps position indicator	57	Auto controls pressure gauge
27	Flaps position indicator switch	58	Pilot's mic/tel socket
28	Throttle levers	59	Windscreen de-icing pump
29	Propeller speed control levers	60	Flaps selector
30	Port master engine cocks	61	Aileron trimming tab control
31	Rudder pedal	62	Elevator trimming tab control

63	Rudder trimming tab control	72	Coolant temperature gauges
64	Undercarriage control lever	74	Fuel contents gauges
65	Undercarriage control safety bolt	75	Inspection lamp socket
66	Portable oxygen stowage	76	Fuel contents switch
67	Harness release lever	77	Fuel tanks selector switch
68	Ammeter	78	Electric fuel booster pump switches
69	Oil pressure gauges	79	Fuel pressure warning lights
70	Pressure-head heater switch	80	Emergency air control
71	Oil temperature gauges	81	Oil dilution buttons

Appendix 6

Fate of the Lancasters
Used by 617 Squadron

Lancasters used on Operation Chastise

Twenty-three Avro Lancaster B.IIIs were converted to Type 464 by Avro at Woodford. Only eleven survived the Second World War and all were scrapped soon afterwards.

Reg	Used on OC	Lost on OC	Lost training after OC	Lost on ops after OC	[1]Used at Ashley Walk	[2]Used on OG	Scrapped
ED765	no		05/08/43		5 Aug		
ED817	no						23/09/46
ED825	YES			10/12/43	5&12 Aug		
ED864	YES	YES					
ED865	YES	YES					
ED886	YES			10/12/43			
ED887	YES	YES					
ED906	YES				5&12 Aug	YES	29/07/47
ED909	YES					YES	29/07/47
ED910	YES	YES					
ED912	YES				12 Aug		29/07/47
ED915	no						08/10/46
ED918	YES		20/01/44		12 Aug		
ED921	YES						26/09/46
ED924	YES						26/09/46
ED925	YES	YES					
ED927	YES	YES					

253

Reg	Used on OC	Lost on OC	Lost training after OC	Lost on ops after OC	[1]Used at Ashley Walk	[2]Used on OG	Scrapped
ED929	YES				5 Aug		07/10/46
ED932	YES					YES	29/07/47
ED933	no				5 Aug	[3]	07/10/46
ED934	YES	YES					
ED936	YES				12 Aug		29/07/46
ED937	YES	YES					
23	19	8	2	2		3	11

OC = Operation Chastise   trg = training   OG = Operation Guzzle

[1] = Ashley Walk Bombing Range Trials – August 1943
[2] = Operation Guzzle – August & December 1946
[3] = Disposal of a single Upkeep April 1945

Temporary Lancaster used on Operation Chastise

Ten Avro Lancasters were supplied from No.5 Group in March 1943 but eight were reallocated during May/June 1943 when dedicated 617 Sqn. Lancasters arrived on squadron.

Reg	Ver	From	Date	To	Date	Comments
W4921	B.I	106 Sqn	26/03/43	619 Sqn	01/05/43	
W4926	B.I	97 Sqn	27/03/43	1654 CU	15/06/43	29/04 Damaged Cat. Ac[34] in landing accident
W4929	B.I	61 Sqn	26/03/43	619 Sqn	04/05/43	
W4940	B.I	57 Sqn	27/03/43	1660 CU	14/05/43	
ED329	B.I	207 Sqn	27/03/43	57 Sqn	09/05/43	19/04 Damaged Cat.Ac
ED437	B.III	50 Sqn	27/03/43	1661 CU	6/06/43	
ED735	B.I	44 Sqn	27/03/43			Remained with 617 Sqn
ED756	B.III	49 Sqn	30/03/43	619 Sqn	13/05/43	
ED763	B.III	467 Sqn	02/04/43			Remained with 617 Sqn
LM309	B.I	9 Sqn	27/03/43	619 Sqn	01/05/43	

Appendix 7

Vickers Type 464 Upkeep

The Upkeep was officially the Vickers Type 464. Originally it had a spherical wooden outer casing which shattered in trials and was discarded to leave a smooth (rivetless) cylindrical drum shaped device 60in long and 50in in diameter. Its overall weight was 9,250lb, of which 6,600lb was the explosive charge Torpex which was designed for use as a torpedo explosive, to provide a longer explosive pulse for greater effect against underwater targets. Training Upkeeps were inert filled with a mixture of concrete and cork to replicate the same density and weight of the live versions.

It had three hydrostatic pistols, set to fire at a depth of 30ft and a self-destruct fuse, armed automatically as the bomb was dropped from the aircraft, and timed to fire after 90 seconds.

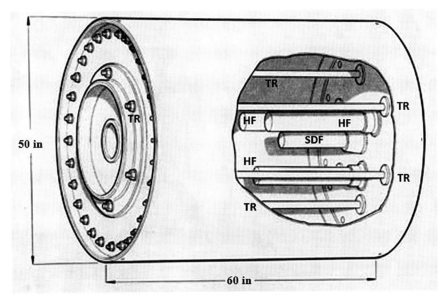

Key: TR = Tie Rod   HF = Hydrostatic Fuse   SDF = Self Destruct Fuse

Final version of Vickers Type 464 Upkeep.

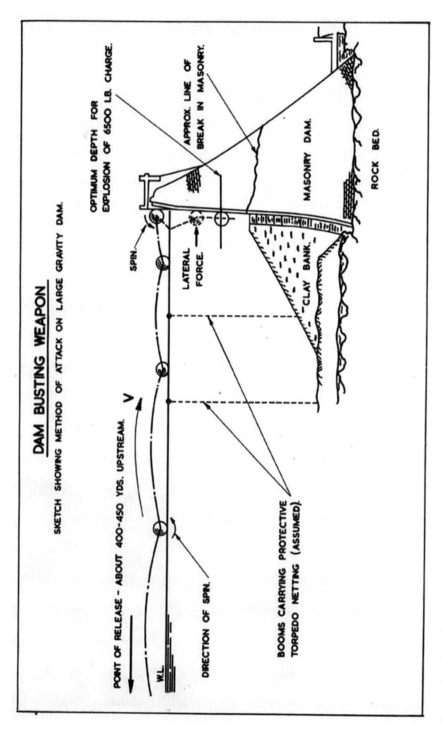

Barnes Wallis's sketch of the use of the Upkeep against a gravity dam (Möhne and Eder dams).

Appendix 8

Medals and Decorations

Decorations and ribbon bar in order of precedence received by crew members following Operation Chastise. Recipient shown with decorations at the time of the raid.

**Victoria Cross
(VC)**

Recipients

Wg Cdr G. Gibson DSO & Bar, DFC & Bar

**Distinguished Service Order
(DSO)**

Recipients

Flt Lt H.B. Martin DFC

Flt Lt D.J.H. Maltby DFC

Flt LT D.J. Shannon DFC

Plt Off L.G. Knight

Flt Lt J.C. McCarthy DFC

Bar to Distinguished Flying Cross (DFC)

Recipients

Flt Lt R.E.G. Hutchison DFC

Flt Lt J.F. Leggo DFC

Flt Lt R.C. Hay DFC

Fg Off D.R. Walker DFC

Distinguished Flying Cross (DFC)

Recipients
Plt Off H.T. Taerum
Plt Off F.M. Spafford DFM
Plt Off G.A. Deering
Flt Lt R.D. Trevor-Roper DFM
Fg Off L. Chambers
Plt Off J. Fort
Fg Off J. Buckley
Fg Off H.S. Hobday
Fg Off E.C. Johnson
Plt Off C.L. Howard

Conspicuous Gallantry Medal (CGM)

Recipients
Flt Sgt K.W. Brown
Flt Sgt W.C. Townsend DFM

Bar to Distinguished Flying Medal (DFM)

Recipients

Sgt C.E. Franklin DFM

Distinguished Flying Medal (DFM)

Recipients

Sgt J. Pulford

Flt Sgt T.D. Simpson

Sgt V. Nicholson

Flt Sgt L.J. Sumpter

Flt Sgt D.A. MacLean

Sgt G.L. Johnson

Sgt D.P. Heal

Sgt S. Oancia

Flt Sgt G.A. Chalmers

Sgt D.E. Webb

Sgt R. Wilkinson

Distribution of Medals within aircraft that attacked and returned

	Captain	P	FE	N	WO	BA	FG	RG
AJ-G	Gibson	VC	DFM	DFC	DFC-B	DFC	DFC	DFC
AJ-P	Martin	DSO		DFC-B	DFC	DFC-B		DFM
AJ-J	Maltby	DSO		DFM		DFC		
AJ-L	Shannon	DSO		DFC-B		DFM		DFC
AJ-N	Knight	DSO		DFC		DFC		
AJ-T	McCarthy	DSO		DFM		DFM		
AJ-F	Brown	CGM		DFM		DFM		
AJ-O	Townsend	CGM		DFC	DFM	DFM-B	DFM	DFM

Key: P=Pilot, FE=Flight Engineer, N=Navigator, WO=Wireless Operator, BA= Bomb Aimer, FG=Front Gunner, RG=Rear Gunner.
DFC-B= Bar to DFC, DFM-B= Bar to DFM.

Jack's Decorations and Medals

Unofficial Bomber Command Medal

No official campaign medal was issued to the aircrew of Bomber Command, despite the loss of more than 55,000 personnel during the Second World War. Following a campaign an unofficial medal was produced in 1985 to a design resulting from a competition in the British magazine *Medal News* and made available for sale to veterans of Bomber Command and their next of kin.

Appendix 9

Phonetic Alphabet

Phonetic alphabet as used in 1943 and as currently used.

Letter	1943	Current
A	Able	Alpha
B	Baker	Bravo
C	Charlie	Charlie
D	Dog	Delta
E	Easy	Echo
F	Fox	Foxtrot
G	George	Golf
H	How	Hotel
I	Item	India
J	Jig	Juliet
K	King	Kilo
L	Love	Lima
M	Mike	Mike
N	Nan	November
O	Oboe	Oscar
P	Peter[35]/Popsie	Papa
Q	Queen	Quebec
R	Roger	Romeo
S	Sugar	Sierra
T	Tare	Tango
U	Uncle	Uniform
V	Victor	Victor
W	William	Whisky
X	Xray	Xray
Y	Yoke	Yankee
Z	Zebra	Zulu

Appendix 10

Operation Chastise Codewords

Cooler	Codeword for Operation Chastise
Goner	Upkeep released (result codewords below)
Pranger	Attack on Möhne Dam
[Gibson's Dog's Name]	Möhne Dam breached proceed to Eder Dam
Dinghy	Eder Dam breached proceed to Sorpe Dam
Mason	All aircraft return to base
Tulip	Hopgood to take over at Möhne Dam
Cracking	Maudslay to take over at Eder Dam
Gilbert	Attack secondary dams as instructed

Goner result codewords

Goner Upkeep released and …

1	Failed to explode
2	Overshot dam
3	Exploded more than 100yds from dam
4	Exploded 100yds from dam
5	Exploded 50yds from dam
6	Exploded 5yds from dam
7	Exploded in contact with dam

with results noted …

8	No apparent breach
9	Small breach
10	Large breach

at target …

A	Möhne Dam
B	Eder Dam
C	Sorpe Dam
D	Lister Dam
E	Ennepe Dam
F	Diemel Dam

Operation Chastise codewords as transmitted to No.5 Group Operations:

Möhne Dam

Time	Wave	Lancaster	Wireless Op.	Dam	Codeword
00:28	1	AJ-G	Hutchison	Möhne	*GONER* 68A

GONER 68A indicating Upkeep had been released and exploded 5yds (**6**), with no apparent breach (**8**) from the Möhne Dam (**A**)

Time	Wave	Lancaster	Wireless Op.	Dam	Codeword
00:38	1	AJ-P	Chambers	Möhne	*GONER* 58A

GONER 58A indicating Upkeep had been released and exploded 50yds (**5**), with no apparent breach (**8**) from the Möhne Dam (**A**)

Time	Wave	Lancaster	Wireless Op.	Dam	Codeword
00:43	1	AJ-A	Nichols	Möhne	*GONER* 78A

GONER 78A indicating Upkeep had been released and exploded in contact (**7**), with no apparent breach (**8**) to the Möhne Dam (**A**)

Time	Wave	Lancaster	Wireless Op.	Dam	Codeword
00:49	1	AJ-J	Stone	Möhne	*GONER* 78A

GONER 78A indicating Upkeep had been released and exploded in contact (**7**), with no apparent breach (**8**) to the Möhne Dam (**A**)

Time	Wave	Lancaster	Wireless Op.	Dam	Codeword
00:49	1	AJ-G	Hutchison	Möhne	*[Gibson's Dog's Name]*

[Gibson's Dog's Name] indicating the Möhne Dam had been successfully breached

Eder Dam

Time	Wave	Lancaster	Wireless Op.	Dam	Codeword
01:39	1	AJ-L	Goodale	Eder	*GONER* 79B

GONER 79B indicating Upkeep had been released and exploded in contact (**7**), with a small breach (**9**) to the Eder Dam (**B**)

Time	Wave	Lancaster	Wireless Op.	Dam	Codeword
01:57	1	AJ-Z	Cottam	Eder	*GONER* 28B

GONER 28B indicating Upkeep had overshot (**2**), with no apparent breach (**8**) to the Eder Dam (**B**)

Time	Wave	Lancaster	Wireless Op.	Dam	Codeword
01:45	1	AJ-N	Kellow	Eder	*GONER* 79B

GONER 79B indicating Upkeep had been released and exploded in contact (**7**), with a small breach (**9**) to the Eder Dam (**B**)

Time	Wave	Lancaster	Wireless Op.	Dam	Codeword
01:54	1	AJ-G	Hutchison	Möhne	*DINGHY*

DINGHY indicating the Eder Dam had been successfully breached

Sorpe Dam

Time	Wave	Lancaster	Wireless Op.	Dam	Codeword
00:46	2	AJ-T	Eaton	Sorpe	*GONER* 78C

GONER 78C indicating Upkeep had been released and exploded in contact (**7**), with no apparent breach (**8**) to the Sorpe Dam (**C**)

Time	Wave	Lancaster	Wireless Op.	Dam	Codeword
03:14	3	AJ-F	Hewstone	Sorpe	*GONER* 78C

GONER 78C indicating Upkeep had been released and exploded in contact (**7**), with no apparent breach (**8**) to the Sorpe Dam (**C**)

Ennepe Dam

Time	Wave	Lancaster	Wireless Op.	Dam	Codeword
03:37	3	AJ-O	Chalmers	Ennepe	*GONER* 58E
GONER 58E indicating Upkeep had been released and exploded 50yds (**5**), with no apparent breach (**8**) from the Ennepe Dam (E)					

Appendix 11

The Dams

Discussions about attacking dams in Germany in the event of conflict in Europe had started before the war. For Operation Chastise, seven German reservoir dams had been identified as potential targets.

Five were in the industrial Ruhr Valley (Möhne, Sorpe, Lister, Ennepe, and Henne) and two further to the east in the Weser Valley (Eder and Diemel). The Möhne, Eder and Sorpe Dams were the primary targets and all the others were secondary, but the Henne was removed from the list of targets prior to the operation.

All the dams, with the exception of the Sorpe Dam, were gravity dams. These dams were a masonry or stone construction with a vertical upstream face to hold back the water. The weight of the dam and its resistance against its foundation opposed the horizontal pressure of water pushing against it.

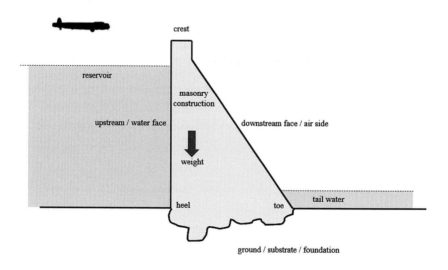

Generalised Gravity Dam.

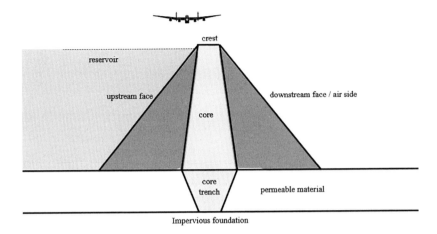

Generalised Earth Dam.

These required an attack straight on with the Lancaster flying perpendicular to the centre of the dam releasing the backward spinning Upkeep to skip over torpedo nets to hit the upstream face of the dam and sinking to 30ft before exploding.

The Sorpe Dam was an earth (or embankment) dam. These typically have a reinforced concrete core with compacted layers of earth, with earth and other more permeable substances on the upstream and downstream faces.

This required an attack along the crest of the dam with the Lancaster flying parallel and slightly to the water side of the dam before releasing the Upkeep without rotating as low as possible to roll down upstream face of the dam and sink to 30ft before exploding.

Möhne Reservoir and Dam

Valley basin	Ruhr
Planning Code	X
Attack Code	A
Reservoir size	135 million m³
Dam type	limestone curved gravity dam
Dam height	112ft
Dam length	2133ft
Width top	21ft
Width bottom	130ft
Towers	two – 639ft apart
Breach size	253ft x 72ft

Eder Reservoir and Dam

Valley basin	Weser
Planning Code	Y
Attack Code	B
Reservoir size	202 million m^3
Dam type	limestone curved gravity dam
Dam height	139ft
Dam length	1310ft
Width top	20ft
Width bottom	119ft
Towers	two – 780ft apart
Breach size	230ft x 72ft

Sorpe Reservoir and Dam

Valley basin	Ruhr
Planning Code	Z
Attack Code	C
Reservoir size	72 million m³
Dam type	concrete core, earth bank & stone slabs
Dam height	190ft
Dam length	1965ft
Width top	22ft
Width bottom	n/a
Towers	none
Breach size	Not breached

Lister Reservoir and Dam

Valley basin	Ruhr
Planning Code	D
Attack Code	D
Reservoir size	22 million m^3
Dam type	masonry curved gravity dam
Dam height	131ft
Dam length	866ft
Width top	23ft
Width bottom	103ft
Towers	One
Breach size	Not breached

Ennepe Reservoir and Dam

Valley basin	Ruhr
Planning Code	E
Attack Code	E
Reservoir size	15 million m³
Dam type	masonry curved gravity dam
Dam height	165ft
Dam length	1050ft
Width top	15ft
Width bottom	101ft
Towers	Two 600ft apart
Breach size	Not breached

Diemel Reservoir and Dam

Valley basin	Weser
Planning Code	F
Attack Code	F
Reservoir size	20 million m³
Dam type	masonry
Dam height	131ft
Dam length	635ft
Width top	23ft
Width bottom	102ft
Towers	none
Breach size	Not breached

Appendix 12

Jack Marriott's RAF Service Record

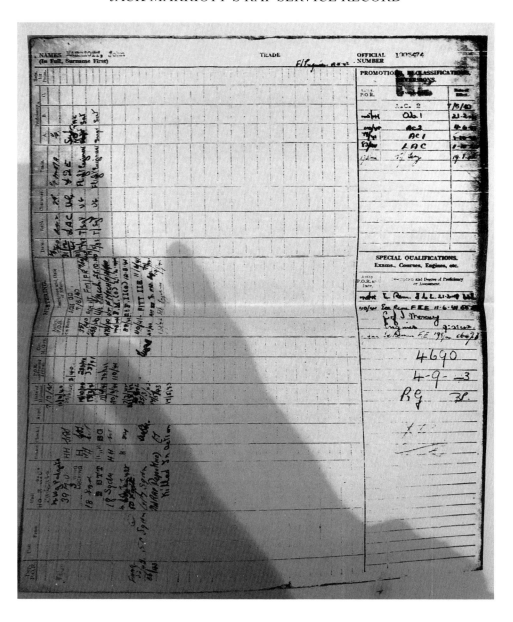

Appendix 13

Avro Lancaster ED933 and ED937 RAF Record Cards

Form 1180 Accident Record Card for ED933 12 May 1943 at Reculver

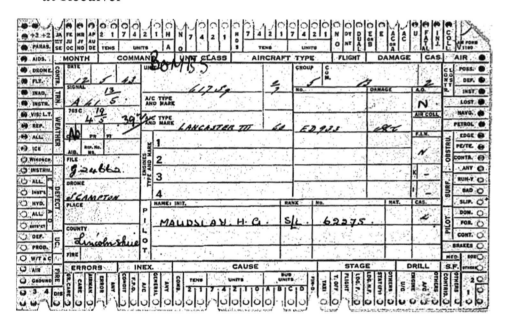

Comments on the second page (opposite):

Underside of a/c damaged by spray from explosion of special

mine dropped by a/c [aircraft]

O/C. [Commanding Officer] *E of J* [Error of Judgements] *pilot misjudged his height*

Stn/Cdr [Station Commander]*: E of J consequent with special training carried out*

Form 78 Aircraft Movement Cards

These cards record movements of aircraft during their time in RAF service.

Date	Comment
04/05/1943	Delivered to 617 Sqn.
12/05/1943	Damaged Cat.Ac (at Reculver) ROS (Repaired on Site)
22/05/1943	Returned to 617 Sqn.
02/08/1944	Repaired by Avro
02/09/1944	Returned to 617 Sqn.
29/01/1945	Transferred to 46 MU
04/04/1945	Returned to 617 Sqn. (for disposal of an Upkeep)
05/04/1945	Transferred to 46 MU
07/10/1946	S.O.C. (Struck off Charge) and broken up on site

Type of Aircraft		Mark	R.A.F. Number
LANCASTER		Ⅲ	ED934

Contractor		Contract No.	Engine Installed :—
A. V. Roe		B692 43/40	Merlin 28
			Maker's airframe No. :—

Unit or Cat'y/Cause	Station or Contractor	Date	Authority	41 or 43 Gp. Allot.
39 MU		6.5.43	1632/29	
617 Sqdn		14.5.43	1623/120	
Cat E (missing)		17.5.43	FB/A60	
S.O.C		26.5.43	1623/141	

A.M. Form 78

Date	Comment
06/05/1943	Delivered to 39 MU
14/05/1943	Delivered to 617 Sqn.
17/05/1943	Cat.E (Missing) – Operation Chastise
26/05/1943	S.O.C.

Loss Card for ED937 17 May 1943 Operation Chastise

Comments:

Crashed Emmerich nr [near] *Düsseldorf*

German (file) just inside German border. All killed and consequently b'd [buried] *at D'dorf* [Düsseldorf] *– now Reichswald Forest.*

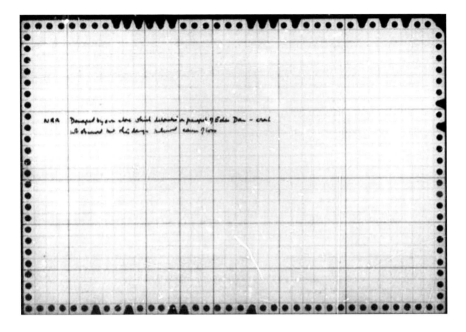

Comments:

Damaged by own store which detonated on parapet of Eder Dam – crash not observed but this damage believed cause of loss

Appendix 14

Book References

Title	Authors	ISBN	Year	Publisher
The Dam Busters	P. Brickhill		1952	Evans Brothers
Enemy Coast Ahead	G. Gibson VC		1955	Pan Books
Lancaster at War	M. Garbett & B. Goulding	0711002258	1971	Ian Allen
Lancaster at War 2	M. Garbett & B. Goulding	071100966X	1979	Ian Allen
Lancaster at War 3	M. Garbett & B. Goulding	071100966X	1984	Book Club Associates
The Dambusters Raid	J. Sweetman	9781854091802	1990	Arms & Armoury
Bygone days of Whitehough & Bugsworth	A. Watson		1993	Alan Watson
Avro Aircraft since 1908	A.J. Jackson	9780851778341	1994	Putnam
AVRO: The history of an aircraft Company	H. Holmes	1853105317	1994	Airlife
Combat Legend: Avro Lancaster	H. Holmes	9781840373769	2002	Airlife
Dambusters	M. Arthur	9780753515730	2008	Virgin Books
No 617 'Dambuster' Sqn	A. Bateman	9781846034299	2009	Osprey
Dambusters: The race to smash the dams 1943	J. Holland	9780593066775	2012	Bantam Press

BOOK REFERENCES

Title	Authors	ISBN	Year	Publisher
Dambuster Crash Sites	C. Ward & A. Wachtel	981844155682	2013	Pen & Sword
Dambusters: Failed to Return	R. Owen, S. Darlow, S. Feast & A. Thorning	9780957116344	2013	Fighting High Ltd
Henry Maudslay: Dambuster	R. Owen	9780992620707	2014	Fighting High Ltd
Dambuster Lancaster: The definitive illustrated guide to the Avro Lancaster BIII Type 464 (Provisioning)	P. Forkasiewicz & M. Postlethwaite	9781906592486	2018	Red Kite
Fuel, Fire and Fear: RAF Flight Engineers at war	C. Pateman	9781781556757	2018	Fonthill
The complete Dambusters: The 133 men who flew on the Dams raid	C. Foster	9780750988087	2018	The History Press
Chastise	M. Hastings	9780008280529	2019	William Collins

Appendix 15

Transcriptions of Letters and Telegraphs

Transcript of the letter from AC Jack Marriott, starting page 13

No 1003474 AC2 J Marriott
Tent No 11
HQ No 39 MU
Colerne, Wilts

Sun 15.9.40

Dear Floss Fred & Norma,

First I must apologise for not writing before but as our letters crossed in the post I thought that perhaps you would have written again. However as I haven't seen anything you must be waiting for me. I told mother in the letter that I posted yesterday that I should write to you Sunday night cum Monday morning. It is my turn on tonight it is now about 9.30. I say about 9.30 because I don't know for sure as I dropped my blue pencil four & sixpence watch on the ruddy floor last Wednesday & needless to say it doesn't. Thanks for the PO you sent I shall be able to put it towards another 4/6 – I don't think. And now to get on to the subject of air-raids.

As you probably know last Friday was Friday the 13th. It was very windy and cloudy down here. It was about 3.30 in the afternoon. I was just going for an early tea as I was on duty at 4. I just happened to look up and I saw a plane come out of the clouds heading this way. I thought it looked a bit different to what I'd been seeing and then I saw something drop from it and then the ruddy whistling. For a couple of seconds I was sorta rooted to the ground, then I came to and flung torso flat on floor at the same time as the do das landed. There was two dropped, so I thought I had better be going towards a bit of cover (there is a sod over now) I set off towards a trench and then suddenly remembered I'd dropped my knife and fork so for some unknown reason I went back for them and ran like a rabbit to the trench while sonny boy was still sticking around. However the ack ack[36] gun started on him so he vamoosed.

When everything had got back to something like normal we found he had missed us by quite a bit but it was quite near enough to be going on with. They must have been fairly heavy bombs as one of them knocked a few trees down and set one on fire. Needless to say no laxatives were needed on Saturday.

We have had very little air raids during the night. It is a bit different to what I expected as it is a full moon tomorrow. I don't expect we shall worry if he fails to come again. It is now ten past one and nothing doing. I wrote to May tonight just before I wrote to you. I went out last night for the first time for nearly a fortnight. I went with two more lads down into Box which is a place a bit bigger than Colerne but we have another of those great hills to climb in fact anywhere we go to from the camp we have to climb a hill to get back.

You will see by my address that I am now in a tent. I don't know for how long but I rather like it although I only sleep there every other night. I have heard that we are to be billeted out. The five of us on our job had some pleasant news on Wednesday. We learned that we were to get 6d. a day extra as we are doing Service Police work. It will come in very handy especially as we shall get the 6d. a day for tobacco. We have also got about 17/6 back pay to come.

I should think by now that Joe has got to where ever he is going. Well Floss I don't think there is anything else just now. I don't think I will seal this now. I'll wait till Monday and see if anything arrives.

Cheerio
Jack

Transcript of the letter from AC Jack Marriott, starting page 19

No 1003474 AC2 J Marriott
Tent No 11
HQ No 39 MU

Sun 16.9.40	*Colerne, Wilts*

Dear Floss,

You will no doubt be surprised to receive another letter from me so quickly after the one I posted this morning.

I told you in that letter I wrote last night that I wouldn't seal it up till I saw whether I got one from you this morning. However there was a fellow going to Bath at 6.30am so I thought I might as well send it down with him together with the one for May. Well I got the one back from you that you wrote on Friday complete with stamps, for which I thank you, but you needn't put any in every letter you send. I shall try and get this posted in Bath tonight so that you should get it the day after the other.

I got the Reporter and a letter from Arthur as well this morning. I was glad to hear that mother has got her money through. It was funny you starting your letter with "Friday 13th" after me writing about same. You are right about us not being able to leave the Guard Room during raids, but I think it is as safe as any place as there is a wall of sand bags in front of it. It wouldn't of course stand a direct hit but there aren't many places that would.

We seem to have one or two firemen in the family. It should be a good show when Chas and Frank Hulley get together.

It will be tough if May has to wait till the cold weather comes before she can have her operation on the thyroid gland. If it is that that is making her lose weight Fred won't have to worry about his, will he? I hope you don't mind that crack Fred but I have to fill up space and get my 2½d worth.

The weather is not too good today as it has rained nearly all the morning. I believe we are moving out of the tents into a big house tonight, but you can put Tent No11 on your next letter as I shall get it OK.

Mother told me about that bloke who was on leave but it is hardly worth it for a weekend as it is all travelling. Well Floss I will close now. You can tell mother I got the Reporter & will write Wednesday unless I get a letter before.

> *Cheerio*
> *Jack*

Letter from AC Jack Marriott, starting page 37

1003474 Sgt J Marriott
Sergeants Mess
RAF Swinderby
Nr Lincoln

(Saturday)
Dear Floss Fred & Norma,

Just a few quick lines to let you know I have not forgotten you although I'll bet you will be thinking I have. But since arriving back here on Tuesday things have certainly moved.

I expect you will know I did my first op on Thursday night. (Monday night) I will try and finish this off now. Up to half an hour ago we were due for a trip tonight but the weather over most of the course was or is lousy so we don't play.

I received four letters today the only ones I've had since I came here apart from one that was re-addressed from Barry [RAF St Athan].

I would have written before but with being moved around so much I didn't get a chance. I have however been to Lincoln once or twice and to Newark which is about the same distance away.

I had hoped to arrange a meeting with Arthur in Lincoln but from May's letters he is going to Scotland. I believe Alf is somewhere near Newark though, so maybe I shall see him. I'm hoping to get a 48 on the 10th or 11th of the month and as I'm not all that far off it should be worth it.

I saw one of Lowes' waggons from Whaley [Bridge] in Lincoln the other night so for once I am within striking distance of home.

Well there doesn't seem much else to say. I'm afraid your parcel is still following me around as I have not seen anything of it.

Being in the Sergeants Mess the grub is quite good. We had bacon, egg and fried bread at 8 o'clock tonight. You only get that these kind of suppers when you are due for ops though. We diddled them tonight with not going.

We get biscuits, chocolate, raisins and chewing gum to take with us and also coffee. We can also take some kind of pill to keep you awake. I had one on Thursday which was OK, but on Friday when we set off and had to come back after a couple of hours the one I had kept me awake so I had to play snooker when we got back at about 12:30 to try and get tired.

Anyway folks I'll call it a day now.

So cheerio
Love Jack

Transcript of the telegram on page 169

Priority Mr T Y Marriott Middleton House
New Smithy Chinley Nr Stockport

Deeply regret to inform you that your son
Sgt J Marriott is missing as a result of
operations on night 16/17th May 43.
letter follows. Please accept my
profound sympathy. OC 617 Squadron

Transcript of Gibson's letter on page 171

No. 617
Squadron, RAF. Station,
Scampton, Lincs.

20th. May, 1943.

My Dear Mr Marriott,

It is with deep regret that I write to confirm my telegram advising you that your son, Sergeant J. Marriott, is missing as a result of operations on the night of 16th/17th May, 1943.

Sergeant Marriott was Flight Engineer of an aircraft detailed to carry out an attack against the Eder Dam. The aircraft was seen to drop its load, and when the captain, Squadron Leader Maudslay, was called by radio, he seemed to be in extreme difficulty. It is possible, however, that the crew were able to abandon the aircraft and land safely in enemy territory, and if this is the case, news should reach you direct from the International Red Cross Committee within the next six weeks. Squadron Leader Maudslay would, I am sure, do everything possible to ensure the safety of his crew.

Please accept my sincere sympathy during this anxious period of waiting.

I have arranged for your son's personal effects to be taken care of by the committee of adjustment at this station, and will be forwarded to you through normal channels in due course.

If there is any way in which I can help you, please let me know.

Yours very sincerely
Guy Gibson
Wing Commander,
Commanding, 617 Squadron, RAF

Transcript of the Forge letter on page 172

Dear Mr Marriott,

It is with very deep regret that the members of the "Union" learned that Jack was missing, and may we extend to you are hope, that you will receive more reassuring news in the near future.

We all realise what a great debt we owe to the lads who are carrying out these operations, without any thought of self, and yet so ready to see that every atom of themselves is put to the job in hand.

It is such thoughts that make us proud we knew Jack, and trust that there will be some good news of him soon.

Yours sincerely
For the "Forge" Social & Athletic Union

W H Markham

Transcript of the Air Ministry letter on page 174

Sir,

I am commanded by the Air Council to express to you their great regret on learning that your son, Sergeant John Marriott, Royal Air Force, is missing as the result of air operations on the night of 16th May, 1943, when a Lancaster aircraft in which he was flying as flight engineer set out for action during moonlight and was not heard from again. This does not necessarily mean that he is killed or wounded, and if he is a prisoner of war he should be able to communicate with you in due course. Meanwhile enquiries are being made through the International Red Cross Committee and as soon as any definite news is received you will be at one informed.

If any information regarding your son is received by you from any source you are requested to be kind enough to communicate it to the Air Ministry.

The Air Council desire me to convey to you their sympathy in your present anxiety.

I am, Sir,
Your obedient Servant,
J A Smith

Transcript of the letter from the Central Depository on page 176

1003474 Sgt Marriott J.

Dear Sir,

The personal effects of your son as listed on the attached inventory have now reached this office from the Unit and will be held in safe custody pending the receipt of further evidence which will enable a conclusive classification of the casualty to be made.

In the case of casualties reported "missing" unless definite evidence comes to light in the meantime, authority to release the effects is not normally received from the Air Ministry until at least six months from the date of the casualty, since official action to presume death is rarely taken before the expiration of this period.

In the case of casualties ultimately reported "Prisoner of War", the Air Ministry will as a general rule, only authorise the release of effects on the written request of the officer or airman concerned. In these circumstances, in order to expedite release, any original letter received from a Prisoner of War in this connection should be forwarded to this office for perusal and early return.

In the meantime, may I be permitted to express my sympathy with you in this period of anxiety.

Yours faithfully,
G Hibbert
Squadron Leader, Commanding,
R.A.F. Central Depository.

Transcript of the telegram from the Air Ministry on page 180

Priority (cc) J H Marriott Middleton House
Chinley Nr Stockport Cheshire
KWY. 706/11 From Air Ministry Kingsway PC 539 11/8/43.
Deeply regret to advise you that according to information received through International Red Cross Committee your son Sergt. J Marriott is believed to have lost his life as a result of air operations on the night of 16th/17th/5/43. Stop. The air Council express their profound sympathy. Stop. Letter confirming this Telegram follows. Stop.
Under Secretary of State. Stop.

Transcript of Holden's letter on page 181

No. 617 Squadron,
R.A.F. Station, Scampton,
Lincoln.
13th August 1943.

My Dear Mr Marriott,

It is with deepest regret that I now have to write to confirm the telegram you have received that your son Sgt. J. Marriott was killed in action on the night of 16/17th May 1943.

Please accept my sincere and heartfelt sympathy and that of all members of this Squadron in the sad loss which you have sustained.

Yours Sincerely
G W Holden
Squadron Leader
Commanding No. 617 Squadron R.A.F.

Transcript of letter from the Casualty Branch on page 182

*Air Ministry
Casualty branch,
77, Oxford Street,
London, W.1.*

17 August, 1943

Sir,

I am commanded by the Air Council to inform you that they have with great regret to confirm the telegram in which you were notified that, in view of information now received from the International Red Cross Committee, your son, Sergeant John Marriott, Royal Air Force, is believed to have lost his life as the result of the air operations on the night of 16th May, 1943.

The Committee's telegram, quoting official German information, states that your son and the six other occupants of the aircraft in which he was flying on that night were killed on 17th May. It contains no information regarding the resting place of their burial nor any other details.

Although there is unhappily little reason to doubt the accuracy of this report, the casualty will be recorded as "missing believed killed" until confirmed by further evidence, or until, in the absence of such evidence, it becomes necessary, owing to lapse of time, to presume for official purposes that death has occurred. In the absence of confirmatory evidence death would not be presumed until at least six months from the date when your son was reported missing.

The Air Council desire me to express their deep sympathy with you in your grave anxiety.

I am, Sir,
Your obedient Servant,
Charles Evans

Transcript of letter from Gwen Maudslay on page 184

Aug 20th

Dear Mr Marriott,

I write to you as the mother of your son's pilot in the glorious but fated Dam operation.

How I hoped & prayed they might all be safe somewhere in those agonising weeks of waiting. Now we have to face life without them.

Henry was so proud of his crew –

What we owe to all their young lives, so full of bravery & courage is immense.

I feel I must be as brave as they were.

Please accept my great sympathy,

L Y sincerely
S. G. Maudslay

Transcript of letter from the Air Ministry on page 188

12 Nov 1943

'Sir,

With reference to the letter from this Department of 30th September, 1943, I am directed to inform you that action has now been taken to presume, for official purposes, that your son, 1003474 Sergeant J. Marriott lost his life on 17th May, 1943.

I am to express the sympathy of the Department with you in your great loss.

I am, Sir,
Your obedient Servant,
D Bent
For Director of Personal Services.

Transcript of letter from Buckingham Palace on page 189

Buckingham Palace

"The Queen and I offer you our heartfelt sympathy in your great sorrow.
We pray that your country's gratitude for a life so nobly given in its service may bring you some measure of consolation.

George R. I. [Rex Imperator – King]

Transcript of letter from Central Chancery on page 198

Central Chancery of
The Orders of Knighthood
St James's Palace, S.W.1.

22 November 1945.

Sir,

I have the honour to inform you that your attendance is required at Buckingham Place at 10:15 o'clock a.m. (doors open at 9.45 o'clock a.m.) on Tuesday, the 18th December, 1945, in order that you, may receive from The King on behalf of your father, the Distinguished Flying Medal awarded to his son, the late Sergeant John Marriott, Royal Air Force.

Dress: Service Dress, Civil Defence Uniform, Morning Dress or dark Lounge Suit.

You may be accompanied by one relation only, who must be a blood relation of the deceased (children under seven years of age may not attend) and I shall be glad if you will complete the enclosed form and return it to me immediately.

Two third class return railway vouchers will be forwarded to you if you so desire, and I shall be glad if you will give the details required on the form enclosed.

This letter should be produced on entering the Palace as no further cards of admission will be issued.

I am, Sir,
Your obedient servant,

Transcript of letter from the Air Ministry on page 204

Air Ministry
2, Seville Street
London, S.W.1.

16 April 1948

Dear Mr. Marriott,

I am deeply sorry to renew your grief in the sad loss of your son, Sergeant J. Marriott, but I am sure you will wish to know of the removal of his grave from Dusseldorf Cemetery, to Reichswald Forest Military Cemetery, Cleve, where he now rests in Grave 18, Row B, Plot 5. You will be glad to know that the comrades who lost their lives with him rest in graves nearby.

I must explain that this reburial is in accordance with the policy agreed upon by His Majesty's and Commonwealth Governments that our fallen in Germany should not be left in isolated cemeteries, but should rest together in special military cemeteries which have been selected for the natural beauty and peace of their surroundings. The graves there will be maintained in perpetuity by the Imperial War Graves Commission who will consult you, later on, regarding the inscription upon the headstone they will erect to his memory. A photograph of the grave will be sent to you although this may not be for some considerable time.

I do hope the thought that his last resting place will always be reverently tended may be of some slight comfort to you in the great loss you have sustained.

Yours sincerely,
G M Haslam

Transcript of letter from the Air Ministry on page 205

Air Ministry
2, Seville Street
London, S.W.1.

26 October 1948

Dear Mr. Marriott,

With reference to this Department's letter of the 16th April last, the Royal Air Force Missing and Enquiry Service has reported that owing to replotting in the British Military Cemetery at Reichswald Forest the Grave of your son, Sergeant J. Marriott is now registered as No.4, Row C, Plot V.

Yours sincerely,

Transcript of letter from the ABPC on page 212

Associated British Picture Corporation Ltd.
Elstree Studios
Boreham Wood

Herts   13th January 1954.

T. H. Marriott, Esq.,
c/o Air Ministry,

Dear Mr. Marriott,

We have for some time been making preparations for a film of the magnificent operation carried out in 1943 by 617 Squadron, Royal Air Force, in which the Moehne and Eder dams were destroyed and which earned for them the title of "The Dam Busters". Our film story, written by R. C. Sherriff, is based mainly on Paul Brickhill's book of the same name but we have also received considerable information, encouragement and assistance from the Air Ministry, Mr. Barnes Wallis, Air Chief Marshal Sir Ralf Cochrane, Group Captain Whitworth, Wing Commander H. B. (Micky) Martin and many others closely connected with the events portrayed, all of whom have now read our script and expressed their approval.

In endeavouring to tell the whole story from the time the idea was first conceived until it was so successfully carried out we are very conscious of the fact that it has not been possible to pay full credit to everyone concerned for their part in this great achievement. In the course of the attack on the dams, however, we propose to show scenes in which members of the crews of most of the aircraft taking part in the main operation will be seen at their duties. We enclose a copy of our proposed script and you will see that some of the scenes will be in the aircraft piloted by Squadron Leader H. E. Maudslay D.F.C., in which your son Sgt. J. Marriott, was Flight Engineer.

We are for that reason writing to you, who have such a close personal connection with these events, as you may read of the intention to produce the film and wonder how it is to be presented. If you will be good enough to read the script, which is entirely fact and contains no fictional material, we hope you will agree that we are setting out to give a simple, sincere account of achievement and heroism which will bring added prestige to the Royal Air Force, and 617 Squadron in particular, wherever it is shown.

After you have read the script will you kindly return it to us; we shall, at the same time, be most interested to have any comments which you may wish to make.

Yours sincerely,
W. A. Whittaker.

Transcript of letter to the ABPC on page 213

Middleton House,
New Smithy
Chinley
Derbys.
12th February, 1954.

W.A. Whittaker, Esq,
Associated British Picture Corporation Ltd.
Elstree Studios
Boreham Wood
Herts

Dear Sir,

Your letter of the 13th January last has been handed to me due to the death, some two years ago, of my father – Mr. T.H. Marriott, to whom it was actually addressed.

I have to say that I have carefully read, with much interest, the script of the proposed film, and return same to you herewith. I would apologise for the delay which has ensued in letting you have this script back but this has been due to the fact that my brothers were anxious to read it and as they live away from here it has taken a little time.

Yours faithfully,
Mrs. M Hawksley

Transcript of letter from the RAFA on page 215

21 March, 1955.

Dear Mrs Hawksley,

We have now finalised plans for the Premiere of the film "The Dam Busters". This is to take place at the Empire Theatre, Leicester Square, London W.1., at 7.45 p.m. on the 16 16th My, the anniversary of the actual raid.

Her Royal Highness The Princess Margaret has graciously consented to attend, and the proceeds of the World Premiere are to be equally divided between this Association, the R.A.F. Benevolent Fund, the R.A.F. Escaping Society, and the Pathfinder Association.

If you would like to have an invitation to attend the Premiere, I should be most grateful if you would let me know so that I can make sure that some very special seats are booked for you. When you write perhaps you will tell me if you would like one or two seats.

Yours sincerely,
G R Boak

Transcript of letter to the RAFA on page 216

Dear Sir,   *5 /4/55.*

Thank you for the invitation to the Premiere of the film The Dam Busters.
Further to my telephone conversation yesterday, due to unforeseen circumstances I would be pleased if you would forward the two tickets as

stated in your letter of the 21st not three as mentioned in my telephone conversation.

Please accept my apologies for the delay and hope this will not cause any inconvenience.

Yours Sincerely,

Transcript of letter from the RAFA on page 217

Dear Mrs. Hawksley,   *19th April 1955*

Thank you so much for your letter.

We would very much like to present one of your brothers to Her Royal Highness Princess Margaret. Unfortunately, owing to the numbers, it will not be possible to present them both.

I wonder if you would like to enquire from them if they would like me to arrange for one of them to be presented and if so, whose name they would like me to submit to the Palace.

Kindest regards,
G R Boak

Transcript of letter from the RAFA on page 221

31 March 2011
Dear Mr & Mrs Bagshaw

I do hope you are both keeping well.

Your unwavering patience has paid off at last – I am pleased to let you know that the remembrance stone commemorating the life of Jack Marriott has now been laid in the RAF Remembrance Garden.

We are currently arranging a service to be held at the National Memorial Arboretum on Friday 20 May 2011 to bless the remembrance crosses and stones. The service, which will take place in the remembrance garden itself, will start at 1130 hours and finish at approximately 1150 hours.

This will be a private service for those people and RAFA branches who have placed a commemoration in the garden and we would therefore like to invite you to attend.

Do let me know if you would like any further details about the service.

With very best wishes
Yours sincerely

Transcript of letter from the RAF on page 223

Dear Mrs Bagshaw   *15 October 2013*

DISTINGUISHED FLYING MEDAL BELONGING TO SERGEANT JOHN MARRIOTT

Thank you for your letter of 4 October, in which you asked what would be done with your uncle's Distinguished Flying Medal, which you kindly presented to the squadron on the 50th Anniversary of the Dams Raid. You may wish to know that it is currently on display in the Squadron's crewroom, alongside medals belonging to other notable members of the Squadron from the Second World War.

All the Squadron's memorabilia has recently been catalogued by the RAF Air Historical Branch in preparation for the Squadron's disbandment in March 2014. They have decided that your uncle's medal will be transferred to the RAF Museum at Hendon for safekeeping. Unfortunately, I cannot say whether the Museum intends to put it on display. However, it will be returned to 617 Squadron when it reforms with the new Lightning II aircraft, which is currently planned to take place in 2016.

Kind regards,
David Arthurton

Endnotes

1. A&AEE – Aeroplane and Armament Experimental Establishment
2. HCU – Heavy Conversion Unit
3. op – operational mission
4. RAFVR – Royal Air Force Volunteer Reserve
5. His RAF Service Record shows T/Sergeant. All RAF VR were assigned Temporary Sergeant status
6. Pathfinder – target-marking aircraft
7. flak – an abbreviation of the German Flugabwehrkanone (also referred to as Fliegerabwehrkanone) meaning aircraft-defence cannon
8. Pink Pansies were one of several 'Target Indicator' (TI) flares. They were converted from standard 4,000lb incendiary bomb casings and loaded with Benzol, rubber and phosphorus and designed to burn with various colours to prevent the German Defences lighting decoy fires
9. CO – Commanding Officer
10. Dead reckoning is a navigational technique of calculating current position from a previous position using estimates of speed, time and direction.
11. H2S – early airborne ground mapping radar system
12. Tinsel tests were an early form of electronic counter measures
13. ILS – Instrument Landing System
14. RAE – Royal Aircraft Establishment
15. AOC – Air Officer Commanding
16. SASO – Senior Air Staff Officer
17. Compass swing: required to determine the effect on the compass before and after loading of the Upkeep so a compensation could be included after the Upkeep had been dropped.
18. R/T – Radio Telephone (or Radio Telephony)
19. Met Officer – Meteorological Officer
20. Peri-track – perimeter track. Now more commonly referred to as the taxiway

ENDNOTES

21. Trolley-acc. Trolley accumulator or Ground starter battery, external batteries on a wheeled trolley used for starting the aircraft so not to waste the aircraft batteries before take-off.
22. Radiator shutters were often abbreviated to RAD shutters
23. Packard built Rolls-Royce Merlin engines under licence in the USA
24. DR Compass or Distant Reading Compass was the aircraft master compass
25. GEE – Early radio navigation equipment
26. Air Speed Indicator. The Lancaster navigator position had a duplicate of the pilot's air speed indicator and altimeter
27. Standard Packard Merlin 28 engines would use +12 psi boost for take-off
28. IFF – Identification Friend of Foe – aircraft identification system
29. API – Air Position Indicator
30. Feathering an engine is to stop the engine and turn the propeller blades in line with airflow to create minimal resistance
31. Möhnesee is a reservoir formed by the damming of the rivers Möhne and the more southerly Heve
32. The Imperial War Graves Commission became the Commonwealth War Graves Commission (CWGC) in 1960
33. OTU – Operational Training Unit
34. Damage category Cat. Ac – Repair is beyond the unit capacity but can be repaired on site by another unit or a contractor
35. AJ-P was identified by its pilot Flight Lieutenant Martin as P–Popsie rather than the official 1943 phonetic name of P-Peter.
36. Ack ack – Anti-aircraft

Other Works by Frank Pleszak

Two Years in a Gulag

At the onset of the Second World War, my father Mikołaj, aged 19, was forcibly removed from his family in Poland by the Russian secret police and exiled to the harshest of the Siberian labour camps, the dreaded Soviet gulags of Kolyma. He spoke very little about it. Only very occasionally would his painful memories allow him to tell me and my siblings a little snippet of information. After his death, I became intrigued and began researching his early life. As I discovered more and more, I became amazed and shocked at the ordeals my father had endured. When Germany invaded Russia, my father was freed from Kolyma but still had many trials yet to face. He survived gulags, torture, and the war, but was never allowed to return home. I followed my father's footsteps on a journey of 40,000 kilometres, through places most of us have never heard of, a journey through despair, fear, hope and disappointment, and in these pages recount everything I discovered along the way. This true story occurred during a largely unknown and poorly documented period of modern history that has

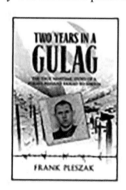

been denied by successive Russian Governments and largely ignored by Western governments and media. *Two Years in a Gulag* provides a valuable insight into not only my father's story but the story of a whole Polish nation.

The Battle of Vileyka

Very little is known in the west about the battles on the Eastern Front in the Great War. The battle for the small town of Vileyka (now in Belarus), about 100km east of Vilnius, at the end of September 1915 is one such battle. It is rarely, if ever, mentioned in English historical text, but it marked the extent of the German advance east at the end of the Russian Army's 'Great Retreat' of 1915. It constituted one of the few military successes of Russia's Army, and was instrumental in defining Germany's Eastern Front for the remainder of the war with Russia.

The Bombing of New Mills and Hayfield

The fatal Second World War bombing raid on two remote Derbyshire villages with an attack on the iconic Chatsworth House after which the German raiders were shot down by Spitfires of the famous Battle of Britain 303 Polish Squadron.

Townscliffe Golf Club

The small town of Marple, formally in Cheshire, now on Greater Manchester's south eastern border with Derbyshire, can still boast two nearby and spectacular golf courses. A short distance to the south west of Marple town centre is Marple Golf Club which was established in 1892. About a mile to the east of Marple, high up on the beautiful foothills of the Pennines, the village of Mellor, often and accurately described as the remotest village in Greater Manchester, is home to Mellor and Townscliffe Golf Club – a club created from the merger of two independent Mellor Golf Clubs. This book outlines the intriguing history of Mellor's two golf clubs and some of the people associated with them, many whose names appear in several different contexts as the story unfolds.

Blog: https://pleszak.blog/
books@pleszak.com

Index